INTO
the
LIGHT

*The Early African American
Men of Colgate University
Who Transformed a Nation
1840-1930*

PUBLISHED BY BOLDER SPIRIT PUBLISHING

Into the Light: The Early African American Men of Colgate
University Who Transformed a Nation, 1840-1930

Cover by Ji Cooper
Designed by Ji Cooper

Expressly edited for the preservation of the
authenticity of the voice of the author.

Edited by
Jane Malloy
Elizabeth Davis

Managing Editor
Roxanne Bellamy

ISBN: 978-1-7328703-2-1

BOLDER SPIRIT PUBLISHING
www.bolderspiritpublish.com

Dedication

To future students and scholars:
remember the past as you create the future

Miriam
Thank you.
We must tell our
stories so others may
learn & grow.

Diane Uccione
June 2019

CONTENTS

AUTHOR'S NOTE ON LANGUAGE

I have chosen not to change the language/names used in various historical documents or the common usage for the particular time period in reference to these men.

Some language/names may offend some readers, but it was important not to sanitize any document or belief, so the reader understands the context of the lives lived by these men.

I have chosen to use Black to refer to these early African/Caribbean men.

PREFACE

This work was inspired by my desire to bring the lives of the early Black men that attended Colgate University out of the shadows and into the light. As they struggled to overcome the footprint left by the slave oligarchy, their courage, and commitment, lay the bedrock for future Blacks at Colgate and within emerging Black communities in the South. The Black men celebrated in these pages worked faithfully to affect change. These men were involved in the abolitionist movement, they educated freedom seekers (runaway slaves), and took a stand against Jim Crow. Regardless of their path, no study of this crucial period of American history is complete without investigating their lives and times. Whether standing up for Civil Rights or sitting down at organized sit-ins planned as nonviolent protests on the Colgate campus, the stories of these men remain familiar and relevant to the students of color who attend Colgate today.

In writing this book, I accepted the challenge to conduct the research necessary to illuminate a part of history that has been hidden from view far too long, and to state the facts in a writing style that seeks to exhibit editorial distance and control. This is a tall order given the underlying circumstances of slavery, Jim Crow segregation, and Colgate's eventual role in promoting eugenics, inviting Nazis to campus, and promulgating the "Colgate Plan" during the controversial Cutten years.

This research of the life and times of early Black Colgate men was occasioned by the Colgate bicentennial and presents a clear opportunity to correct a 200-year oversight. This oversight, the product of neglect and marginalization, made these men of color practically invisible. It not only deprived them of their rightful place in the Colgate community, it deprived us all.

The facts emerged only after the arduous task of piecing together various original source documents, newspaper articles, journals, and Colgate and non-Colgate records, many of which were unpublished. The task of identifying early Black men without the benefit of photographs (photographs are helpful, but not determinative in cases where racial identity is sometimes ambiguous) or references to their ethnicity was often daunting. However, strong evidence supports the proposition that Jonas Holland Townsend and Henry Livingston Simpson were the first Black men at Colgate. Merely identifying the names and dates of attendance of these men doesn't necessarily tell us what life was like for them during their time at Colgate, in particular where the time period was tumultuous. The preservation of first-person narratives are useful, but the first-person narratives are often subject to many silent variables such as education, financial resources, access, and predilections of individual archivists that threatened to compromise reliability. In view of the gravity of the endeavor at hand, we tried in earnest to sweep aside those variables to reach bedrock factual statements. In rare instances, first-person narratives of some of the early Black men have been uncovered, but generally, their narratives were scant with respect to their time at Colgate.

The period between 1840 and 1930 was a time of transformation in American history. President Lincoln decided to bring the idea of transformation to the doorstep of the South, and the Union Army prevailed in what is regarded as the bloodiest war on American soil. Although the signing of the Emancipation Proclamation ended slavery in measured stages by prescription, the legacy of the slave oligarchy was extended and perpetuated through America's racial caste system, in Jim Crow.

The early Black men who attended Colgate were not merely passive observers of arguably one of the most transformative periods of American history, they were active participants and agents of that transformation. In short, they committed their lives and education to surviving and resisting the atrocities of the slave oligarchy and its poisonous legacy. It was this commitment to education and transformation that became the blueprint of their lives.

Colgate's admission of Black men began in 1840 with the enrollment of Jonas Holland Townsend, the first admitted Black to Colgate (1840-1842), and then later in 1847 when Henry Livingston Simpson became the first Black Colgate graduate (1847-1855). The impressive line of men of color at Colgate includes such legendary figures as Townsend, the confidante of Frederick Douglass; Samuel Howard Archer Class of 1902, the mentor and role model of Martin Luther King, Sr. and Dr. Martin Luther King, Jr., and Adam Clayton Powell, Jr. Class of 1930, a colorful member of the body politic and a notorious firebrand of the United States House of Representatives, as well as many others.

Proponents of liberation politics have argued persuasively that the underpinnings of the American cultural, economic, and political spheres were steeped in the rape and pillage of the land and the forced enslavement of African men and women. From the first landing of settlers at Jamestown, Virginia to the progress made by the Pilgrims at Plymouth, Massachusetts and beyond Black Codes (laws specifically designed to keep the Black bodies and minds enslaved as second-class citizens) were embedded in the legal lexicon as early as the mid-1600s. The U.S. Constitution, widely regarded as the foundation of modern liberal democracy, carved out the status of the enslaved African, and provided the judicial precedence that designated Black men (whether slave or free) as only three-fifths a man. Thus, the status of the enslaved African was ensconced in the Constitution and accommodated the White man's representation in the new American government and provided the blueprint for other equally suspect classifications on the socio-economic hierarchy. Little would change in 19th century America and the use of Black bodies to grow a fledgling nation was interwoven with the seemingly insatiable thirst to grab land from indigenous people. Blacks of all classes were victimized by the Fugitive Slave Act of 1793, especially those who were not enslaved or were freedom seekers. The newly formed Congress enacted laws that required every state in the Union to return, by force if necessary, any enslaved person who escaped from their owners, regardless of the law of the land in the state from which they fled.

When the ever-increasing resistance to the notion of enslavement began to take root, the question of what to do with the growing population of Black people permeated the country's otherwise suspect moral conscience. Colonization societies formed with the hope of liberating the enslaved and returning them to Africa and anti-slavery societies called for the gradual abolishment of slavery. While historians primarily recorded the White men and women of the abolitionist movement, many of the Black voices who risked life and limb to fight to free their enslaved brethren were erased or minimized.

Times changed after the Civil War, and emancipation became the 'official' law of the land. Formerly enslaved men could actualize their desire to seek and receive a formal education and return to teach the masses of similarly minded Blacks from the pulpit and the classroom. Although bondage was no longer an obstacle, the very act of seeking education placed the lives of Black men and women at risk. There was a climate of terrorism fueled by White supremacists for any Black person who dared to teach or minister to Blacks in the South. Similarly, during this period of White terrorism, lynchings and other atrocities were sanctioned to discourage Black men and women who dared to stand up. It was in this climate that these early Colgate men summoned courage, stood up and opened doors. The full measure of the Colgate experience of the early Black men comes to life only when it is considered in this larger historical context.

Samuel Howard Archer, a perfect example of a strong Black man or as is often said, a man of color 'through and through,' became the pillar and created the great legacy of the 'Morehouse Man.' George Jackson, another distinguished Black man at Colgate, broke the color barrier when he became the first Black to pass the Foreign Service Test, join the Foreign Service, and serve at a European post, only to lose his posting during the Woodrow Wilson presidency. Enoch Gousse, still another pioneer at Colgate, railed against the racism that manifested itself in the medical admissions process. He challenged a system that was tainted by racism and had repeatedly blocked his admission and the admission of other highly qualified Black candidates. In many respects, the Colgate experience of Archer, Jackson, and other early Black men at the University is emblematic of the struggles of Blacks as a whole across the larger historical continuum. The threshold question is where these legendary Black men fit into this continuum. The answer is, of course, practically everywhere.

With expanding opportunities, Black Colgate men spread their influence into medicine, law, politics, and the arts. Colgate men continued to be firsts and influencers: the Mayor of Washington, D.C., a member of Congress, a vocal opponent of Jim Crow, a physician and a contributor of the civil rights movement. This legacy of Colgate's Black men who influenced the transformative landscape of the American culture, economy, and politics is rich indeed.

Against a backdrop of slavery, Black codes, Jim Crow, segregation, lynchings, and second-class citizenship these men rose and were leaders in the quest to transform this nation into a more 'perfect nation.'

Given the nature of record keeping at the time, we hesitate to characterize our efforts as exhaustive. However, we are convinced that we have exercised our best efforts to pursue every reasonable lead and even some leads that were considerably less than reasonable. This book is the result of those best efforts.

*LIST OF KNOWN BLACK MEN WHO ATTENDED COLGATE
BETWEEN 1840-1930*

Jonas Holland Townsend* +
Henry Livingston Simpson
William J. Simmons*
Price Alpheus Leftwich
Sterling Gardner
Armstead Mason Newman
Jospeh Endom Jones
David Nathaniel Vassar
Gilbert Raiford*
Wesley Ely*
Peter Verdier Hazel
Lucius Hippolyte
Castle Brewer
Matthew Gilbert
George H. Jackson
Jeffrey Livingston James
Gregory Bond*
Peter Carter Neal
Samuel Howard Archer
George Lewis Hayes
John Brown Watson*
Everett Booker Jones
Lloyd Newton Gilbert*
Burwell Townsend Harvey
Ira David Pinson
Garnett Langton Hegeman
Gordon Blaine Hancock
William Tucker Parker
Howard Franklyn Lewis
Reginald Osborn Tullock
Leon Bogigian
William Henry Arthur Booker

Henry Morrison Smith
James Robert Bess
William Ravenell
Granville Hamilton
William Maynard Allen
George Edward Allen
Henry Shields Robinson, Jr.
Enoch Abel Gousse
Pierre Gousse
Merton Blair Anderson
Raymond "Ray" Vaughn
Daniel "Major" Crosby
John Edward Enoch
Adam Clayton Powell, Jr.
*- attended but did not graduate
+- first Alumni of Color of African American descent

LIST OF COLGATE MEN WHO BECAME COLLEGE PRESIDENTS

Samuel Howard Archer – Morehouse College
Matthew Gilbert – Selma University
Ira Pinson – Morris College
William J. Simmons – Simmons College
John Brown Watson – University of Arkansas at Pine Bluff

CHAPTER I
A Nation, A School

The 1840 United States Census listed the following:
2,487,335 Slaves
377,942 Free Blacks
- United States Census, 1840

Early Black students who arrived on campus did so during, arguably, the most transformative period in American history. The men enrolling at Colgate between 1820 and 1860 were from the American Indian tribal nations, (given the time period, different names have been used to identify these men and they have been referenced as Native Americans, Indians, American Indians, savages, or indigenous people) and Burmese students. Included in this number are Jonas Holland Townsend and Henry Livingston Simpson; the first Black men to enroll and graduate from Colgate, respectively in 1840 and 1853. The lives and contributions of these early Black men are a part of the forgotten Colgate legacy.

It is virtually impossible to understand with particularity what went through the minds of these early men. Therefore, it is difficult to fully understand the experiences and obstacles faced by them while attending a predominately White institution before the Civil War. Questions arise as to how were they received, embraced, ignored, or rejected? Unfortunately, answers to these questions are difficult to find. There are some basic historical markers that can be used to give a broad overview of American life, economics, culture, politics, and its impact on Black people.

When referencing primary source material of the period, monikers like 'colored,' 'Negro,' 'sable son,' and 'Black' are commonplace. There are also several instances where the term 'nigger' is used.

It is useful to consider race relations in the nation to understand what Jonas Holland Townsend and Henry Livingston Simpson faced and how their lives of activism and service were shaped. Slavery was legal in many parts of the United States when Townsend and Livingston attended Colgate.

Both men were born free, Townsend in Pennsylvania, and Livingston in New York. At the time of their birth, early years, and adulthood slavery had come to dominate the legal system and global economy. It has been estimated that by 1860 there were 4 million enslaved people in bondage with a value of approximately 3.5 billion dollars; the largest single asset in the entire U.S. economy.[1] The founding fathers and first presidents were slave owners, and the Bill of Rights and the Constitution were written with the slave economy, culture, and politics embedded in its foundation. The enslavement of men and women for free labor to build this country was not only accepted and tolerated, it was legalized. One can scarcely imagine the courage it took for Townsend and Simpson to pursue an education when the majority of the country saw Blacks as either property or second class citizens.

In 1780, Pennsylvania was one of the first states to enact legislation to abolish slavery. This law mandated a gradual emancipation of its indentured and enslaved populations by gradually allowing for emancipation up to the age of 28, and the length of time any person born after 1780 could be indentured was changed to 18 or 21 years, effectively reducing the waiting period by 7 to 10 years. However, 'masters' of the indentured and enslaved began to shift away to hired help and wage labor. The influx of European immigrants changed the landscape, suddenly making wage labor more attractive. Wages were more cost effective, by providing low wages eliminated the need to house and care for the sick and old enslaved. This extended the years of indenture which included both Whites and Blacks. Seeing profit and greed, many slave owners freed their enslaved, changed their status to indentured servants, and shipped them to Philadelphia to be sold at auction back into slavery in the rural South.

In 1799, New York State enacted gradual emancipation, the second to last northern state to do so (New Jersey was the last, abolishing slavery in 1804). In New York State, the new law freed any slave child born after July 4, 1799, but males remained 'indentured' until the age of 28 and females until the age of 25. The law was modeled to parallel the Pennsylvania law allowing 'masters' to retain their young slaves during their most productive years to maximize their investments. In 1817, at the urging of the governor, the New York legislature enacted laws that provided an economic benefit to the 'slave masters' by mandating the freeing of all slaves born before 1799 as they had little value to their owners. However, many slaveholders in the late 1780s saw that gradual emancipation was coming and began to sell off their enslaved down 'the river' to the South to make money. Neither law prevented slaveholders from other states from bringing their enslaved into the state as long as it was for no longer than 9 months. It wasn't until 1841 that the law dictated that no enslaved person could live or be present in New York State. However, these laws gave little comfort to the free Blacks living in the state.

Near the time of Townsend's birth, the 1820 census records of Pennsylvania listed 211 enslaved Blacks and 30,202 free non-whites. Similarly, near the time of Simpson's birth, the 1820 census records of New York State listed 10,088 enslaved and 29,278 free Blacks. Blacks lived near Colgate at the beginning of the institution. Rev. Robert Powell, one of the founders of Colgate, noted in his autobiography that he would often preach in a Black church in a small Black community near Hamilton, called Mud Flats. The community consisted of a tract of 300 acres that had been given to the former Mohawk Valley enslaved around 1800 from the Stockbridge Indian Reservation[2]. His journal acknowledged the existence of free Black communities residing within geographical proximity to Hamilton and Colgate[3].

In the 1840s, the conversation surrounding the enslaved communities in the southern United States began to increase and take on an urgency. Most of the northern states had already abolished slavery or adopted gradual emancipation acts that would free the remaining enslaved in due course. This gave rise to numerous free communities of Blacks that began to dot the American landscape. Free Blacks were mobile, and freedom seekers took refuge and built new lives in the North, Canada, Mexico, and Florida. The New York cities of Auburn, Syracuse, Rochester, Buffalo, Schenectady, and Albany all had thriving Black communities while other smaller Black communities were scattered along the hillsides of Central New York, and within geographical proximity to Hamilton, New York. These free Black communities used their proximity to Canada and the Underground Railroad routes to become an integral part of the movement to assist freedom seekers (runaway slaves) traveling to the free northern states and Canada.

These communities continued to grow with freedom seekers from the South seeking refuge until the passage of the Fugitive Slave Act of 1850, when the federal government, under pressure from the southern states once again enacted laws that allowed for and sanctioned the pursuit and re-enslavement of Black men and women wherever they were found. This turn of events intensified the debate on how to deal with 'that peculiar institution.' It was a debate that would divide the entire continent and Colgate was not immune.

The piecing together of references in letters and newspapers uncovered two 'colored,' 'Big Black,' or 'Sable Sons of Africa' students prior to the Civil War: Jonas Holland Townsend, who attended Colgate from 1840-1842 and a second, Henry Livingston Simpson, who attended from 1847-1855. Simpson was the first to receive degrees: 1853 (AB) and 1855 (Theology degree). It is noted that each man had never been enslaved. However, that was not the case for some of the other men who attended Colgate after the Civil War.

➤ CHAPTER II ➤
The Debate Over Slavery

The petition for an A.A.S.S. (American Anti-Slavery Society) was taken up and it was resolved that the petitioners be informed that the Faculty. see no reason for departing from the grounds of this former action is similar cases; and that, therefore, this request cannot consistently be granted. Prof. Eaton to inform them.

Professor and later President, George Eaton, and Gerrit Smith, the abolitionist, maintained very public differences on the issue of slavery and abolition. Their differences were illustrative of the debate on campus, (as well as the country) during the years the first two Black men attended Colgate. One can only imagine what it was like to be a student during the very time when others in the Colgate community zealously made arguments pro and con about one's humanity, or whether members of one's racial group were entitled to share in the reservoir of human rights inherent in the dignity of the human condition. As it was in the rest of the country in the 1830s, the question of slavery and what to do with the 'colored' came to Colgate and Madison County. Active Anti-Slavery and Colonization Societies existed in Hamilton, New York and the surrounding areas, and on campus a group of students at Colgate sought to form anti-slavery societies.

The faculty and Administration were consistently opposed to the formation of any anti-slavery societies on campus, leading to the faculty denial of anti-slavery societies on three separate occasions in 1834, 1837, and 1841. The faculty gave the students a simple choice:

renounce or leave. Isaac K. Brownson Class of 1838, a regular visitor to Peterboro, New York (a few miles from Hamilton, New York and the hometown of Gerrit Smith), kept a diary and recounts some of the events in the late 1830s on the question of forming an anti-slavery society at the University. In an August 1837 diary entry, Brownson writes:

> There has been some incidents to break the dull monotony of things since my last date. An Anti-Slavery Society was formed in the institution in the early part of the term which was the second formed here. Though consisting of upwards of twenty members and prospering, the faculty pronounced it a nuisance and labored zealously for its dissolution. They wished to compel on one's conscience or restrain liberty in any respect save this the society was noxious to the best interests of the institution and must be dissolved. Hence the individuals composing it were presented with an official request to withdraw their names from the constitution within a fixed period or as an alternative leave the institution. The society was dissolved, all withdrawing their names except three, who left 2 for Hamilton College (near Hamilton, NY and where Gerrit Smith was a trustee). The young men composing this society (Anti-Slavery Society) immediately attempted to form an association in the village and were successful enlisting several citizens and adopting a constitution. This measure however drew upon them the indignation and opposition of the young men and twice they have interrupted entirely the progress of the meetings.[4]

According to the faculty minutes of 1841, (Townsend was a student at this time) the issue of the formation of an Anti-Slavery Society was yet again before the faculty. "A petition of certain students for have [sic] to form an Abolition Society in the institution, was laid on the table for one week." At a faculty meeting, they reiterated their position to not allow an Anti-Slavery Society on campus.

Gerrit Smith, a wealthy landowner who resided several miles from campus, was an outspoken abolitionist, and supported the cause publicly and financially. He was an influential figure in Central New York, at one time was a financial supporter of Colgate, a trustee at Hamilton College, and a financial and spiritual patron of Oneida Institute and Central New York College, and regularly spoke on Colgate's position on slavery.

Oneida Institute was founded to train men, Black and White for the ministry and to be vocal advocates of the abolition movement. The Oneida Institute (a Presbyterian institute) was formed in 1827 in Whitesboro, New York, as a manual and higher education institute. Founded by abolitionists, it became known as a school that admitted both Black and White men. Lead by Beriah Green in 1833, some of the leading voices of Black abolition were trained there, such as Reverend Henry Highland Garnett. Incredibly, Oneida Institute enrolled more Black students than any other school in the country. The institute closed in 1844 due to a lack of funds.

Central New York College was founded by several Colgate alums who were disappointed at Colgate's position. The school was supported by White and Black abolitionists. The school admitted Blacks, women, and hired a Black man as a professor it however also closed for lack of funds. Both schools were in the general vicinity of Colgate.

Smith often challenged George Eaton on Colgate's position in support of slavery. George Eaton came to Colgate in 1833 as a professor of Mathematics and Natural Philosophy, then Ecclesiastical and Civil history, Intellectual and Classical Philosophy (1850), Christian Theology (1856), and in 1860 Homiletics and Practical Theology. Eaton served as president of the Theological Seminary from 1856 to 1868 and often spoke for the school on its position on slavery. Colgate's position on slavery was a high-profile controversy, one that challenged the moral fiber of the University. The underlying question that would have been conspicuous to both Townsend and Simpson, who were enrolled during this time, was whether a Baptist school founded to prepare young men for the ministry, would show the moral inclination to defer to reason and accept enlightened change or cling to the narrative of slavery.

Local press published the Smith/Eaton letters and carried reports on their verbal battles; however, despite the heated rhetoric between Smith and Eaton, the Colgate faculty and administrators attempted to remain neutral on the question of slavery. This position was due, in part, to the schism between the Southern and Northern Baptists; Northern Baptists denounced slavery, but Southern Baptists did not. This schism forced a split of the Baptist hierarchy into two groups; a Southern and Northern Baptist organization. Colgate attempted to appease both sides of the issue by not openly supporting either position and seeking to remain neutral; however, this was a difficult position to maintain as the debate over slavery came to dominate the national narrative. It is impossible to know what went through the minds of students of Townsend and Simpson while attending classes on a campus, with faculty and students who did not denounce slavery and in many instances openly supported it.

Smith openly accused Colgate in letters published in the local papers of hypocrisy for allowing students to form organizations on behalf of heathens of other lands, but not the heathens of this land. After all, Smith argued, the University trained men to be missionaries to preach in Asia, Africa, and the western frontier of the United States. In addition to underscoring his point about hypocrisy, Smith's letters provided evidence of the existence of the two earliest Black men at Colgate. In one letter he made reference to the Black men who attended Colgate and pointed out that one of Colgate's professors was teaching that slavery was not sinful and that if the opportunity arose to give counsel to a fugitive slave, the students should promote his return to his master.

Smith obviously was not the only critic of Colgate's position on slavery. Anti-slavery newspapers often made reference to Colgate's position on abolition. Colgate received negative press when Colgate alum, William Carey Crane, was noted as the person partially responsible for the enslavement of a Black minister, Caesar Blackwell. The defenders of Crane and his cohorts rationalized that the enslavement of Blackwell was for his own good. Incredulously, the Colgate brain trust did not question the morality of the argument that Blackwell would benefit more, and have greater mobility to preach in Alabama and other southern environs as an enslaved person that he would as a free man. This did little to put Colgate in a favorable light with abolitionists.

Further damage to the Colgate reputation came when a Colgate faculty member, John S. Maginnis, a professor of Biblical Theology, invited Jonathan Davis from Georgia to address faculty, students, and others to defend slavery. Davis, who owned thirty enslaved Black people on his plantation was touring northern states to justify the slave oligarchy. Davis spoke at a local church in Hamilton, New York that was widely attended by faculty and students alike and this alone caused sharp divisions within the Colgate community. Colgate received criticism for inviting Davis to Hamilton to champion slavery, yet conversely, several Colgate faculty members came to the defense of the invitation, citing that Davis technically had not spoken on campus on the issue of slavery. They argued that it would have been 'unchristian' not to welcome a Christian minister regardless of his stance on slavery. It was further argued that the Southern Christians were doing the best they could to accommodate change under a political system that sanctioned slavery.

Davis described his experience in Hamilton as friendly. He observed that he felt welcomed, spoke to a large crowd, and was grateful for the kind treatment of Professor Maginnis and his students who attended the talk. Hearing word of Colgate's "kind treatment" of Davis, an Albany abolitionist changed his will and bequeathed $1,000 to a different Baptist school in Rhode Island. This loss, coupled with the withdrawal of financial support from Gerrit Smith, is evidence of how Colgate suffered financially due to its flawed position of neutrality, and its flaccid effort to frame the slavery debate as a political issue rather than a moral one. Despite the school's position on the question of slavery, it was one of the few White institutions of higher education that admitted Blacks prior to the Civil War. Remarkably, it was against this backdrop that the first 'colored' students began their studies at Colgate.

← CHAPTER III →
Jonas Holland Townsend

In other States, though nominally free, they are deprived of the benefits of real freedom…And where the law does not operate against them, prejudice steps in by proxy and treads them to the earth; never faltering nor tiring, but pursuing them like an evil genius, and giving them no respite.[5]

> Letter to William H. Seward, NYS
> Governor co-authored by Jonas H. Townsend

Jonas Holland Townsend 1840-1842

Jonas Holland Townsend, the first Black student to enter Colgate, was from Phoenixville, Borough of West Chester (county), in Pennsylvania. His Colgate acceptance of August 6th, 1840 is recorded as being 'by letter,' a recommendation from a qualified individual, (his minister) recognized by the administration of the school. Townsend was 21 years old when he arrived in Hamilton. Suggestions are that he had some earlier education qualifying him for admission. Information about his early years is vague.

Phoenixville, near Philadelphia, was an area with a large Quaker population with free Blacks more common than slaves. "Blacks had been present from the borough's earliest days, including a few slaves"[6]. Pennsylvania's gradual emancipation act was passed in 1780, and by 1820, there were only 211 slaves living in all of Pennsylvania. Therefore it is presumed that Townsend was born a free Black.

Rev. Dyer A. Nichols, Colgate, Class of 1829, was living and working in the Borough of West Chester, PA. and the Phoenixville area from 1833-1843.[7] Nichols, originally a Quaker, converted to Baptist as a young man, and he was a tireless organizer of Baptist churches in the region for over thirty years. It has been suggested that Rev. Nichols in some measure, influenced Townsend to attend Colgate.

In the 1800s, the geographical location of birth or residence of free Blacks during slavery provided little safety. Free Blacks in the North and the South remained under the same oppression, none sharing the same status as White citizens under state and federal laws.

Townsend came of age intellectually as tensions were growing over the issue of slavery. The plantation economy, the economic engine of the South and the North, fed northeastern factories used in processing the cotton produced by southern slave labor. The shipping industry thrived as well by filling the demands of what is known as the slave trade triangle, with its human cargo and commodities transported from Europe to Africa, to the Americas, and back to Europe.

During Townsend's childhood small communities of free Blacks were beginning to appear in northern states. Many in these communities, under threats of death and worse, worked tirelessly to provide shelter, food, education, and passage to Canada and Mexico for those escaping slavery. This climate profoundly influenced Townsend and contributed to the shaping of his character and life goals. As a free Black man seeking an education, Townsend was carrying an extremely heavy burden.

When he arrived at Colgate, slavery had all but disappeared in the northern states. The 1840 Federal Census recorded 2,457,355 enslaved persons in the United States. New York State accounted for 50,027 of the total number of free Blacks. Four such Blacks who lived in Hamilton, New York.

By this time the landscape on the slavery question was rapidly changing. In 1800, in South Carolina, Denmark Vesey, a Black man purchased his freedom. Unable to purchase the freedom of his wife and children, Vesey engaged in various very public abolitionist activities. Eventually, Vesey was captured, tried, and hanged. In apparent retaliation to the actions of Vesey, the South Carolina legislature passed laws severely restricting the movement of free Blacks.

A highly promoted rebellion in Virginia in 1831 was organized by Nat Turner, a slave, who believed he was divinely driven to lead an insurrection. Unproven reports estimated that more than 60 White people had been killed during the fight. Six weeks later Turner was captured, tried, and hanged. His body, and those of his 'co-conspirators,' was left hanging from a tree as a deterrent to others. Strict laws prohibiting slaves from learning to read and write were enacted across the South to try to suppress the number of uprisings.

In 1836, Francis McIntosh, a free Black boat worker, born in Pittsburgh, moved to St. Louis. In the process of arresting a co-worker, Police demanded that McIntosh assist them. McIntosh refused, was arrested, and given five years in jail. While escaping, one of the officers who had arrested McIntosh, was killed. McIntosh was hunted down by Whites who tied him to a tree and burned him alive while thousands watched. This was only the beginning of the sanctioned murder of Blacks by White mobs.

The number of those seeking freedom increased. Joined by sympathetic Whites, more Blacks became involved with Underground Railroad activities. However, westward expansion pressured the growth of slavery. Violence broke out over the question of new western states coming into the Union as a slave holding or 'Free States.' In return the abolitionist movement grew.

As the voices to abolish slavery were growing, Colgate attempted to force students to change their anti-slavery stances or face expulsion. Colgate student, Samuel Silsbee, challenged the faculty's position on slavery during 1838-1839 and was expelled, but later readmitted when he publicly renounced his position.

It was against this backdrop that Townsend officially enrolled at Colgate on August 6, 1840. A fellow Colgate student in 1840 wrote a letter to a friend who referred to Townsend as "a colored brother at the institute from Philadelphia."

In an 1841 letter from Gerrit Smith addressed to Professor Eaton, Smith mentioned that Townsend shared his thoughts on his experience at Colgate. Townsend reported that the faculty and students treated him well. Smith, of course, took the opportunity to stress to Eaton that the institution should let a few more colored students enroll at the University.

In the summer of 1841, Townsend was listed as a supporter of the Hamilton Anti-Slavery Convention. The historical situation at Colgate, a period of rapid transformation involving controversial racial issues, likely influenced the entirety of Townsend's intellectual experience. Although Townsend had impressed Gerrit Smith, his presence managed to offend someone in a position of power at the Academy, presumably for trying to promote abolition or just by being on the campus.

In May of 1842, the faculty disciplinary committee recommended that Townsend be "separated from the institution."[8] Townsend left Colgate in May of 1842 under a 'cloud' of gossip and innuendo. Records have not been found that revealed the reason for his separation. In the 1840s, the range of possible acts or reasons for expulsion were limited to sexual misconduct, thievery, or not following authority. It is not known if any of the above reasons applied to Townsend, or perhaps an unpopular position on the issue of slavery and abolition was the cause of Townsend's expulsion. It is known, Townsend visited Smith at least once while attending Colgate, and was listed as a supporter of the Hamilton Anti-Slavery Convention held the summer before his expulsion. It was not the first nor the last time the University expelled a student for their anti-slavery stance. Mysteriously, however, the 'cloud' followed Townsend every time he came near to pursuing advanced education.

Townsend's life after Colgate was one of activism. He was a pivotal agent in the fight for freedom of his enslaved brethren, equality for free Blacks, and education of the newly freed Blacks after the end of the Civil War. Townsend used his pen, his intellect, his voice, and his organizational skills to influence the transformation of the racial and racist landscape in America for the next thirty years of his life. It is plain to see that the trajectory of his activism over that period mirrored the transformation of the American landscapes as a whole. It was instrumental in adjusting the climate of change that would dismantle slavery and, inspired the fight for civil and equal rights for all Black men and women.

Townsend moved to Albany, New York where he was ordained in 1843, and became the 6th Pastor of The First African Baptist Society, for one year.[9] The First African Baptist Church had been founded in Albany in 1820 by Thomas and Nathaniel Paul, brothers from the influential Black activist Paul family from Boston. The church was known for its activism in the fight against the 'peculiar institution.'

At Albany he found the Albany-Schenectady region already had a thriving activist community. In the 1840s, vigilance committees were forming around the country. These committees were dedicated to assisting freedom seekers by offering temporary shelter, food, money, jobs, and work within Anti-Slavery societies[10]. Vigilance committees worked with other local Anti-Slavery societies, such as: The Liberty Party and the Eastern New York Anti-Slavery Society in Albany and its surrounding areas. In the area there were already two anti-slavery newspapers in Albany: *The Tocsin of Liberty* and the *Albany Patriot*

In 1831, The American Society of Free Persons of Colour held the first national convention of free and freed Black citizens in the U.S., in Philadelphia. It was held for the purpose of improving the condition of free Blacks in the United States, and a goal to purchase land for the establishment of Black settlements in Upper Canada. National Conventions were held annually in Philadelphia through 1835.

The next national convention was not held until the meeting in Buffalo, New York on August 3, 1843, for the purpose of securing the enjoyment of inalienable rights. The 1843 Convention was an important moment and pivot to dismantle the slave oligarchy. It was attended by all of the important abolitionists of the day, including Frederick Douglass and Rev. Henry Highland Garnet. Townsend was also an active and vocal participant.

Townsend, as the delegate from Albany, represented some 700 Black men and women. On the first day of the convention, Townsend was placed on the committee to nominate convention Officers, as well as on the business committee, with Rev. Garnet, as the chair. Townsend came to the attention of Governor William H. Seward, when his persuasively worded resolution in support of abolition was delivered to the governor, an outspoken abolitionist. Townsend chaired the meeting[11] that adopted the resolution and offered support for Governor Seward.

The convention revealed a schism in the Black community as to the direction to be taken in their efforts to end slavery. After several days of very difficult and heartfelt work by the participants, the convention chose to support Douglass's position. Douglass believed his strategy would prevail over time to emancipate the enslaved. Garnet felt the enslaved should demand their freedom by "any means necessary." Townsend supported Rev. Garnet and introduced the motion to accept the Address. The full text of the address was printed in 1848 (see Appendix).

After the vote, Townsend requested the opportunity to address the convention floor. The minutes recorded his words, words that have resonated throughout the years as urban Blacks struggled to eat and Black farmers had their land stolen from them. Townsend's remarks were not only cogent, they were prophetic: Self-reliance was the key to liberation. Townsend was not advocating that Blacks should be farmers. Rather, he argued Blacks needed to address basic needs in order to be able to elevate the race. In the decades since his remarks, we can see how the lack of control of the Black communities' basic needs for access to food, malnutrition, and poor health have affected progress; from the stealing of Black farmer's land to the current food deserts (lack of access to quality food) in the urban area have been a factor to effectively keep millions of people in the Black community in poverty and unable to scale the ladder out.

... he thanked the committee for bringing in that report-it was just what we wanted; just what this Convention ought to send out to the world; he believed that our people would have to turn their attention to Agriculture before they would ever be an elevated people; he spoke of the great evil in our people's clustering about the large cities, and picking up just what they could get to do, and never having any thing [sic] permanent; he had lived in some of those cities, and had seen much to convince him of the bad policy of so clustering about them; he said he hoped, as he doubted not, the report would be unanimously adopted.[12]

The 1843 convention minutes clearly demonstrate Townsend's organizational and writing skills. Townsend's 1843 Convention experience provided important tools for future work during the remainder of his life.

While working in Albany, Townsend attempted to continue his formal education, applying to Brown University and Colby (formerly Waterville) College. Black newspapers in the Boston area were routinely reporting the efforts of Blacks to gain admissions to white institutions. Schools such as: Williams, Amherst, Bowdoin, Dartmouth, Columbia, and Lafayette College were among those schools having policies of not admitting qualified Black students at that time. The *Liberator,* reported in 1845, without mentioning Townsend by name, that a Black man had studied for the entrance exams at Brown and was denied admission. The reason reported was thought to be the fear of the loss of southern patronage, and the withdrawal of southern students if a colored man became a student at the institution.

Townsend then applied to Waterville (Colby) College, in September of 1845. Given the political climate, Townsend's effort to simply enroll at Colby was met with controversy. He was accepted with a caveat, that if he did anything that resulted in serious injury to the College, he would be immediately expelled. Townsend's presence at Colby is documented. While there, he joined the Erosophian Adelphi Society, a literary society at Colby, as well as literary, debating, and social clubs. During this period, he was very proud to become a Mason, reaching the highest levels in the organization. He remained a much respected Mason all of his life.

In 1847, Townsend spent the summer in the South preaching. As a free, educated, Black male preaching in the South, during that time there still existed inherent dangers to his life. The 'cloud' of rumor and innuendo had returned. It was rumored he had spent his preaching earnings drinking and gambling. Returning, Townsend spoke at the Colored Men's Temperance Convention in Great Barrington, Ma. in 1848.[13]

Colby cut all ties with Townsend...forced him to immediately leave the premises before nightfall...none of the other students who may have accompanied Townsend were expelled. This representation of Townsend does not seem plausible, that a man who would risk his life to go slave state to teach his Black brethren would subsequently squander that hard earned money drinking and gambling.

After his failed attempts to obtain a degree, Townsend's public life focused on his activism as an abolitionist, journalist, preacher, suffragist, teacher, and advocate for Black legal rights from New York to California. Townsend was to spend his life working for and on behalf of the freedom, equality, and dignity of Black people.

Townsend's journalism career emerged in 1848 in New York City, with the creation of a monthly magazine called the *Spirit of the Age*. The Black periodical instructed its readers to direct, "all communications be sent to the General Agent J.L. Townsend of No. 61 John Street New York, New York." The purpose of the publication was to advocate for the rights of those not included in the Declaration of Independence. Black abolitionist newspapers were the primary source of information concerning the efforts of Blacks and their friends to abolish slavery in the United States, prior to the Civil War. Townsend's voice reporting on those actions in the struggle was often found in abolitionist papers. *Spirit of the Age*, appears not to have survived past its first issue.

Townsend went on to publish the *Hyperion*, also short-lived. As editor, Townsend argued Black cultural nationhood was a necessary prerequisite to political and social equality. The *Hyperion* was described at the time as, "a gratifying exception to the mass of papers started in the country by Black people, both in regards to its size and ability."[14]

Finding opportunities elsewhere, in 1849[15] Townsend sailed to California in a group with several Black men who went there during the Gold Rush. He quickly established himself as a leading voice of the Black community in San Francisco. It is not clear if he established the first Masonic Lodge in San Francisco on that trip, but he was a member of it while there.

Townsend, and his colleagues, organized the San Francisco Athenaeum in July of 1853, to focus energy on fighting for equal legal status for the Negroes of California. Despite the small Black population in San Francisco in the 1850s, the Athenaeum attracted 70 members. The organization acquired a two-story brick building having a library and reading rooms. These provided opportunities to engage in political discourse and debates, as well as access to books and national newspapers. Subscriptions to anti-slavery newspapers such as, the *Liberator* or *The Northern Star,* kept communities abreast of events and the progress towards full equality for all Blacks.[16]

The first California Colored Convention was organized in 1855. As in New York, Townsend was an active participant and organizer of the Colored Conventions in California. His experience with the New York Conventions served as a model for a leadership role in organizing the California conventions. A key figure at the 1855, 1856, and 1857 State Colored Conventions, Townsend was chairman of a statewide Black executive committee. The focus of the 1855 convention was twofold. One was to petition the California Legislature to change the law to allow the testimony of 'colored people' in Courts of justice. And the second focus was to improve educational opportunities for the 'colored population'. Townsend was a leading member of the convention; and a member of the rules and business committees. He reported and authored several resolutions. The minutes of the convention recorded some of his thoughts on the issue of 'coloreds' being called as witnesses in Court proceedings:

"I deny that the pitiful support which the law offers can be called a *protection*. Are we heard before the bar of justice? Are we recognized as having souls, and comprehending the nature and responsibility of an oath? "Tis but a few months since a negro was stabbed in the streets of San Francisco, in the presence of twenty witnesses. The murderer was a Spanish man, he was arrested, and discharged on bail. On the day of his trial his counsel ridiculed the idea of his being punished, and said he had '*only killed a nigger*' who attempted to strike him down." What was the result? The murderer was cleared, and in a few hours he was walking the streets openly. There is indeed a semblance of protection, but it is not real."[17]

In response to calls by the Athenaeum members and the 1855 convention attendees, Townsend helped establish the first Black newspaper in California, *Mirror of the Times*. He edited it from 1856 to 1858 as a platform for the equal rights campaign.[18]

Townsend wrote of his impressions of California and they have survived.
"I have become so much of a Californian, that the refinement of the Eastern States would almost present a novelty to me. San Francisco has arisen from a miserable village of a few huts to become a great city, covering areas of some six square miles; and it is now the fourth among the great commercial emporiums of the Union, all within the short space of six years, showing a spirit of energy that is unsurpassed in the world's history.

California, to use a vulgar phrase, has in a great measure, ('caved in,') become like the older States; her palmy days are numbered! The poor man's chance is like the money on the Monti Bank, very uncertain. We are overrun with hordes of Chinamen and Spaniards, who have reduced wages to almost New York prices. The country is full of speculators the hirelings of the rich in the Eastern States, who monopolize all the avenues that open with any favorable prospects for the poor man.

As to the colored people who are always poor, they are scarcely recognized among the human family in this country. We have no vote, no oath against a white person, no protection against the insults and brutal barbarity of the common street loafers and vagabonds, of which numbers there is not a few; yet there is a good state of public sentiment in our behalf in this city. We are subject, it is true, to most degrading laws; but here we meet with but few insults from the better class of the community.

The colored people here are very active and energetic. They are in almost every class of business, from the highest to the lowest. Some are doing a good business, while others are getting along very poorly. It is the height of my ambition to see colored men take a bold and decided position before the world a stand upon the platform of truth and justice, and act like men. It will command respect from our most inveterate enemies, and eventually obtain our rights."[19]

Townsend returned to New York City, and then to Rochester, at the end of the 1850s resuming his journalistic career writing for the *Anglo-African Magazine.* He was asked to edit *Frederick Douglass' Paper* during Douglass' 1859 tour of Europe. He continued to fight for Black voting rights as a member of the New York State Suffrage Association, and secretary of the 1858 Black Suffrage Convention.

A rare glimpse of Townsend's character by a person who knew him is found in the abolitionist papers.

"...Mr. J.H.T., formerly editor of the Hyperion, a literary periodical of considerable merit, which had an ephemeral existence here some seven or eight years ago. Brother T was educated in one of the Eastern colleges, and was, I believe, destined to the ministry. He came to this city about ten years ago, a tall, sedate, prim, puritanical, intellectual looking young man. We soon took the starch out of him, i.e., his Puritanism, and transformed him from an embryo country parson to a regular New York businessman. A happy transformation."

Townsend and other Black abolitionists viewed the Civil War in apocalyptic terms—an epic confrontation between the forces of liberty and slavery, the fate of humanity in the balance. As an example of their views was the reaction to Governor Horatio Seymour's reluctance to enlist Black troops in New York. The group issued a manifesto on the meaning of the war. The document which was drafted by a committee consisting of: P. B. Randolph, *Jonas H. Townsend*, N. B. Thompson, Peyton Harris, Benjamin F. Randolph, and Isaac Deyo rejected the notion of the war as a narrow "fratricidal conflict", and portrayed it as a cataclysmic struggle to determine the fate of civilization and human progress. It warned that "failure to end slavery would inaugurate" "a reign of horror as never yet has been known on earth."[20]

He was appointed to the Customs' House on the New York City docks, a respected, well-paid, and coveted position.[21] In 1863 Townsend returned to Albany, New York, and as previously mentioned he was one of the authors of the Manifesto of the Colored Citizens of the State of New York in July of 1863. The manifesto was a reaction to New York Governor Seymour's reluctance to enlist Black soldiers from New York in the Civil War.

On March 6, 1860, at the Hood African-American Methodist Episcopal Church in Oyster Bay Long Island, Townsend was married to Miss Clara Seabry of Port Washington, NY.[22]

Moving to Waco, Texas, in early 1870, among other things, Townsend became District Administrator of Freedman Schools, in addition to being the Principal of and teacher at the Freedman School in Waco.[23] He continued to be active in politics. In 1871, he was elected to represent the Second Congressional District of Texas at the Southern State Convention.[24] He was selected as a Republican presidential elector in 1872.[25]

Townsend had, years earlier, proudly become a Mason.[26] He carried on his membership wherever he lived. A Masonic Lodge was just being organized when Townsend arrived in Waco, Texas (1869/70). No records of Masonic membership from this period in Texas survive.[27] We presume that Townsend would have been a member of the closest Masonic lodge he could find in Texas. Generally, the Freemasons were defined as an organization whose members value moral, spiritual, self-improvement, and charitable work in their communities., believing that "freedom of thought, speech, and actions belong to every man."[28]

Townsend held many very important positions in the various lodges he belonged to as he moved around the country, such as: worshipful Master of Olive Branch No. 5 in San Francisco; and Right Worshipful Jonas H. Townsend, Grand Master, (the Grand Master is the head of the Lodge and the leader of all Masons in a Masonic jurisdiction) of the Most Worshipful United Grand Lodge.[29] He was also one of the signatories on the formation of the Adelphic Union Lodge charter, issued by the United Grand Lodge of the State of New York, May 11, 1863.[30]

Townsend's leadership roles in the Masons is further evidence of his stature and character in any organization he was associated. Townsend's life demonstrated his work to transform the Black community and the American landscape into a nation that provided equal access and equality to all of its citizens. A goal and struggle that persists to this day.

Townsend died in Galveston, Texas in, 1872.[31] Townsend's obituary contained a glowing tribute to the man.

Jonas H. Townsend we would state that he was one of the most talented Black men in the United States. He resided in this city from 1849-1859 (San Francisco) and Editor of the Mirror of the Times in conjunction with the late William H.

Newby- it being the first newspaper published by Black men in this city, existing from 1855-1858, and did good service in the advocacy of the repeal of the laws then existing in this State preventing Black persons from testifying in courts of justice against white persons. Mr. Townsend during this period, was Worshipful Master of Olive Branch Lodge. No.5, of this city. He subsequently went to New York, became an active Mason, and was elected Grand master of the United Grand Lodge, Free and Accepted Masons of that State; after the close of the rebellion, he was induced to go to Galveston, Texas, to take charge of a school, as principal where he held that position until just before his death, Mr. Townsend was a ripe scholar, a fine gentleman, and was the leading spirit of the State Conventions held by colored citizens in this State in 1855-6-7-8 for the repeal of the disabling testimony laws, and was one of the principal founders of the Athenaeum Library Company, composed of Black men, and which was in successful operation in this city, from 1853 to the Frazier River, Victoria and British Columbia exodus in 1858. We extend our condolence to the brethren of the United Grand Lodge of New York, for the demise of Past Grand Master Jonas H. Townsend.[32]

An image of Jonas Holland Townsend has not been found. An unbiased description of Townsend is found on his application for a passport when he traveled to California. Given the time, during the height of the 1850 Fugitive Slave law, passage by boat may have been for personal safety reasons. Traveling by boat necessitated passage through what is now known as the Panama Canal.

The description was: "Age 30, height 6 feet, complexion-dark, eyes-black, face-oval, nose-straight, mouth-middling and chin-round."[33]

In contrast, the physical description of Townsend offered a

different picture than referenced in the Colgate narrative as a "Sable Son of Africa", "Big Black", "Colored Brethren."

Jonas Holland Townsend, the first Black man to attend Colgate, used his pen, his intellect, his voice, and his organizational skills to influence the transformation of the racial landscape in America. His life's work was dedicated to the moral calling of freeing the enslaved, fighting for social justice, and equality for Black men and women of this nation. His actions or words were never on the 'wrong side of history.' His words were prophetic and served as a blueprint in the continued fight for social and equal justice over the last two centuries. His legacy may have been in the shadows of Colgate and American history, but his life and deeds have had a profound effect on the trajectory of building a more 'perfect nation.'

✦ CHAPTER IV ✦
Henry Livingston Simpson

...Mr. Henry L. Simpson,...is every inch a man and a gentlemen-whose acquaintance we deem an honor, and of whose friendship we are proud...

Frederick Douglass Paper, April 8, 1853

Henry Livingston Simpson, Class of 1853 and 1855

At the age of 23, Henry Livingston Simpson enrolled in the Grammar School (also known as, the Academy) at what is now Colgate in 1847.[34] He established a reputation for himself in the larger world and received high praise from Frederick Douglass.[35] Simpson entered the Academy program and after his success there was promoted into the University where he earned his Advanced Bachelors (A.B.) in 1853 and his Theological degree in 1855, thus becoming the first Black person to do so at Colgate.

> Henry L. Simpson, is a young man of African descent—of decidedly dark complexion – about 24 years of age – of medium size – an exceedingly modest demeanor, an easy and graceful elocution and a style of speaking direct and forcible...[36]

Simpson was the fifth of nine children born to Francis and Elizabeth Simpson, of Clermont, New York who were "colored domestics of Gen. Livingston of Clermont."[37]   Later, the family moved up the Hudson Valley, and then to Schenectady, in the center of a sophisticated, active abolitionist community involved in the movement from its earliest days, including the Underground Railroad.

Francis Simpson, Henry's father, was a Baptist Minister by profession and a barber by trade. He was a prominent minister becoming a respected advocate for Black men and women, both enslaved and free. Barbers were among the elite businessmen in their communities, and 'the secret keepers' with respect to the protection of Underground Railroad intelligence. Barbershops were deemed a common, respectable, and safe gathering places where men could meet and, in many instances, strategize abolition activities. Francis Simpson, like Townsend, diligently maintained his efforts to lobby for improving the condition of free and formerly enslaved citizens, which included organizing and attending the New York Colored Conventions.[38] The well-recognized abolitionist, Senator William H. Seward and his Black coachman, Nicholas Bogart were also very active in the capitol district abolition activities.

In the years between Jonas Holland Townsend's leaving the campus and Simpson's arrival, the faculty and administration's views on the formation of anti-slavery societies or permitting students to engage in anti-slavery activities had not changed. As noted earlier, the faculty denied students the right to form an Anti-Slavery Society on three separate occasions (1831, 1837 & 1841). In 1846, White student, George Gavin Richie, who started the first Colgate school newspaper, *The Hamilton Student*, wanted to publish an editorial on the issue of slavery, however, he was directed to not publish the editorial. Despite this directive, Richie published the editorial and as a result was expelled for his defiance of the faculty. Meanwhile, the slavery debate continued to intensify across the state and the country, and it was against this backdrop that Simpson attended and completed his course of study at Colgate.

At the time of Simpson's enrollment, students were often supported by scholarships or working on campus. Simpson's records show he received scholarship funding from the Jackson Bequest during his years at Colgate. Life as a Black student at Colgate from 1847-1855 is unclear and the few references of Simpson's existence at Colgate are through the lens of the White community. A series of exchanges in newspapers provide the context on how Whites felt about having Simpson in their presence. His presence in the White space was objectified by those who abhorred it, as well as by those who were supportive of his presence.

In February of 1853 (months before Simpson graduated, but several years after his arrival) comments were recorded in the Religious Herald:

> A big Black negro is now in this institution, reciting, debating and eating with white students...I attended the literary societies...and heard this negro perhaps I ought to give the gentlemen his title, Prince Henry, as he claims to be descended from atavis res [something like born of Kings past], read in a loud, course, bluff voice...

There was also a comment from a southern student who questioned Simpson's right to be enrolled.

> ...why is this negro received into their classes, and placed, in every respect, upon an equality with the white students. [39]

There were also students who defended Simpson's presence on campus as evidenced in the words of a student identified as "Junior":

> ...the simple facts...individual...is somewhat below the medium size, and competent judges...there is little to choose as to *whiteness* between his complexion[40] & that of 'Herndon'. It is, at most, but a slight shade darker, and his cranial surmounting are not much more inclined to deviate from right angles.[41]

European scientists had developed a system of studying the

cranial size of men to differentiate and justify their belief and claim the inferiority of darker hued humans from those with lighter 'white' skin tones.[42] Junior continues his back-handed defense of Simpson's presence on campus by questioning if his 'unassuming modesty' was a "deliberate ploy in order to blend in and obtain the goal of the education and degrees."[43] Junior's defense of Simpson continues, noting that Simpson was "a candidate for the Baptist ministry, a *man, a Christian, and a* gentlemen, every inch of him."

Like Herndon, Junior objectified Simpson's body and intellect. Despite Junior's seemingly positive tone, he fails to humanize Simpson until half way through his response when he calls Simpson by name.

> . . . no apologies are due pro-slavery men...for having such a man as *Henry L. Simpson* among our students...but it is uncontestably [sic] true, that African blood mingles with the Anglo Saxon, in the veins of Mr. Simpson...[44]

It is telling that the defense of Simpson's presence on campus consist solely of one-way references based on a White students' perceptions of Simpson's appearance, and its effect on those who observed him. In this respect, Simpson was viewed as little more than a racial object. It also provides a glimpse of what it must have felt like for Simpson as one of the few free Black men in the country seeking higher education at an institution that still defended the slave oligarchy.

After obtaining his degree in 1853 and with the support of donations, Simpson joined the theological class at Colgate.

When Simpson graduated from Colgate with his A.B. in 1853, he was one of only nine students. Simpson received public recognition in the local papers for his graduation speech on *Wilberforce*.[45] The news article reads:

> We can not from year to year go into an analysis of several exercises of Commencements. We shall particularly allude

to only one of the young men. There was great applause at the announcement of the name of Henry L. Simpson. The reason was obvious when he appeared. He is of African descent.- His physiognomy and entire personal appearance are good...The rareness of such occurrences led us thus to notice this address, and we do it without insinuating that it was in advance of others, or even equal to several of them in ability.

Still another report appeared in a separate newspaper:

Henry L. Simpson, the speaker, is a young man of Africa descent.... His subject was "Wilberforce" and a...theme he could not have chosen...we were subsequently informed that he is quite a favorite with the professors and students and with the community generally, having won their confidence and esteem by the modesty of his demeanor and the purity and propriety of his life.[46]

The journalist's belief that Simpson did not choose his topic suggests several possibilities: a) The journalist believed that Simpson was incapable of choosing a topic of his own, b) Ignoring the impact such a topic could have on Simpson, or c) The journalist's inherent bias with respect to the intellectual capacity of a Black man. Speaking as one of the early Black men to receive a college degree in the United States, Simpson's choice to speak on Wilberforce revealed something of the trajectory of Simpson's life's work.

William Wilberforce, an English politician, who was a leading voice in the movement to stop the slave trade was also a devoted Christian, who wrote several books on the practical aspects of Christianity. Simpson prepared, and delivered, another graduation speech when graduating with his theology degree in 1855. His speech was entitled: "Africa—Its Destiny." It is not known why Simpson chose this topic. Perhaps it was the donation by the Society for Inquiry, or the University encouraging graduates to do missionary work. Other than his brief time in Canada with his second wife, Emmilie Shadd, Simpson spent his entire life and career in Ohio, Tennessee, and Georgia. There were no known trips to Africa.

Simpson, as Townsend before him, used his gifts and skills in his life work in the Black communities in this country and in Canada. The presence of an educated, articulate, and free Black would have been an inspiration. In 1856, Henry Simpson interviewed for a position as minister of the colored First Baptist Church of Cincinnati. The church was known for its sustained efforts to assist enslaved persons. Cincinnati, separated from the slave state Kentucky on the Ohio River, and was one of the first ports of entry for many freedom seekers from the South. The free Black and many White communities in Cincinnati were actively involved in assisting freedom seekers headed to freedom either in northern states or Canada. Union Baptist Church had a dedicated fund that was used to assist enslaved persons who were able to reach Ohio. An example of the church's commitment is when it provided money for Rev. William P. Newman, a predecessor pastor to Simpson, for his studies at Oberlin College. Newman was offered the position as pastor in 1848, but left with the passage of the 1850 Fugitive Slave Law and accepted a position with a church in Chatham, Canada. There were several pastors after Newman before the church asked Simpson to come and preach for a week. Following his visit, a vote was taken to offer Simpson the position of pastor. Although accepted as the new pastor, Simpson was told he needed to be ordained by his home church before taking charge of Union Baptist Church.[47] Simpson was ordained in 1856 at his home church, the First Baptist Church of Schenectady, and among those in attendance was Colgate Professor Eaton. The local papers reported at the time that Simpson was the first "of his race" to take a full course at Madison University.[48]

Simpson returned to New York in 1857 to marry Harriet E. Bogart of Auburn, New York. Harriet was the daughter of Nicolas and Harriet Bogart. Harriet's mother worked in the Seward household, and her father Nicolas Bogart, was the coachman for Seward both in Albany and Washington, DC. The Bogart's were a prominent family in the Auburn Black community known as 'New Guinea,' and had a long relationship with the Seward family of Auburn. Nicolas was instrumental in bridging the Black and White communities involved in the Underground Railroad through his standing in his community and his long-term relationship with Seward. Nicolas Bogart was a prominent man in New York and served as the delegate from Albany at the Colored Conventions in New York and the church sexton.

William Henry Seward was a lawyer, a New York State Senator, the New York State Governor, a US senator from New York, and the US Secretary of State under President Lincoln. Seward as an abolitionist, used his law license to defend cases involving the 1850 Fugitive Slave Laws.

It is unknown how or where Simpson met Harriet Bogart; however, it may have been through their family's obvious stature having hailed from prominent families in central New York or their work in the abolitionist movement. He and Harriet were married in 1857, their wedding guests included all levels of Auburn's Black and White society, including most of the Seward family. Seward's wife, Frances wrote to her husband about the wedding:

Hattie Bogart viz Simpson had a beautiful wedding and party... The church was filled-about 100 guests, white & colored....[49]

Harriet joined Simpson in Cincinnati where he pastored the Union Baptist Church for 4 years, with an annual salary of $400. During his years at Union Baptist, the church prospered by increasing the membership. Simpson resigned in 1860. The minutes from the church are silent as to the cause of his resignation.[50] It was noted that in the 1850s and 1860s in Ohio, the Rev. Charles Satchell, the Rev. David Nickens, the Rev. W.P. Newman, the Rev. James Poindexter, and the Rev. H.L. Simpson were the leading clergymen in the Colored Baptist churches.[51]

Simpson's wife Harriett died after the birth of their daughter, Mary, who went on to live with her Bogart grandparents in Auburn. Following Harriett's death, Simpson accepted an appointment from the American Missionary Association to the Shrewsbury Baptist

Church[52] in Shrewsbury, Kent, Ontario.[53] The area had been settled and developed by enslaved and free Blacks from early in the 1800s. As early as 1815, the Lieutenant Governor offered Black veterans of the War of 1812 land grants. In 1834, the British Parliament abolished slavery in their colonies which included Canada, making it a place where free Blacks could build community and help those free and enslaved Blacks migrating to Canada. After the Fugitive Slave Act of 1850, the migration of freedom seekers to Canada increased significantly.[54] It has been estimated between 30,000 to 40,000 freedom seekers and those born free migrated to Canada. In Canada, Henry met most of the immediate Shadd family who were all committed abolitionists. Mary Shadd, a journalist with the *The Provincial Freeman*, and Emmilie's sister, was a vocal advocate and urged many Blacks to migrate to Canada. The family had been living for years in West Chester, Pennsylvania and Delaware, where education for Black children was common before moving to Canada, as a result of the Fugitive Law of 1850.[55]

Henry married Emmilie Shadd, a college educated teacher and eventually had four children.[56] Their first child, a girl, was named Harriet.[57] While traveling in Canada, William Wells Brown (a leading Black abolitionist), had the opportunity to hear Rev. Simpson preach. He wrote about Simpson's sermon stating that is was well received and eloquently delivered. He mentioned Rev. Simpson's pedigree, and that he was an honor to his race, calling him the most "polished preacher, colored or white, that he had heard in years."[58]

According to his Colgate biography, Simpson was listed as being in Memphis, Tennessee in 1865-1866 with the Baptist Free Missionary Society, the anti-slavery Baptist splinter group. However, after the sudden death of Rev. Newman in Cincinnati, Simpson was called to return to Cincinnati where he took over the pastoral duties once again from 1866-1869. Simpson left a second and final time to become the minister of the Second Baptist Church of Savannah, Georgia from 1871 until his death in 1881.[59] The Second Baptist Church of Savannah was formed in 1802. The church was made famous as the site where General Sherman's order, which was commonly referred to as the '40 acres and a mule' order, was read by General Saxon. The order provided that 400,000 acres of land across the low country and coastal islands, that had been confiscated from the Confederates, would be distributed to the recently freed enslaved. Predictably, the order was rescinded after more than 40,000 families had settled on the land, making them ownerless sharecroppers.[60]

Under Simpson's leadership, the church membership would increase, making it the second largest 'colored' Baptist Church, with a robust membership roll at its height of over 3,000 members. Many of the Black pastors, who attended Colgate were credited with increasing the memberships of their churches. In addition to his pastoral duties, Simpson was actively involved in colored Baptists' organizations.

Simpson, as did Townsend and the others who followed them, understood the value of organization. Simpson served as the president of the American Baptist Consolidated Convention, in Richmond, Virginia from 1869-1871. The objective of the convention was the advancement of missionary work among the Black people. The conventions were held under the auspices of various organizations and provided an opportunity to exchange ideas, work collectively towards common goals, and provided power in numbers.

Rev. Henry Livingston Simpson, like Townsend before him, understood the unique position he held as an early educated Black man, and his duty to assume a role in the transformation of America by working to help freedom seekers, provide spiritual substance, organize to fight against slavery, demand equal rights for all Black people, and cultivate the narrative of the Black intellectual. Simpson, as did the Colgate men after him, understood the power of the pulpit. Their ministries and churches were the seeds for the rise and leadership of the Black church in the civil rights movement of the 20th century.

✦ CHAPTER V ✦
Freedom, Reconstruction, and a New Hope

There were approximately 4,084 lynchings from 1877 to 1930 in the 12 southern states and an additional 300 in other states.[61]

Slavery in the United States 'officially' ended with the surrender of the Confederacy at the conclusion of the Civil War, and the ratification of the Thirteenth Amendment to the US Constitution. From the moment the Europeans came to North America, the southern economy was built on the backs of the free labor of Black men, women, and children. Many of the early framers of the United States Constitution were from the gentry aristocratic class, and many were from families who held enslaved Blacks for their pecuniary benefit. Several early presidents such as Washington, Jefferson, Madison, Jackson, Van Buren, Harrison, Tyler, Polk, Taylor, Johnson, and Grant owned enslaved persons. And more than a few of the founding fathers of this country made their money and political capital from the slave oligarchy. The United States Constitution was drafted to appease and allow the southern states to count their 'Black bodies' for purposes of representation in the federal government. This enabled the early presidents to be elected from the slave states, as the Electoral College (the actual process that elects a president) favored the South. It was not only the southern states that benefited from the slave oligarchy, but the northern states did as well. From the shipbuilders and the factories in the North, the plantations of the South, the insurance industry in England, and the trade from the Caribbean and South America; the global economy thrived on the free labor of enslaved Blacks. The Civil War disrupted these systems, and a new paradigm had to rise from the ashes. As the country struggled to redefine itself, the challenge became how to 'integrate' the newly freed, uneducated, and landless Blacks, who had no visible means of support into society.

Instead of acknowledging its debt, the country chose to deny the newly freed enslaved Blacks and their descendants, the same liberties as its White citizens. A battle for equal justice and access under the law began and continues to today. Regional differences developed on how to deny equality, but the American psyche did not, and has not, accepted the Black populace as equal and entitled to the same privileges as its White citizens. The South had to be rebuilt to replace the slave culture with a new economy, infrastructure, and social structure. Alongside these events were the millions of formerly enslaved men and women who needed education, housing, jobs, and a voice in the rebuilding of the political system and economy of the South.

The Freedmen's Bureau (The Bureau of Refugees, Freedmen and Abandoned Lands Act) was formed in 1865 by Congress to assist in the transition from slavery to freedom. The Bureau created banks, hospitals, and schools for the formerly enslaved. The restructuring of the economy and the southern society as a whole was not a smooth transition, and many were resistant to integrating the millions of formerly enslaved and free Blacks into the rebuilding of the South. President Johnson, a former slaveholder, ensured the federal government's involvement with the rebuilding effort was anemic, temporary, and overshadowed by the strong resistance of the South to accept defeat. More importantly, there was resistance to move from a slave oligarchy to a society that provided the avenue for the formerly enslaved to obtain and be paid for their labor. The '40 acres and a mule' mantra was a mythical aspiration that was never realized or even seriously considered. What emerged in its place was a systematic legal, political, and social construct that would keep the formerly enslaved Black masses continuously enslaved via various *de facto* and *de jure* methods. Laws were created to imprison Black men and women for petty crimes or no crimes. Once imprisoned, the state would lease the 'convict' to various companies for pennies on the dollar to do the hard-manual work of rebuilding the southern infrastructure.[62]

Black families, in many instances, were unable to buy land, so they were forced to lease the land, and became known as tenant farmers. All of the basic, daily needs of a farmer were bought on credit against the value of the harvest at the end of the season. This system was designed to keep the family tied to the land as tenants who could never make enough money to get out of debt.

For a brief moment, the southern Black vote produced Black politicians on the local, state, and national level. Understanding the power of the vote, southern Whites systematically began to suppress the Black vote. Poll taxes, grandfather clauses, intimidation, and violence were among the many ways used to deny the Black vote and perceived rise of Black power and without the vote, White supremacy would rule. The systematic introduction of legislation, White hate groups, and societal norms created what was known as 'Jim Crow,' which worked to subjugate the Black masses of the South. White terrorism became rampant against the Black community with the rise of the Ku Klux Klan (KKK). The KKK, White mobs, and lynchings operated as a means to create fear and deny Blacks the same freedoms as their White counterparts.

Despite the iron grip of Jim Crow, Black progress was made, and the Black men who attended Colgate after the Civil War became active warriors in the fight for education and equality against this new form of oppression that replaced slavery.

Education has always been viewed as a ladder of opportunity and advancement in the American lexicon and with the end of the Civil War, and reconstruction efforts in the South, the education of the formerly enslaved took on a new urgency. Freedom schools, and what became known as 'Historically Black Colleges and Universities' (HBCUs) emerged to fill the void and educate the uneducated Black population. It was at this juncture in American education that predominately White institutions began to slowly enroll or minimally increase the number of Black students at their schools. W.E.B. Du Bois, an early graduate of a predominately White institution, did a study to determine which colleges educated Blacks attended prior to 1900. Du Bois' study on Black college graduates as of 1900 notes nine (9) Colgate graduates, which tied Colgate at #8 among predominantly White colleges on Du Bois' list.

Figure 1 - Du Bois List of Blacks at White Universities and Colleges

Among the Larger Universities:
> Harvard, 11.
> Yale, 10.
> University of Michigan, 10.
> Cornell, 8.
> Columbia, 4.
> University of Pennsylvania, 4.
> Catholic University, 3.
> University of Chicago, 2. (?)
> Leland Stanford, 2.   Total, 54.

Among Colleges of Second Rank:
> Oberlin, 128.
> University of Kansas, 16.
> Bates College, 15.
> Colgate University, 9.
> Brown, 8.
> Dartmouth, 7.
> Amherst, 7.
> Ohio State University, 7.
> Bucknell University, 7.

Colgate University was among the leaders of the predominately White schools of its size and stature that admitted Black students. After the Civil War, the number of Black students began to increase from the early days of when Jonas Townsend and Henry Simpson attended. Still small in numbers, for several years after the war there would be at least one Black per class (accurate numbers are difficult to assess, particularly if a student left before graduating). Many of these early men were formerly enslaved, unlike their predecessors Townsend and Simpson. They would, however, use their education and talents in the pulpit and classroom to become leaders in their communities. Like Townsend and Simpson, they would endeavor to help other Blacks as part of their life's work. The known list of men who attended Colgate from 1865-1900 is as follows[63]:

William Simmons' 1869 (attended but did not graduate)*
Price Alpheus Leftwich' 1875
Sterling Gardner' 1875*
Armstead Mason Newman' 1876*
Joseph Endom Jones' 1876 *
Nathaniel Vassar' 1877 *
Gilbert Raiford' 18— (exact date unknown)
Peter Verdier Hazel' 1880
Lucis Hippolyte' 1882
Castle Brewer' 1885
George Jackson' 1887
Matthew M. Gilbert' 1887, 1890*
*Formerly enslaved
 These men became part of the Black educated elite. They left their familiar surroundings and family to attend Colgate during a time when the Freedmen's Bureau, a group of northern Whites and Blacks, was organized to support Black schools and colleges in the South. These men understood and took on the challenge, of using their education and status to work toward educating the minds and souls of fellow Black men and women, who had only recently been released from their physical bondage. Still not free of the economic, social, educational, and political bondage created by generations of slavery, these men were instrumental in uplifting Black men and women.

✦ CHAPTER VI ✦
William J. Simmons, the First Post Civil-War Black Man to Attend Colgate

I wish the book to show to the world—to our oppressors and even our friends that the Negro race is still alive, and must possess more intellectual vigor than any other section of the human family...[64]

William Simmons, Men of Mark

William J. Simmons, 1867-1868

Simmons only attended for one year; therefore, he is technically not an alumnus. However, his profile is in some respects prototypical of the men who were educated at Colgate and elsewhere, after the Civil War. They were members of what was known as the 'First Generation' or as Du Bois famously called it, the 'Talented Tenth.' These men accepted the challenge and burden to use their talent, skill, and education to educate the formerly enslaved masses and to provide them with skills to grow and become productive members of the American landscape. Unfortunately, there was resistance to the efforts of the Black men and women to take their rightful place on the American economic, political, and cultural landscape and Simmons understood the importance of this historical movement.

The importance of recording the transformative narrative of the Black men who attended Colgate remains invaluable. Simmons documented the men who took on this challenge in his book, *Men of Mark*. Simmons' life provides a rare glimpse into the life of the

Black men who would lead and educate a nation, while fighting for equal justice in America. In *Men of Mark*, the introduction is a sketch of Rev. Simmons written by Henry M. Turner.

William J. Simmons was born to slave parents, Edward and Esther, in South Carolina on June 29, 1849. Turner writes of Simmons' flight to freedom:

> At an early period in his life, interested parties hurried the mother with three small children northward, without the protection of a husband or father, to begin a long siege with poverty.[65]

In his own words, Simmons wrote about his early life in a letter printed in the Anti-Slavery Reporter (Office of the Commissioner, Bureau of Refugees, Freedmen, and Abandoned Lands).

> I was born in Charleston, Louisiana County, June 29th, 1849 (into enslavement). My mother came to the north shortly after my birth, and brought me and two sisters. Since then we have lived in Philadelphia, Pennsylvania, and Bordentown, New Jersey.... I...apprenticed to a surgeon-dentist,...in Bordentown. I despaired.... I left and joined the army a private in the 41st Regiment U.S.L.I. I enlisted in Philadelphia at Camp William Penn; I served thirteen months, doing service in the 'Army of the James' and participated in the battles of Hatches Run, Petersburg, &c.- in fact, all through the last spring campaign of the war my brigade figured conspicuously. Simmons was present at the surrender of General Lee. After the war I was dispatched to Texas, where I did garrison duty in Edinburg on the Rio Grande River. Discharged at New Orleans, I hastened home.[66]

On the advice of his pastor, and with the financial support of the New Jersey State Educational Society, Simmons entered

Colgate University in 1867.[67] We are treated to a privileged glimpse of his experience through his own eyes in the lines of a letter he wrote describing his time at Colgate (a rare first person narrative):

> I entered the grammar school of Madison University in Hamilton, New York. When I got there the junior academic class was two terms ahead, so took private lessons in Latin and Greek, and made sufficient progress to enter the class in the following fall. Before I had gone there I had attended no school in my life. I learned the English branches at home under the instruction of an uncle.... At the close of my academic course I entered the Freshman class at Rochester University, at Rochester, New York. Not liking Rochester, I left, and have come to Howard University. I wished from the beginning of my course to enter a college among coloured students, but my pastor overruled my wishes, and all this while I have been isolated from my people. I can complain of no ill-treatment, but I left both institutions because I was the only coloured student there.[68]

According to Turner, Simmons graduated from Howard University in 1873 (an HBCU in Washington, D.C.) and he took Horace Greeley's advice, and went west to Arkansas.[69] With the idea of making Arkansas his home, he secured a State certificate from the Honorable Superintendent of Education, J. C. Corbin, but soon returned to Washington, D.C. and taught at Hillsdale.[70] After marriage, he returned to the South and became an ordained deacon and was licensed to preach.[71] He dabbled in politics and taught school in Washington, D.C. before settling in Lexington, Kentucky to accept the pastorate of the First Baptist Church. In Kentucky, he became the president of the Normal and Theological Institution, a school under the auspices of the General Association of the Colored Baptist of Kentucky. As Turner writes:

Few men of Professor Simmons ability and standing would

have been willing to risk their future in an enterprise like the Normal and Theological Institution; an enterprise without capital and but a few friends. But it can be truly said of Professor Simmons, that he has proven himself master of the situation. The school had been talked of for nearly twenty years but no one ever dreamed of its possibility. When he was elected president, every cloud vanished, and the sunshine of success could be seen on every side. Some of his students already ranked among the foremost preachers, teachers and orators of the State. As an educator, he has likely no superiors. Discarding specialism in education, he claims that ideal manhood and womanhood cannot be narrowed down to any one sphere of action, but that the whole being—every faculty with which we are endowed—must receive proper development (an educational philosophy that would be shared and followed by man Colgate men who succeeded Simmons). No boy or girl comes under his influence without feeling a desire to become useful and great. He infuses inspiration into the least ambitious. He has a knack of 'drawing out' all there is within. No flower within his reach 'wastes its sweetness on the desert air.[72]

Simmons demonstrated great involvement in his community and Turner describes the diversity of Simmons commitment to community.

Dr. Simmons activities are prominently identified with the most affairs of the race. Several years he has been chairman of the executive committee of the 'State Convention of the Colored Men of Kentucky.'[73]

Simmons was extremely concerned about the refusal of White Southern Baptists to recognize their Black counterparts. The Civil War did little to change the attitude of the Southern Baptists and the White Southern Baptists were not as welcoming of the

Black Baptists, and this attitude prompted the National Baptist Organization to vocally decry this treatment. Simmons and other Black ministers advocated the establishing of African missionaries to help unify the denomination.

Simmons assumed the leadership of Normal and Theological Institute of Louisville, Kentucky at a time when the institution was floundering; however, under his leadership the school flourished. As an educator, Simmons believed his responsibility should be to inspire students and he was credited with being able to 'draw out' all that was within a student. He found the usefulness of each student and worked to train the students to apply their talents. The Normal and Theological Institute of Louisville, Kentucky was posthumously renamed Simmons College of Kentucky, to honor the impact of his tenure.

Simmons wrote *Men of Mark: Eminent, Progressive, and Rising,* which was a compilation of biographical material on 177 prominent Black men from across the United States. In the preface, Simmons describes his commitment to the education and assisting of Black men and women:

> I desire that the book shall be a help to students, male and female, in the way of information concerning our great names.... It is a suitable book, it is hoped, to be put into the hands of intelligent, aspiring young people everywhere, that they might see the means and manners of men's elevation, and by this be led to undertake the task of going through high schools and colleges. IF the persons herein mentioned could rise to the exalted stations which they have and do now hold, what is there to prevent any young man or woman from achieving greatness? Many, yea, nearly all these came from the loins of slave fathers, and were the babes of women in bondage, and themselves felt the leaden hand slavery on their own bodes; but whether slaves or not, they suffered with their brethren because of color. That 'sum of human villainies' did not crush out the life and manhood of the race.

I wish the book to show to the world—to our oppressors and even our friends that the Negro race is still alive, and must possess more intellectual vigor than any other section of the human family, or else how could they be crushed as slaves in all these years since 1620, and yet grappling with abstruse problems in Euclid and difficult classics, and master them? Was ever such a thing seen in another people? Whence these lawyers, doctors, authors, editors, divines, lecturers, linguists, scientists, college president and such, in one quarter of a century?[74]

The book was a best seller and the single largest collection of Black biographies of its time. Therefore, it was no surprise that several Colgate Black men would be listed in Simmons's book. (Appendix - of Simmons' sermons titled "The Lord's Supper" published in 1890.)

✦ CHAPTER VII ✦
The First Formerly Enslaved Men to Attend Colgate

Some brother asks what I mean by 'putting him in'. It was putting me in a place known as the whipping room, and on the floor of that room were rings. The individual would be laid down, his hands and feet stretched out and fastened in the rings, and a great big man would stand over him and flog him.

Rev. Armstead Mason Newman, Class of 1876

The increase in the number of educational institutions for Black people was a direct result of the mandate under the Federal Reconstruction Act, and the efforts of various religious and civic organizations. The American Baptist Home Mission Society (ABHMS) supported Black schools throughout the South and the involvement of ABHMS provided opportunities for several of the men who attended Colgate after the war. From the 1870s until the end of the century, several formerly enslaved men who attended Colgate via schools in Virginia were supported by the Baptist Home Mission Society or their patrons: Sterling Gardner, Armstead Mason Newman, Joseph Endom Jones, David Nathaniel Vassar, and Matthew Gilbert. These men traveled from the South to attend Colgate, to study and return to be part of the transformation of the South, and to educate other Black people.

When the Emancipation Proclamation of 1863 immediately

freed thousands of men and women, the ABHMS understood the need and opportunity to meet the spiritual and educational needs of the newly freed men and women by building churches and schools.[75]

It was a natural path for men who were supported and/or educated by the ABHMS benefactors or institutions to study at Colgate. Colgate, a respected Baptist college was a natural fit to provide the academic and spiritual training of these men. Furthermore, Samuel Colgate's relationship to Colgate and his leadership positions in the ABHMS may have been the connection between the southern schools funded by the Society and the path to continuing study at Colgate.

One such institution that educated several Colgate men before attending Colgate was Virginia Union University. The school opened shortly after the Civil War and the surrender at Richmond in April 1865. In November 1865, the Mission Society began holding classes for the Richmond Theological School for Freedmen, one of the four institutions forming the Union that gave the University its name. The Mission Society proposed a National Theological Institute designed primarily to provide education and training for Black men to enter into the Baptist ministry. A branch known as the Wayland Seminary was set up in Washington, D.C. with the mission to offer courses and programs at the college, high school, and preparatory levels. In Richmond, at the sight of the old Lumpkin Jail, (once used as a holding pen/punishment and breaking center for enslaved people), became the site of the Richmond Theological School for Freedmen. In 1867, under the direction of the ABHMS, Nathaniel Colver leased the land and Lumpkin Jail buildings and opened the Richmond Theological School for Freedmen. Colver remained for one year and after his departure the school was known as Colver Institute, in honor of Dr. Nathaniel Colver.[76]

The brick building that housed the school had formerly been the jail that was used to imprison and punish disobedient enslaved Blacks. The windows had metal bars, and there was a room with whipping rings. Ironically, as will be described later, Armstead Newman Mason had been punished in the Lumpkin's jail as a child. Colver Institute was incorporated in 1876 under the laws of the State of Virginia as Richmond Institute. It was the first Institute in the South to employ Black people teaching assistants and faculty (several men who had attended the school before attending Colgate returned to teach). In 1886, it was re-established as Richmond Theological Seminary and in 1899 Wayland Seminary and Richmond Theological Seminary merged and became Virginia Union University.[77]

After the war a group of men from the schools established by the American Baptists Home Mission Society made their way to Colgate: Sterling Gardner, Armstead Mason Newman, Joseph Endom Jones, David Nathaniel Vassar, and Matthew W. Gilbert

Sterling Gardner, Class of 1875

Gardner was born enslaved in Augusta, Georgia and was one of the first students at Richmond Institute. The ABHMS financially supported his education and he was the first student from the Richmond Institute to attend Colgate. His excellent record of achievement while at Colgate was called *A feather in Richmond's Cap*, as stated by the corresponding secretary of the ABHMS in a letter dated July 19, 1869 to his mentor and tutor Rev. Corey.[78] His academic success opened the doors for several to follow him.

The archives at Virginia Union University have several letters Gardner sent to Dr. Corey while attending Colgate. Dr. Corey supported and helped Gardner secure admission and financing to attend Colgate and the letters provide a narrative of the life of a Black man at Colgate before the turn of the 20th century.[79]

Prior to attending Colgate, not only did Gardner study at the Richmond Institute, he also taught at Richmond. He was sixteen when he traveled to Hamilton, New York to attend Colgate; however, it is not clear why Gardner was sent to complete his studies there. Gardner's enrollment may have been precipitated by the fact that Colgate had already established itself as a Baptist college of distinction or perhaps it was Samuel Colgate's association with the ABHMS and the work they were doing.

Gardner wrote to his mentor and tutor, Rev. Corey, about his attempts at finding students and his desire to teach. In one of his letters he expresses his loneliness at the death of his sister, a loneliness that is palpable in the letters he wrote while studying at Colgate. When Gardner arrived on campus, there was one other student, Armstead Mason Newman, who studied at Wayland Seminary in Washington, D.C. before enrolling at Colgate (The Academy) from 1869-1871. The reference in one of Gardner's letters about taking a room with Mr. Newman most likely refers to Armstead Mason Newman. Newman graduated Colgate in 1876. The letter mentions his fellow Richmond Institute classmates and how they are managing financially and what they do to support themselves...

> I had the notices of my school read in the different churches and asked the pastors to recommend me, but when the time to open school came, no one was present. I went to the schoolroom three mornings to see if anyone would come, but no body [sic] came.... I have received a letter from home last week stating that my sister (name Susan) was dead, she was a member of Springfield Church. We both were baptized the same day. I was very home sick, and have not gotten over it yet. I feel very sorry, but she was willing to go, and I thank God that He took one, who was ready to go. I can't express with my pen how I feel because I love my sisters, and just think I will not see her face again on this earth.[80]

In a letter to Rev. Cory on May 7, 1870, Gardner gives his impression of the environment and the habits of fellow classmates at Colgate and his lack of money:

> I am well and hearty, but I cannot say I am pleased with the school. Things are very loose. There is no rule to govern the

students. They go out or come in when they please. They stamp and hollorr (holler) in the hall at night, and also out in the yard. They just have their own fun. The unoccupied rooms are **very** dirty.

The window and door framers and washboard are in such a state, that in most every room students, had to have them painted. Over some of the hall doors, glasses are broken. The steps are made of stones; they are tumbling down; if you are not very careful you will fall.

So I only have money enough to pay for board one month, and school bill of this term.... So unless I can get some money by the last of this month I will not have any where to board. Love to all.[81]

In his May 15, 1870 letter to Dr. Corey, Gardner worried he might have offended Dr. Corey for complaining and not being grateful. Gardner also reiterated the shortcomings of the physical environment of the school, his financial woes, and his observations of fellow classmates:

My opinion of the institute, when I first arrived (and has been so ever since) was not good. I got Mr. Newman to let me room with him this term, on which account.

After I had written you the letter concerning the school, I was afraid you might get affronted at it, but I did not intend it, I will not say anything about the teachers yet awhile. The hallways, in which the students sweep the trash out of their rooms, are swept out only once a week. Old papers, hats, boots or shoes, collars, and other things are thrown from the windows, and remain around the building. The Gymnasium is very dirty and needs repair.[82]

Later, his opinion of the school and habits of the students would not improve. In his March 13, 1871, letter to Dr. Corey, he recounted the 'reasoning' surrounding what he perceived as a denial of his receipt of honors. It is important to underscore the fact that Gardner was formerly enslaved, approximately age 17, the only 'colored' student on campus and from all accounts, an exceptionally bright and gifted student. It is not unthinkable that his fellow students and professors had doubts about his capabilities or were uncomfortable with his strength academically. His preference to discontinue his studies at Colgate may have stemmed from what appears to be the lack of support and encouragement from professors and the absence of a bond with his classmates. These things were not an issue at Richmond. Despite this preference, he mentions the advantages of studying at Colgate or a similar northern (white) college in his remarks about Jones and Vassar, students who followed him from Richmond to Colgate:

Dear Sir;

Your letter was received this afternoon. It arrived here last Saturday, 11th inst., but one of the students took it from the Post Office and forgot to give it to me. I have thought that the class wished to abolish the honors because I was in it and I have told some, in a way to avoid an appearance of pride, that I thought thus, but they deny that was the thing which moved them and they think that no one was moved by such a motive. There is no outward appearance of such a thing just now, but I am afraid that it is in some. Some of the other classes speak of doing the same think, but my class was the first. The reason why they do it is, to promote the good feeling and friendship of the classmates, so that when we graduate we will not despise one another on account of honors, as it usually is. But the thing is settled in my class now. The honors are given up. I did not vote either way and another one voted against. I gave reasons for not voting. But I think I can study without reward as well as any one and I

think I will sign the resolutions, provided that the motive is pure. I have not had an opportunity of ascertaining my standing from the professor's since I rec'd your letter, but some of the class members say that I stood a chance for the valedict[orian]. I stand among the best scholars in everything, except speaking. It would be glad to see Jones and Vassar in some northern college; it would be a great advantage for them. They couldn't well enter the lowest class in the preparatory department next term, for that class will have reviewed the common English branches and studied Greek two terms. Jones and Vassar know more about Latin then the class and therefore might be able to make up; they would also have the Summer vacation for this. If they come, I have no doubt but that they will be disappointed in respect to some things, but I don't know where they can get a better preparation for college. I would not like to remain here another year, but it is not as I please. I would like to see Jones and Vassar, but I think I would feel about the same way as I do now about remaining. You are going to close school very early this year. I hope you will come here at the Commencement if possible. My regards to all. Please reply soon.
Yours humbly,
Sterling Gardner[83]
(see Appendix for original, handwritten letter)

In his April 17, 1871 letter, Gardner clearly was elated about the prospect of not being the only colored student at Colgate and unlike Simmons before him, he stayed and graduated. However, while elated that Jones and Vassar would be joining him, he again expressed his desire not to stay in Hamilton. His letters revealed his struggle to fit in and achieve the financial wherewithal needed to remain in attendance long enough to graduate:

I am glad that you decided to send Jones and Vassar next term. I will be overjoyed to see them. Although Madison Uni- is not as good looking as your building and things are not kept as nice and clean, I hope they will content themselves and be glad that [they] are in a place known as a university

I did want to go home next vacation, but if J & V come, I suppose, I can't go, I do hate to stay in H-during vacations and really do not want to stay again, but as I made the proposal I guess I will have to stand to it.

A great many people think that students, who try to live savingly, can get along very cheaply here, but if a person lives comfortably it takes money, especially on account of inconveniences. It takes all the money I have, and then I deny myself and economize.

I know I get along among the students pretty well and friendly and sociably, but elsewhere I don't know much about. I try to act gentlemanly and keep myself in a decent manner.
S.G.[84]

Still in his teens in his freshmen year at Colgate in 1870, he placed fourth out of 12 students in the Dodge Prize.[85] The Dodge Prize was established by President Ebenezer Dodge (1869-1890) and awarded to the top three freshmen who successfully completed five 3 hour courses, which included Latin and/or Greek. Gardner was focused and committed to succeeding at Colgate. In a letter dated September 2, 1872 from Augusta, Georgia, Gardner writes to Professor Lewis and requests the professor send him the reading list so he can begin to prepare for the upcoming year:

Prof. J.J. Lewis
Dear friend,
Having been unable to call by your house to get that list of books for my course of reading, I write to you to ask you to send it to me. I wish you would place them in the order that

you think they should be read.

I am going to leave Augusta on the 12th instant, so I hope you will send it to Richmond Va, and, as I want to begin to read as soon as I arrive at Richmond, you will oblige me by forwarding it immediately.

I have spent a pleasant vacation and now I feel fresh for another year's work.

Yours truly,
Sterling Gardner[86]

Gardner was a young man only a few years emancipated out of the bowels of bondage; therefore, he clearly understood the burden he carried to be successful. Despite his loneliness and desire to leave Colgate, it was his recognition of that burden to succeed that inspired him to remain. He persevered so that others could follow and create opportunities for the larger Black community. Gardner was well aware of the serious role he played in propelling other Black people following their recent release from bondage. The letters reveal a dedicated and studious young man desperately working to establish himself academically in order to benefit the entire Black community.

In his junior year he was ranked second and fourth in the senior class. In his junior year he presented "Man and Action-Inseparable" and graduated with honors in Classics in 1875.[87] Gardner's classmates reluctantly acknowledged his intellectual gifts upon completion of his studies. He was mentioned in the class prophecies as, " a cloud no shades the vision and Sterling Gardner appears as the President of a flourishing Freedman's College The literary world is still enriched by his ready pen, while his latest eulogy of Charles Sumner has become the admiration of the ages."[88]

Gardner returned to Richmond Institute during his college years and taught in 1872-1873, and 1875.[89] In 1876, Gardner was an assistant at Augustus Institute. Still in its formative years, Augustus Institute would later be renamed Atlanta Institute and then became the world renowned Morehouse College. Tragically, Gardner took ill at the tender age of 23 and died of consumption and heart disease in 1877. Of his untimely death, Dr. Roberts, president of Augustus Institute, called him a "great Christian and a scholar of great promise." Gardner is credited with helping to establish two historically Black colleges and universities: Virginia Union University and Morehouse College.

Armstead Mason Newman' 1876

Armstead was born enslaved in Virginia. He attended Wayland Institute before attending Colgate. The value of first person narratives puts the experiences that shaped his life into the context of the broader narrative of the community, culture, and nation. In addition, the personal narrative provides insight into how one experienced that broader narrative. On a personal level, it reveals the character of the person. At an ABHMS meeting held in Nashville, Tennessee in 1888 Newman wrote of his experiences at Lumpkin's Jail in a speech titled, "History of Richmond."

> … gives us a picture of one kind of work carried on in the Lumpkin Establishment and also furnishes an illustration of the truthfulness of the remark sometimes heard, that truth is oftentimes stranger than fiction. Brother Newman, the former neglected slave boy, after graduating at Madison University, became the influential pastor of large and important churches.

> Dr. Corey and Brother Holmes were talking last night about Richmond and Lumpkin's jail, and wondering at the change that had taken place. I thought of one of those changes that took place in my own individual history. About the year 1862, the person with whom I was living called me and said 'Take this note and carry it down to Mr. Lumpkin.' Well I took the note, went off down Broad street just as happy as a little fellow could be. I handed Mr. Lumpkin the note,

I presented the note and Mr. Lumpkin looked at it and said: 'Here John, take this boy, carry him back there and put him in.' It seemed to me that my heart went right down. I could not understand it, but there may be some of my brothers here to-day who understand what it means by 'putting him in'.

Some brother asks what I mean by 'putting him in'. It was putting me in a place known as the whipping room, and on the floor of that room were rings. The individual would be aid down, his hands and feet stretched out and fastened in the rings, and a great big man would stand over him and flog him. I out of there in 1862, and went home.

Time passed on. By and by great things came to us. We were all free. Prison walls were broken down. As soon as possible I went to Wayland Seminary, D.C. From there I went to Madison University, and then in 1873, to New Orleans to take charge of a church.[90]

Newman became the Chaplin for the Louisiana Senate in 1874[91] and returned to Colgate to finish his degree and graduate. After graduation, Newman returned to Louisiana. There, he helped draft the address of the colored citizens of Louisiana in 1879.[92] He was also the editor of the semi-monthly magazine "The Evangelist"[93] and pastored several churches in Louisiana before taking over the duties at the Antioch Colored Baptist Church in Shreveport, Louisiana in July 1889.[94]

Gardner was noted as one of the greatest preachers of his time and yet his name is buried in the lost history of numerous Black men and women who worked tirelessly for their communities. As mentioned in Gardner's letter to Rev. Corey at the Richmond Institute, V & J as they were known, Joseph Endom Jones and Nathaniel Vassar followed Gardner from Richmond to study and graduate from Colgate University. Jones and Vassar attended Richmond Institute and Colgate at the same time, married biological sisters, and later taught at Richmond and Virginia Union University. They were leading members of their communities and educated some of the finest minds scarcely beyond the first generation of the formerly enslaved.

Joseph Endom Jones, Class of 1876

Jones was born in Lynchburg, Virginia in 1850. He and his parents were enslaved and he gained freedom with the surrender of the Confederacy, at the end of the Civil War.

Despite his mother's protestations, he was sent to a tobacco factory to work at the tender age of six. Pre-Civil War Virginia had enacted some of the toughest laws designed to continue to control the body and mind of Black people in the South. Therefore, unable to control her son's body, and understanding the importance of her son being able to read and write, his mother was determined to make sure he was educated to ensure he would maintain control of his mind. In order to ensure that Jones was educated, his mother initially had a fellow enslaved African teach her son. However, when the man was sold away for teaching her son to read and write, she exchanged food with an ill Confederate soldier near the end of the Civil War to continue his lessons. After the end of the war, she sent her son to private schools.[95]

In 1868, after being called to the ministry and baptized, Jones enrolled at the Richmond Institute. From Richmond he went to Hamilton, New York to enroll first in the Academy followed by a full course at the University. He received his AB in 1876 and a Divinity Degree in 1879. His financial support to attend Colgate came from Hon. Henry Bill of Norwich, Connecticut. Norwich was also interested in supporting students at the Richmond Institute and provided books and financial support for Jones and others during Jones's tenure at Colgate.[96]

As with Gardner, several of Jones' letters have survived. In a letter addressed to Dr. Corey in November 1872, Jones shares his melancholy feelings over losing his mother, feeling abandoned by Dr. Corey and others, and enduring some of the challenges of life at Colgate:

> …I ask you to write me at once and to give any advice which might suggest itself, but as yet, have not had a line from you whom I look up as being my parent intellectually, I am aware that you have been quite busy and can make all necessary palliative, but I think that you might have written me a short letter.

> I wrote you under peculiar circumstances, just after the death of my dear mother that gave rise to many thoughts for when one is afflicted by the hand of providence he looks to his fellow man for sympathy and when those who have been his faithful friends prior to his affliction turn their backs upon him he does not know where to go for succor.

> I am getting on finely, but find plenty work in the freshman year. Vassar sends love to you all, he is getting on pretty well also. I had good success in Norwich (Norwich had an established Black community that predated the Civil War) last Sept, and found many kind and generous friends which seemed to sympathize with me in my affliction.[97]

Jones graduated Colgate with honors and after graduation was appointed, by the ABHMS, to a professorship at Richmond Theological Seminary. At Richmond Theological Seminary, Jones held the Homiletics and Greek chairs. He was a member of the staff of "The Baptist Companion," was elected corresponding secretary of the Baptist Foreign Mission of the United States in 1883, and edited "African Missions."[98] Jones was respected by his peers across racial lines as evidenced in "The Religious Herald," an organ of the White

Baptists of Virginia:

> He is one of the most gifted colored men in America….He has the ear and heart of his people and fills with distinction the high position to which his brethren, North and South, have called him.[99]

Throughout Jones's career, he worked for the educational and spiritual enrichment of the 'Negro race.' This was evident in 1880 Saratoga Springs, New York address titled, "The Desire and the Need of the Freedman for these schools to the Home Mission Society":

> In concluding my remarks, let me ask this Convention, in behalf of five millions of human beings, and in the name of our denomination and in the name of our common Christianity, do all in your power to remove the great hinderance to the progress of the Negro race, - the prevalent belief that they can never rise above the condition of servants or serfs or political tools. Educate and Christianize them as you do the Indian, the Burmese, the Chinese, and the other races of the world. Do not check and modify their efforts to rise higher in the scale of being by telling them that they cannot become the equals of white men. Encourage and stimulate them, as you do other peoples, by providing for and assisting them in a high course of intellectual and moral training; remind them of the great responsibilities they are soon to bear in the State, the business world, the Christian church and the great battle of life. Do not hang on the necks of the young men of the race who are buffeting the waves of poverty, adversity and prejudice, the leaden weights which are too often thrown upon them, by telling them that God never intended that they should be anything else than what they find themselves now; that neither they nor any of their race can ever amount to anything; but rather extend to them

the hand of Christian sympathy, and say to them: "We are willing to help you to help yourselves, and to do all in our power to lift you from ignorance and darkness into the light of intelligence, culture, pure religion, and into the honorable and responsible position of American citizenship." Then will your duty have been done, the Negro race redeemed, and God honored.[100]

While the idea of converting Richmond Institute to a university was still in its infancy, Jones wrote to Rev. Corey to share his insights on the need for a university in Virginia to train and retain the talented Black men and women of the first generation. He observed that this generation was hungry for education, and a full-fledged university would give them an incentive to remain in the South. Left unsaid was the racialized experience the students would encounter as he and others who traveled North would inevitably experience without such a school. He was also concerned that if Richmond did not seize the opportunity as a Baptist institution then other denominations would fill the void. (See Appendix for letter). Jones followed up his June 28, 1893 letter with a letter dated July 10, 1893 to Rev. Corey on his reaction to the decision to convert the Institute to a university.

I am glad to learn that it has been decided to have a University.

I am satisfied, too, that I voice the sentiment of the great majority of my people.

J.E. Jones[101]

Additionally, "The Crisis" magazine[102] wrote about Jones's death:

Virginia Union University has lost a distinguished land mark through the death of Professor Joseph Endom Jones, A.M., D.D....one day before his seventieth birthday... he was one of the first colored men of Virginia to receive a college education, receiving the degrees of Bachelor of

Arts and Master of Arts from Colgate University (then Madison University).... He was immediately called to the Chair of Greek and Church History at Richmond Institute subsequently Virginia Union University where he has since served with distinction.[103]

William Simmons praised Jones in the book, "Men of Mark: Eminent, Progressive and Rising," he echoed the praise of many when he called Jones a man who was divinely ordered and superintended.

Jones and his childhood friend, David Nathaniel Vassar, not only studied together at Richmond Institute, but attended Colgate together and returned to Virginia and taught at Virginia Union University after their respective graduations. Jones was also a member of the Emancipation Club that held an Emancipation Celebration at Newport News; this serves as a testament to his civic work and dedication to the academic liberation of his race.[104]

David Nathaniel Vassar, Class of 1877

David Vassar was born free in Virginia in 1847; however, he was subsequently stolen and sold into slavery at the age of 3 (the same year of the Fugitive Slave Law of 1850). He taught himself how to read by reading commercial signs in Lynchburg, Virginia. In 1868, he began his formal education at Richmond Institute[105] and eventually followed fellow Richmond students Jones and Gardner to Colgate. Vassar and Jones were inseparable at Colgate and their professional and personal lives mirrored each others. As mentioned previously, they both attended Richmond Institute and were sent to Colgate to study together, and alongside Gardner. They spent their careers teaching at Richmond and were members of the Richmond Black elite. Their wives were sisters and their children were sheltered from the hardships that they encountered growing up enslaved in the South. Vassar, as with Jones and Gardner, was an exceptionally gifted student at Colgate. During his senior year, Vassar humbly wrote to Rev. Corey regarding his academic success:

> My year's work, so far, has been very pleasant and on the whole I think I have gained more than I have in any former year. This not only my opinion but it seems to be both the opinion of my class and professors.
>
> I do not mean to boast of any things that I have done but simply make the statement that you may know how I am getting on.
>
> I have always remembered the least as well as the greatest favors that you done for me. What I am as far as learning or education is concerned, you were the first cause, and I may saw [sic] also that your kindness and friendship for me have aided me all through my course" As my college course is almost complete, I feel that I ought to express my true feelings to you in regards to your self. For this reason, then, I have written you this simple, plain letter.[106]

This letter sums up how Vassar (as well as Gardner and Jones) felt about the opportunity Rev. Corey opened to these men to first attend Richmond, and then to go on to Colgate. Each of these men returned to the South to 'pay it forward' and bestow the opportunity for academic liberation to other Black men. These men believed that an educational foundation and support to obtain that education had the potential to uplift other Black men beyond the legacy of slavery. Some have argued that the opportunities for these men were limited and returning South was their only realistic option. That rather narrow viewpoint ignores the broader context of these men and their personal narratives in a time of great change and need in the Black community and the nation at large. To begin, many of these men had either personal experiences with enslavement and/or had family members who had been enslaved. They understood the destructive nature of slavery, knew the limitations placed on them and their brethren to live free, become educated and enjoy the fruits of their labor. There were Black communities in all regions of this country where, as educated Black men, they would have prospered; however, they chose to return South where they saw the greatest need. Furthermore, contrary to the argument that they had no other options except to return South, it is important to note that they were committed to their communities and uplifting their race. Regardless of any perceived limitations, these men understood the opportunities they were given and devoted their lives to helping others achieve similar opportunities. They worked and engaged in the vision to build strong, viable Black communities.

After graduation, David Vassar returned to Richmond Theological Seminary (later to become Virginia Union University) and taught classes from 1877 to 1899 in natural science, mathematics, bible and church history. He was appointed by the Foreign Mission Convention of the Colored Baptists of the United States to visit and oversee their missions in Liberia. He traveled and stayed in Liberia from February to July in 1891. He returned from Liberia for health reasons; however, he continued to be an advocate for missionaries in Virginia to help educate Black ministers.[107]

Jones and Vassar were educators, pastors, community leaders, and also involved in local politics. They dabbled in the newspaper business and formed a short-lived paper, "Virginia Baptist" to replace the "Virginia Baptist Companion," which was burned and destroyed.[108]

Matthew W. Gilbert, Class of 1887 and 1890

Gilbert was born in South Carolina in 1862. Prior to his education at Colgate, he attended Benedict Institute (Benedict College) in South Carolina for three years, completing college preparatory classes before entering Colgate University in 1883. Gilbert entered Colgate after passing rigorous entrance examinations and ranked third among twenty White applicants for matriculation; he was the only Black man in his class. In 1885, while still a student, Gilbert attended the 53rd Annual ABHMS and gave a brief address at the afternoon session. An interesting aspect of Gilbert's address is that he was preceded on the dais by William Simmons who had also attended Colgate, and who spoke on the industrial worth of the 'colored people.'[109]

Undaunted by his racial isolation, Gilbert was the class secretary and treasurer each of his four years at the school as well as being named the class historian his senior year. During his sophomore year, he was selected to compete for the merit-based Kingsford prize. The Kingsford prize was established in 1881 through a gift of one million dollars by Thomas Kingsford. The prize recognized the top two public speakers in each of the freshman, sophomore, and junior classes. Not only was Gilbert the first Black man at Colgate chosen to compete, he won the prize.[110]

He graduated from Union Theological Seminary of New York City in 1890.[111] The "New York Globe's" 'Stray Notes' reported:

The only colored person in the college department of Madison University at Hamilton New York is Matthew W. Gilbert, though there is a colored boy in the academy and also one in the theological department. Mr. Gilbert says he likes the institution and is treated as well as can be expected. He is a member of one of the college literary societies, of the YMCA, the students' Blaine and Logan Clubs and secretary and treasurer of his class (87) Being "treated as well as can be expected" is either Gilbert had low expectations of how he expected to be treated and/or the treatment was obviously different from how his white classmates treated each other and were treated.[112]

Like his predecessors at Colgate, Gilbert devoted his life to the ministry and the education of the Black community. After graduation, Gilbert pastored in various Baptist churches in the South and in New York City. He was involved with the Baptist State Convention of South Carolina and pastored the first colored Baptist Church in Nashville, Tennessee. He was also a member of the White Baptist Conference in Nashville, being one of the first to be invited to join. Gilbert's accolades were numerous and included serving as the founder and principal of the Florida Baptist Academy of Jacksonville, Florida, the editor of several newspapers in the various communities he lived, and vice-president and professor of history, political science, and modern at the Colored College at Orangeburg, South Carolina. His poor health eventually forced him to decline an appointment to the presidency of the State University at Louisville, Kentucky. He, like many of his fellow Colgate men, published many articles.

> The late Matthew W. Gilbert was born in South Carolina in 1862. He was educated at Benedict College, South Carolina, and at Colgate University, Hamilton, where he received his bachelor's degree. He afterward received the honorary degree of Bachelor of Divinity from Union Theological Seminary. Entering the active ministry of the Baptist church he held charges at Nashville, Tenn., and Jacksonville, Fla. He was the founder of the Florida Baptist College at Jacksonville. Several years' work followed as pastor, missionary and college teacher until finally Dr. Gilbert became pastor of Mt. Olivet Church, New York City, where he had a hard fight to hold together a divided church. He then went South again and at the time of his death was pastor of the First Baptist Church of Nashville, Tenn., and dean of the theological department of Roger Williams University. He leaves a widow and three children. His oldest son, a young man of great promise, died while a student at Colgate University.[113]

Gilbert was one of the five Black men from Colgate that went on to become college presidents. He was also a gifted minister and one of his sermons from 1890 can be found in a collection of sermons and papers: " The Negro Baptist Pulpit. A collection of Sermons and Papers on Baptist Doctrine and Missionary and Educational Work" edited by E.M. Brawley, D.D. (see Appendix).

While the lives of some of these men have been lost to Colgate and the nation's history, what has been uncovered about them reveals the extraordinary achievements of their lives as the first generation following the legal end of slavery. These men understood the importance of their role in the transformation of a nation that constructed its commerce, political, and cultural self-worth on the plunder of the slave oligarchy. However, as these men were aware of the urgency to build a new image and narrative; history has revealed, the nation was not ready. Today, one must beg the question if the United States is ready to seek repentance from its history of the subjugation of Black bodies for profit.

There still remains reluctance to acknowledge that the foundation of this country rests in the blood, sweat, and tears of centuries of free labor by enslaved Black men and women. Erasing the contributions of these men and other men and women to their rank only feeds the false narrative of an intellectually dishonest history. The narrative that minimizes the contributions of Black men and women in order to swing open the doors of marginalization is not only reactionary, it subverts the value of Black people in the past, present, and future of the country as a whole.

Top: Class of 1894, James Jeffery Livingston
Bottom: Colgate Academy class 1900, Everett Booker Jones and Sherman Smith
Courtesy of Special Collections and University Archives, Colgate University Libraries

Matthew M. Gilbert'1887
Henry Hill photograph collection, A1297

Top: Matthew W. Gilbert in class photo, 1887
Bottom: Samuel Archer'1902 with other commencement speakers
Courtesy of Special Collections and University Archives, Colgate University Libraries

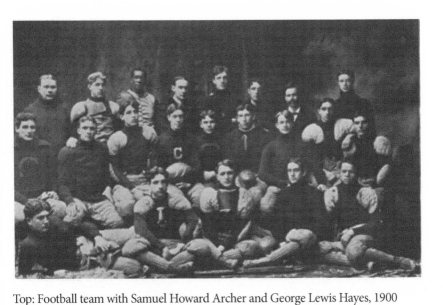

Top: Football team with Samuel Howard Archer and George Lewis Hayes, 1900
Salmagundi yearbook
Bottom: Everett Booker Jones, 1905
Courtesy of Special Collections and University Archives, Colgate University Libraries

Everett Booker Jones with Professor MacGregory and other chemistry students by coal stove
Courtesy of Special Collections and University Archives, Colgate University Libraries

George Lewis Hayes, 1903
Courtesy of Special Collections and University Archives, Colgate University Libraries

VAUGHAN, '29

Raymond "Ray" Vaughn, 1929
Courtesy of Special Collections and University Archives, Colgate University Libraries

Rev. Henry Livingston Simpson (1860s)
Courtesy of Chatham-Kent Black Historical Society & Black Mecca Museum

✦ CHAPTER VIII ✦
The First Generation

The enslaved were not bricks in your road, and their lives were not chapters in your redemptive history. They were people turned to fuel for the American machine.

Ta-Nehisi Coates, "Between the World and Me"

Not all of the African American men who attended Colgate after the Civil War were formerly enslaved as were Simmons, Newman, Gardner, Gilbert, Vassar, and Jones. There were other men who attended Colgate between 1865 and 1900, who never knew living as an enslaved person. However, like their predecessors they, too, moved into the ranks of the African American elite and worked to better their communities.

George Jackson, Class of 1887

Jackson was born in 1863 in Massachusetts. In 1886, his senior year at Colgate, Jackson was sent to the Inter-seminary Missionary Alliance held at Oberlin College to serve as a senior delegate. He was one of two speakers at his Colgate seminary commencement, and received special mention by denominational papers as the first graduate in many years to receive applause on such a "glorious occasion." With several opportunities available to him after graduation, Jackson was called to pastor at Immanuel Baptist Church in New Haven, Connecticut. He stayed at Immanuel for six years and doubled the membership during his pastoral duties. Jackson assisted in the organizing of four new Baptist churches in

Connecticut as well. Simultaneously, he attended the Yale medical school, and eventually became an assistant instructor there after graduation.[114] Jackson pledged to do missionary work in the Congo, a promise he would keep.

In 1893, under the auspices of the American Baptist Missionary Union, he fulfilled his pledge and went to the Congo Free State as a medical missionary. Illness, however, forced him to return to the states in 1895.[115] Jackson broke the color line and became the first career Black person in the foreign consular services to be stationed in a European country. Jackson was stationed in Cognac, France in 1897. He was transferred to La Rochelle, France the following year.[116] Jackson occupied one of the more important political positions held by a Black person in the William Taft administration and served in France for President Taft from 1897-1917.[117]

Unfortunately, Jackson was a casualty of President Woodrow Wilson who put racism and White supremacy ahead of patriotism by 'cleansing' the federal government of all Black people despite their laudable contributions to America; that 'cleansing' included relieving Jackson of his duties. It was irrelevant that the department inspectors commented that Jackson was highly regarded in his district and should not be dismissed. It did not matter that Jackson served his position with professionalism and distinction. It was of little significance that he received praises from his superiors and that the French he served loved and admired him. All that seemed to matter to the Wilson administration is that his vacated post was filled by a white man.

> George H. Jackson, who was appointed consul at Cognac, France, by President Taft, has been dismissed. Kenneth F. Patton, a white man, succeeds him. This position is perhaps the best in the consular service ever held by a colored man and was supposed to be protected by the civil service.[118]

During his tenure in France, Jackson immersed himself and his family in the local community and in 1928 he authored "The

Medicinal Value of French Brandy in 1928.[119] Jackson loved sports and was president of Stade Rochelais, a sports club in La Rochelle. He was credited with developing the club's rugby section and the French did not forget Jackson. In 2014, Stade Rochelais opened a new stadium and in recognition of Jackson's service to the club, a section of the stadium was named in his honor.[120]

Jackson was also, unsurprisingly, a Niagarite.[121] The Niagara movement, which lasted three years, was organized by W.E.B. Du Bois and William Trotter in 1905. It was a civil rights movement that stressed the need for immediate equality, unlike Booker T. Washington who took a more conservative approach. Du Bois organized the National Association for the Advancement of Colored People (NAACP) in 1908 after race riots broke out in Springfield, Illinois when a White mob was thwarted in their attempt to lynch two Black inmates in the Sangamon County Jail. The mob destroyed hundreds of Black-owned properties and businesses, and two Black men were lynched as well as other related deaths.[122]

Price Alpheus Leftwich, Class of 1875

Leftwich was from Newark, New Jersey and he attended Colgate from 1869-1871 in the Academy.[123] Leftwich transferred and finished his studies at Howard University and after Howard, he attended Andover Newton Theological School.[124] Occasionally, the prejudices of some or perhaps most of the student body, faculty, and administration at Colgate regarding their Black classmates bubbled to the surface and was expressed publicly. This duality of harboring racist notions of superiority while praising a fellow classmate as an 'exception to his race' is found in tangible and undeniable terms.

In a program offered by the Beethoven Society Chorus, Leftwich was noted as singing: "I'm the Blackest Nigger that ever you did see." Next up on the program was "How could they do Without Me" by Tristram Tupper, who was from a White Confederate family[125] (see Appendix for image of the program page).[126] Leftwich died in 1881.

A more disconcerting sign of the lack of respect for the Black man's presence on campus was the absence of any meaningful record or acknowledgement of the existence of their time at Colgate or their contributions to the history of the institution. In researching the early men, more often than not, their lives were recorded by other Black outlets; newspapers, books written by and about Black people, archives at HBCUs, publications sponsored by Black abolitionists, and local archivists who had sizable Black populations and documented them. Sadly, much of the history was recorded only after it became fashionable and deemed 'scholarly' to do so. The Colgate archives have some information about the early Black men while on campus and after graduation. However, records of student life in general can only provide an imagined experience for these men. The lack of documentation of the specific experiences of the Black body and mind from their perspective is a challenge. Often, when their presence is known it is not in their own words, but through the lens of others, or as Du Bois described it as the 'double consciousness,' describing an experience through the viewpoint of another. It becomes important to understand that these men were pioneers, active participants of a changing world, and faced insurmountable odds to attain an education. These men used the education and talents to work towards transforming the nation, and offered to forge a 'more perfect union.' The dream of a 'more perfect union' eluded the early men of color, despite their best efforts, but it is important to at least know their names. Thus, understanding the Black body in a White space throughout the early years of this nation and institution provides a perspective that is unique and amplifies their experiences.

Lucis Hippolyte, Class of 1882

Lucis Hippolyte was born in Haiti in 1857. At Colgate he was a member of the Aeonans Society[127] and was ordained in New Haven, Conn. in 1884. He attended and graduated from the Newton Theology Institute 1884-1886 as a nonresident. He went to Paris from 1885-1890 before returning to Haiti to lead the Cap Haitian Church. It was reported in various magazines and journals that Rev. Hippolyte lead the independent sole Baptist Church in Port au Prince without support from any of the Baptist organizations at a time when there were only approximately 1,300 Baptist on the island of Haiti.[128] It was also noted that the church thrived during his leadership.[129] Hippolyte is another example of Colgate men who were responsible for leading thriving churches that increased in membership.

Peter Verdier Hazel, Class of 1880

Hazel was born in South Carolina in 1856. From 1874-1876 he attended Atlanta University (later renamed Morehouse) before transferring to study for the ministry at Colgate.[130] In his freshman year, he roomed with Lucis Hippolyte. His education was supported by two women from Clarendon St. Church and Captain Morgan of Connecticut.[131] A local paper commented on his commencement speech: "The Elements of Power in Abraham Lincoln." He was a pastor in various churches in North and South Carolina.

Castle Brewer, Class of 1885

Castle Brewer was from Babylon, Long Island and attended Worcester Academy in Worcester, Massachusetts and Richmond Institute prior to enrolling at Colgate. At Colgate, he was also a member of the Aeonians Society. Colgate records described the physical characteristics of his body (athleticism), but nothing of his mind (scholarship). It was noted that Brewer won the running backward race in the annual field days.[132] After Colgate, Brewer became the pastor of St. Paul Missionary Baptist Church in Stanford, Florida and he served in that capacity from 1894-1936. Under his leadership, Brewer grew the church from a cabin sanctuary to a thriving parsonage.[133] This was yet another example of the power of the mind, spirit, and commitment of Brewer and other Colgate men who went into the pulpit and grew their churches. The work of Brewer was not forgotten. A scholarship day, housing project, and a street have all been named in his honor in Stanford, Florida; commemorating how Brewer touched and enriched the lives of the people he served.[134]

The church was an important staple in the Black community. It provided spiritual sustenance at a time when the harshness of segregation and discrimination were often overwhelming. It was a safe and sacred space. The Black church became the bedrock of the early resistance movement in the struggle for civil rights and equality in the 20th century.

Gilbert Raiford

Gilbert Raiford was born in South Carolina sometime after the Civil War. Little is known of his early life or times at Colgate. Records indicate he was in the Academy, but no further details have been uncovered as to when he graduated or transferred. It is known that he became one of the leading Baptist ministers from Florida and was president of one of the Baptist State Conventions in Florida (see the Appendix for one of his sermons).

The common thread of these men who attended Colgate before the turn of the 20th century was that they were all exceptional students who prevailed against meager beginnings and succeeded in a hostile environment. They also became respected members of the ministry who through their leadership expanded their churches. All were well regarded and their communities honored their legacies by naming buildings, streets, or churches after them. The hope was that future generations would know, remember, and understand their contributions to their communities, and the fight to transform this nation into a nation, speaks volumes with respect to their legacy.

The other Black men who have been identified as attending Colgate during this period are as follows:

Wesley A. Ely, Class of 1879

James Jeffrey Livingston, Class of 1894 (transferred and graduated from Shaw University)

CHAPTER IX
Debate Over Educating Black America

. . .for the problem of the Twentieth Century is the problem
of the color-line.

W.E.B.Du Bois, "The Souls of Black Folk"

The new century and its White citizenry, both in the South and
North, worked to construct a society that sanctioned and codified
the American psyche with respect to the political, cultural, economic,
and social degradation of Black men and women. While at the same
time, America benefitted politically, culturally, and economically
from the systematic discrimination and the second class citizenship
of Black people. W.E.B. Du Bois wrote and argued persuasively that
the controversy of the 20th century was the issue of the color line.

The South enacted pernicious legislation that prevented Black
people from advancing politically, socially, or economically.
Moreover, that same legislation authorized a brand of domestic
terrorism designed to subject Blacks to substandard conditions and
permanent underclass status; thus, denying an entire race of people
their basic human rights. This period of pernicious southern laws and
cultural division was known simply as 'Jim Crow.' Needless to say,
Jim Crow was more than a stone's throw away from the 'American
Dream' enjoyed by its White citizens.

The North decided to remain complacent and turned a blind
eye to the terror unfolding in the South. Instead of intervening
on moral grounds, the North managed to perfect its own brand of
discrimination in housing, employment, and education that also

subjected Black people to a second-class status. The racial divide was ugly; it was violent, morally impoverished, and it appeared to be in America to stay.

Nonetheless, where there is oppression, there is always resistance. Resistance is a phenomenon that manifests itself in many forms, yet historians often revise, dilute, or ignore the men and women who were the agents of resistance and actively fought against discrimination and institutional racism. Resistance for the Black men of Colgate would take the form of educational advancement as an important step towards equal access to the American political, economic, social, and cultural spheres.

The classic public debate within the Black community was over the best educational path for African Americans to follow on the way to righting the wrongs of the slave oligarchy and achieving the 'American Dream.' Booker T. Washington famously argued that Black people should focus their educational efforts on learning a trade or technical skill (manual, practical skills). Washington believed that there was honor and victory in working hard, and saving money in order to obtain success and help Black people rise from the legacy of slavery. However, these efforts did not include an aggressive push for social equality.

Conversely, W.E.B. Du Bois argued that Black people should use education to develop advanced intellectual skills in order to enter the social mainstream as doctors, lawyers, bankers, accountants and other professionals. Du Bois' focus included an exigent push for economic, political, and social equality. Du Bois called the intellectual elite who would achieve these educational goals the 'talented tenth.' According to Du Bois' theory, the 'talented tenth' would receive an elite education and lead the rest of the racial group to the bright light of equality. The difference in approach between Washington and Du Bois would be played out in the public as they represented opposite poles in the tactical struggle for civil rights. However, it would be Du Bois' point of view with which these early Black men would ultimately side.

Booker T. Washington was born enslaved in 1856. He rose to

prominence as a 'Negro' educator who was the founder and president of Tuskegee Institute in Tuskegee, Alabama. Washington's early formal education began at Hampton Normal and Agricultural Institute. The school was started by Whites who believed it essential to teach the recently free Black men and women trades in the interest of providing them with the means to support their families.

Washington took academic classes and worked on a farm, the work at Hampton had a dual purpose: 1) To educate Black people with practical skills and, 2) Finance their education and provide needed work to build the school. When the Alabama legislature passed laws to fund a school for Blacks to train teachers, Washington was tapped to be its first principal.

Tuskegee Normal School (later Tuskegee Institute) trained men and women in practical skills such as carpentry, farming, domestic help, and cabinet making. The school was built by the labor of its students who made bricks, constructed buildings and farmed food that fed the student population. Under Washington, Tuskegee thrived, and in its twenty-fifth year it trained students in thirty-seven industries and had over 1500 students in attendance.[135] Washington's success and philosophy for educating Blacks attracted the southern and northern Whites, and in 1895, he was invited to deliver a speech at the Atlanta Convention. The fact that Washington delivered his speech to a predominately White audience was historic. While many Whites applauded his speech and his stance on not pushing for social equality as well as training Blacks to be available to fulfill trade jobs; Washington's views were very controversial among many Blacks, including Du Bois. Washington's speech, also called the 'Atlanta Compromise' noted, <u>inter</u> <u>alia</u>:

> … the fact that the masses of us are to live by the production of our hands, and fail to keep in mind that we shall prosper in proportion as we learn to dignify and glorify common labor, and put brains and skill into common occupations of life; shall prosper in proportion as we learn to draw the line between the superficial and the substantial…. If need be, in

defense of yours, interlacing our industrial, commercial, civil and religious life with yours in a way that shall make the interests of both races one. In all things that are purely social we can be separate as the fingers yet one as the hand in all things essential to mutual progress.[136]

There was a level of comfort to many Whites in Washington's philosophy. It was safe and it kept Black people subordinate to Whites by advocating to maintain the status quo of pre-Civil War southern life. Black people would be useful in helping to build the economic strength of the nation by staying in their place as second class citizens on the economic and social ladder. This would protect the status quo and keep the Black body and mind subjugated to tyrannical discrimination. Not all Black people felt this approach was acceptable.

W.E.B. Du Bois was a leading opponent of Washington's methods for the advancement of the race. The two came from decidedly different backgrounds. Du Bois was born in Massachusetts and never experienced slavery first hand as Washington had. Du Bois went to predominately White primary schools and received his first degree at Fisk (an HBCU in Tennessee). It was at Fisk that Du Bois first experienced Jim Crow. He earned a Masters degree from Harvard and was the first Black person to earn a Ph.D. from Harvard. Du Bois also completed advanced graduate studies at the University of Berlin. He taught at Atlanta University and was a prolific writer and lecturer. Along with others, Du Bois organized the Niagara Movement, the National Association for the Advancement of Colored People (NAACP), and was founder and editor of "The Crisis" magazine. He prepared and presented the 'Negro Exhibition' at the Paris World Fair in 1900 which highlighted the progress Blacks had made in the decades following emancipation. Du Bois countered Washington's approach advocating it was imperative that education do more than just teach Blacks to do manual and semi-skilled labor. Du Bois argued that Blacks were needed to become politicians, doctors, lawyers, educators, and other professionals to help raise the economic, political, and social status of the race in order to achieve real progress.

In the "Souls of Black Folk," Du Bois voiced some of his criticism of Washington's 'Atlanta Compromise' :

> ...compromiser between the South, the North and the Negro...represents in Negro thought the old attitude of adjustment and submission.... Mr. Washington's programme [sic] practically accepts the alleged inferiority of the Negro races...asks that Black people give up...political power, insistence on civil rights, higher education of Negro youth.... This policy...disfranchisement of the Negro...legal creation of distinct status of civil inferiority...steady withdrawal of aid from institutions for higher training of the Negro.... His doctrine has tended to make whites North and South, shift the burden of the Negro problem to the Negroes shoulders and stand aside as critical and rather pessimistic spectators; when in fact the burden belongs to the nation, and the hands of none of us are clean if we bend not our energies to righting these great wrongs.

Du Bois believed that Black people needed to be educated and take on professions such as law, medicine, and business to build the race economically, socially, politically, and culturally. The 'talented tenth' encompassed the elite vanguard for the civil rights movement, and it was no surprise that the Black men who attended Colgate during this period were part of this elite.

The Black men of Colgate, at the turn of the century, dedicated their careers and lives to advancing educational opportunities in the Black community against staggering odds. Black people were met with discrimination, segregation, violence, and terrorism in both their scholarship and daily lives. The Black men who took up Du Bois' fight against political oppression, economic exploitation, and social degradation began to appear on the Colgate campus against all odds.

The following is a list of Black men who graduated and/or enrolled at Colgate from 1900-1921:

Peter Carter Neal- 1900-1901
Samuel Howard Archer- 1902
George Lewis Hayes- 1903
John Brown Watson- 1904
Edward Booker Jones- 1905
Newton Lloyd Gilbert- 1915 (1st legacy student, died before graduation)
Burwell Townsend Harvey- 1916
Ira David Pinson- 1918
Garnett Langton Hegeman- 1919

✦ CHAPTER X ✦
Samuel H. Archer

I am pleading for an education which will take the undeveloped soul and make, not a carpenter or a Blacksmith, but a MAN.

Samuel Archer, 1904

Samuel Archer, Class of 1902

Archer was born in Virginia in 1870 and attended Wayland Seminary where he was an outstanding scholar and athlete. Colgate alums, Rev. Joseph Edom Jones and David Nathaniel Vassar, recognized his brilliance and encouraged him to attend Colgate. In his letter of recommendation, President Hovey of Wayland Seminary and College wrote:

> He was one of our most faithful and trustworthy students, as well as one of the most gifted intellectually.[137] (See the Appendix for entire letter.)

Unlike Sterling Gardner, who came to Colgate at the young age of 16, Archer was 28 years old upon his arrival on campus. At Colgate, Archer continued to excel as a scholar-athlete and studied logic, ethics, classics, mathematics, the teachings of Jesus Christ, and church history. He was the first Black person to play football for Colgate, lettered in 1899, played basketball in his sophomore year and earned the coveted golden 'C'. Archer served as class president in his sophomore and senior years and in 1901 (his junior year), he took first place in the Grout Oratorical Contest. The contest was founded by the class of 1884 member Edward Grout to award prizes to the top speeches given by members of the junior class. Archer's speech topic was the disenfranchisement of the 'Negro'. The speech not only provided a glimpse of his superior oratorical skills, but it also provided the philosophical and spiritual underpinnings that would become the guiding principles throughout his life.

Archer's speech was written and delivered several years after the Supreme Court handed down the decision in the landmark case, Plessy v. Ferguson, 163 US 537, (1896). Plessy v. Ferguson upheld, as law, that segregation was legal as long as it was equal and, for decades, provided the political, economic, and social cover that allowed Whites to segregate all aspects of Black life in the South.

Archer's speech titled, "Disenfranchisement of the Negro" was presented in front of a predominately White audience at a time when White supremacist groups like the KKK were on the rise. The speech analyzed racial controversies prevalent in America and not only highlighted Archer's powerful intellectual skill but also challenged White supremacy.

When the din of strife had ceased, and the object of the Civil War had been accomplished, statesmen turned their attention to the emancipated slave. What should be his status? How far should he be man, how far serf? Conservative men who knew that social and political qualities are the last fruits of civilization, argued that to bestow these rights upon the negro [sic] in his primitive state, would endanger the institutions of the country. Men with more radical views who prized highly the freeman's rights, mindful of the cost in treasures, in blood, in tears, insisted that this privilege was the necessary complement of Freedom.

Bitterly was the contest waged and radicalism won. When the need of the negro was sorest it mocked him with the ballot; when his ignorance was densest it satirized him with the election franchise. It was the political blunder of the century and has led to the present political crime. This movement has affected a large part of the South. It has advanced by legal and illegal methods; sometimes by force, fraud, bribery, and corruption; at other times by laws which divested of the tricks and snares of diplomacy stand out as flagrant violations of constitution. The chief feature of these laws is the property and educational qualification, which official jobbery can so manipulate that ignorance, poverty, and venality may share in the government, provided they are the misfortune of any save the negro. Now character is the only true measure of a man; and it is a narrow and ignoble spirit which measures a man according to the color of his skin and the texture of his hair.

Disregarding the unjust administration of these laws, let us in charity say that they were conceived in the overzealousness rather than in sin and iniquity. They are the outcome of the effort to express openly what statesmen of other sections have thought in secret; that manhood suffrage is not a signal success; that men must be trained for citizenship; that the ballot is too sacred a privilege and too fraught with the possibilities for lasting harm to be left in the hands of those who know not how to use it. What else does restricted immigration mean?—the refusal of full citizenship to Chinese and Indian! The future will find intelligence general in this country or the ballot restricted, North, West, East as well as South.

When men lay aside sentimental considerations and theoretical dreaming they are ready to assert that wealth of mind and worth of soul are the essential qualifications for the elective franchise; they are willing to grant that the right to vote is not inherent in citizenship, else women would have the right. Promptly they concede to Anglo-Saxon that superiority in governing which comes from a long continued struggle for the highest civilization, and that the mere accident of boundary line should not jeopardize his intellectual, moral, and financial interest. The logical inference from these concessions, is that laws which without discrimination disfranchise ignorance and incompetency, whether from the Orient or Occident, the Shannon, the Rhine, or the Congo may be for the best interest of all. If the operation of such laws, impartially administered, bars the negro, it is assuring to know that the barrier is not insurmountable, gratifying to know that worth is the open sesame of every political avenue.

The contention for an unqualified ballot is based on the equality of men. This doctrine of equality is a dangerous and inviting fallacy. Equalities have no dwelling place outside of mathematics; to the last degree men are unequal in character, reputation, power, wealth, influence, achievement. The granting of civil rights to all does not imply that all have rights to equal things, but that all are entitled to equal opportunity to develop and preserve what is best within them. Civil rights raised the negro from the level of chattel to the high plane of manhood. Without these freedom would have been the bitterest irony. That which in the bane of equality bestowed political rights upon a people who in their poverty and ignorance considered the ballot a privilege to be sold to the highest bidder or a means to pay a debt of gratitude, was not wisdom. It was rash perverseness and reckless statesmanship.

Under such circumstances the negro made the same mistake that others would have made under like conditions. There was no genie of the lamp to accomplish for him in a night what it took Anglo-Saxons centuries to develop.

These recent enactments, unjust though they be, will

contribute to the prosperity of the negro by forcing him out of politics. The future irradicated [sic] by the past and present offers no cause for alarm. The critical period in the history of my people is passed; they have looked the most advanced civilization of the world in the face and despite the predictions of scientists, and the maledictions of foes they still live. Years of bitterness taught them the alchemy by which they change difficulties and obstacles into stepping stones. Disfranchisement gives this undeveloped people needed rest from the consuming excitement of the political arena, it removes the conditions which have militated against them and gives opportunity for growth. The energy given to politics may now be put into industrial and educational effort thus enabling the negro to develop a character strong enough to bear the strain of civic life. Since the laws demand an educational qualification, education becomes a political right and the State must in justice provide better educational facilities.

Too long has the negro been holding the stirrup for vaulting ambition, too long has he been a slave of political creed, too long has he been contemplating his ideal. The present situation bids him leave his low vaulted past and seek an embodiment of his hopes and dreams. It gives him incentive to rise above the limitations of his personal life, above the prejudices of his age and country, to break the fetters of environment and show to the world that he is a man and the master of his fate.

He has had all the rights which legislation can give; yet withal he has been a citizen in name only. He has been an independent voter but his bare feet, tattered garments, untutored mind, and wretched home tell in unmistakable terms how vain, how futile, how illusive, how fatal is any short cut to citizenship. Coming years will bless the movement which taught the negro that political rights are not rewards nor honors, but opportunities and advantages, that political life is not the mere casting of the ballot, but the interval during which issues are weighed and merits of candidates decided, so that the ballot may be a symbol of political conviction. It is too late to repeal the amendments; little can be gained by harsh words; less by imagining what might have been if a different policy had been adopted; nevertheless it devolves upon us all to forward any movement which will harmonize equality and liberty, right and might, and render this government just to the humblest and safe for the noblest citizen.

Southern benevolence is as wide as the world of want, deep as the heart of sorrow, boundless as the kingdom of need. They sympathy which it has vouchsafed to the oppressed of every race and clime is due to the negro. If the South despises negro intellect, let it remember the character that he would and should form. If there is no admiration for his capacity then think on what his unrequited toil wrought. Is his talent contemptable! [sic] Then remember his constancy and devotion to the helpless and innocent. In the late unpleasantness between the States, the able bodied men of the Confederacy were fighting to perpetuate negro slavery while their mothers, wives and children were entrusted to the care of the slave. Nobly did he perform that trust. When he might have destroyed, he protected; when might have cursed, he blessed; when malignant foes urged him to direful revenge, he said nay. In all of that eventful period, history does not record a single act of violence by ebony hands; there is no room for treachery, or perfidy in the negro's dusky bosom. Is he loyal to his country? Gall the roll of army and navy. Hear that mighty response from three hundred thousand sable throats. Is he brave in conflict: Let Shafter, let Wheeler tell, let that negro solider tell who on the eve of battle said of his country's flag, "I'll bring it back in honor or report to God the reason why."

Faithful in slavery, trusty in freedom, loyal in war, and patriotic in peace, to this same race, tidings of a better and nobler life have come. If the negro seems impulsive in his struggle to attain this desired goal, direct his energy, do not fill him with despair. If the outburst of his native forces seems uncontrollable, regulate but do not stifle the longings of and earnest soul. Grant to him an equal opportunity with others to weave about his soul a character noble, exalted, divine.[138]

As a graduating senior, Archer was one of only six seniors to win the Roland speech prize.[139] In his Roland speech, entitled "The Ethical Ideal in American Life," Archer referenced the need for the country to live up to its ideas:

The American nation was born at a time when the world was poorly prepared to receive it. The prerogative of royalty, the divinity of the King, and the privilege of the Nobility had lost little of their charm. Wide and sweeping was the change from the divine right of kings to the rule of the majority. Government by the people was called a vain and idle dream; prophets of evil predicted a military government, critics expected a reign of anarchy and misrule.

Their predictions are unfulfilled and their expectations unrealized, because enshrined in glorious harmony in the national life are ethical ideals and moral principles, the rich legacy, the priceless heritage of our Puritan Fathers. The Puritanism of our heroic and creative period with its intolerance, spiritual despotism, superstition and sanctimoniousness may have merited derision and ridicule, but since it has had time to manifest itself in men, to work out in life and to crystallize into principles and institutions, every man should be a Puritan and every age should zealously foster Puritanism. Puritanism proudly conscious insists that spirit is more than form, and character more than ceremony. The Puritan stood in the twilight in the name of the ample dawn, he never feared, never faltered in his purpose to secure a land hallowed forever with principles well nigh holy, with sentiments almost divine.

If this nation is to be prominent in the great Anglo-Saxon movement of ruling the world and moulding [sic] its thought, fitness and qualification must be proved; if it deserves to win, the claim must rest on something more than power, wealth and achievement. That spirit which garlanded Plymouth Rock with hope and promise must direct racial ambition, regulate commercial aspirations and control political desires. It must pervade our political, economic and social life.

The ethical ideal sounds its vital note throughout our political life, giving the glowing assurance that the history of man is the history of divine progress. The two great problems of government, permanence and progress, have been [sic] solved despite the fact that each man is an uncrowned king. Amid tumbling systems, new rising questions and growing horizon, the vested rights of all are secure, not because the majority is always right but through that sincere respect for law and order which the minority may safely advocate. Americans with their willingness to fight precedent, overturn statutes and bring conditions into correspondence with their will would be the most daring revolutionists, did not the garnered thought of the race liberalize and transform their impulsive radicalism into calm potent evolution. Not with panoplied [sic] hosts is the fortressed might of corrupt government assailed. Truth and reason batter down the stronghold and implant in the civic breast sentiments of municipal virtue. Religion alone might be insufficient, for barbarians are religious, knowledge alone might give zealous visionaries, liberty alone might give France with her Reign of Terror. The ethical idea undivorced [sic] from the Christian religion is our plea.

It may be our pride that the times have produced large and flourishing cities, but it is to our everlasting honor that they are founded on the nobility of man, woman and child; that the great reform movements may summon to their aid men free from fanaticism, free from egotism and indifference, men in full sympathy with the many-sided progress of mankind. Verily the new world has a new political creed. Behind courts, behind legislation, behind devotion to party and party leaders is a force that finds its embodiment not so much in national law as in national character. If there is nothing but political machinery, mere form of government, to meet the political problems of the expanding country, then we are fundamentally unfit for the task before us. We shall go down in the presence of our opportunities.

The indomitable will, the untiring zeal and the inventive genius of Americans have qualified them to win and take a masterly position in the rivalries of the day. Men blinded to all save the magnitude of the results say that commercialism has dwarfed the soul and limited the nobler aspirations; but the world has not yet learned to make nice distinctions, it judges men and things in the gross. Since there is a lack of aristocratic titles and patents of nobility, the purse is made the standard.

This period of industrial development is not alarming; the individual passion for wealth gives no dismay. The interpreters of God in man can see the ideal rising in our economic career, rising not to fight but to utter its word of life and translate itself in terms of love, equity, and justice.

Already Capital is refusing to grow rich at the expense of child labor; unreasoning greed and cupidity are giving place to the perception that it is a privilege to be instrumental in changing the poverty of despair of labor into comfort and hope.

The ideal always supplements the practical. Employment of some kind is the best ethical condition of man. Ignorance of work and inability to earn a living are no longer the boasts of a gentleman but the harmful and expensive traits of a social parasite. The ideal has removed the primeval curse pronounced upon labor. The Son of Man has shed a halo around the workshop and the cause has become too sacred to be conducted by criminal agitators. The workman may make his crusade against convict labor but the growing spirit of the day urges him to reduce the number of convicts and lessen crime. Rates of wages and hours of labor are minor problems. To establish a bond of sympathy between the contending forces so that defenseless humanity with no voice but a sigh or grievance may find a responsive heart,-that is the great problem.

Great economic upheavals are always deplorable and pathetic if on either side there is absent the spirit of justice. The Civil War was such an upheaval. True, political and social conditions ere present but had the industrial feature been eliminated the triumph of right would have been far less costly. The price paid in men to establish a principle of national ethics in our economic life, you know. And whenever we scatter the rosemary upon the graves of those who fought and fighting fell, or stand with bred heads at the altar of the nation where are carve their deeds, it is fitting to turn the mind to the ideals which have preserved us, and join the musical voices of the living with the blessed memory of the dead.

The twentieth century marks a definite stage in the evolution of Western civilization. The eighteenth century witnessed the struggle for political freedom; the nineteenth century saw human freedom; the twentieth century finds science, business and government studying the moral sentiment and ethical framework of society. They are endeavoring to solve the problem set by philosophy that Truth, Beauty, Justice, Goodness and Humanity are all factors of one equation; striving to realize the prophecy of the ser that out of strife shall come harmony, that the dirge and lament of the unfortunate shall be changed into a song of joy, that the dark night is but the prelude and pledge of a more radiant day.

Our social problems are not, as many suppose, the result of the sordid character of the rich nor will they be settled alone by the wealthy. Wealth is an opportunity to which some are false, just as poverty is an opportunity to which some are untrue. Into the adjustment of the difficulties must enter a prompt recognition of the unity of humanity in hope and need.

Never before in all our history has there been less cause for the cry, "The rich are growing richer and the poor, poorer". I am not unmindful of "man's inhumanity to man" nor of the triumph, victory, conquest of avarice, greed and selfishness; but the evolutionary process at work in society bids us hope that they are but pillars of fire and clouds of sorrow leading on to humanity's Promised Land. Rich men are trying to discover not how much they own but how much they owe. The discovery stirs the rich to action, the poor to reflection. Hospitals and asylums were former means of helping the needy, the present tendency is so to change conditions that each man may have an opportunity to help himself; it seems far more charity in building an industrial school than in supporting a community by almsgiving; it is not content to build beautiful home but seeks to form a beautiful character to dwell therein.

From the Academy and the Lyceum comes the thinker whose wisdom completes the visible segment into a circle. The philosopher entering that realm in which Divine Mind supremely dwells, and searching reverently for the infinite and the eternal behind humanity emerges with the whispered secret, Man is not from dust but from God. For ages dust has been emphasized; the truth has been distorted. Man from dust, human passions "scourge him to his dungeon"; man from dust, insatiable greed lashes him to his task; man from dust, covetous wealth throws contemptuously to him the dole symbolic of his dependence. Man from God, womanhood and childhood dependent upon him become sacred objects of tender care; man from God, just wage, decent home, equality of privilege and opportunity are his; man from God, human brotherhood becomes the goal of the race. Base passions and low motives may prevent its present realization, but it hangs in the heavens glorious with the announcement that it shall be fulfilled on earth.[140]

Archer graduated in 1902 with a B.A. and teaching certificate. Ralph Thomas, Professor of Rhetoric and Public Speaking, in his letter of recommendation wrote:

> ...he has maintained an excellent character. I believe in him, and in his future. His work is not to be confined to the classroom, but his power over men will become an influence for good.[141]

After graduation, he returned to the South to teach and in a 1904 letter addressed to the 1902 Class Notes, Archer writes:

Roger Williams University
My Dear Classmates- Two years out in the "cold, cold world" has not made very much change in me. Added responsibilities may have brought some seriousness. Were I inclined to dignify my position here I would say that I am holding the Chair of Mathematics. The required work in this department is the same as that at Colgate. In a small way I am trying to do some work in public speaking among the students; trying to supplement genius with 'gab' and help logic with lungs.

I have some of the brightest students I have ever seen. They tackled Taylor's Algebra in magnificent style-appreciating fully his rigorous proofs and keen discrimination. They are not prodigies, for the classics and sciences are mastered by them just as easily.

But you should see my football team-fastest backs in this section. Win? Well, sometimes they do and again they play like 'preps' (better known here as Q's).

Baseball is our best hold. In the triangular contest between the three negro colleges of Nashville we are sure to lead. The team is banking on that. Next year we expect to have a track meet; in the meantime I shall learn to vault and throw the hammer.

The longer I live in the South the prouder I grow, because necessity and choice have identified me with this Black people. The opportunity for growth, development and service is immense; the outlook is very bright for me and mine. Last summer I spent two months in the rural districts in the interest of the school, and what I saw was revelation to me. It was no unusual sight to meet a family living in very comfortable homes with carpeted floors and curtained windows. Farmers, with property worth $800 to $6,000, can be seen in every county. Negroes without education in very many instances have bought and paid for homes and farms. It was my chief joy to sit and talk to such people; it was an inspiration to me to know that in the distribution of brain and native talent that while God thought of the Shannon and the Rhine he was not unmindful of the Congo. After what I have seen, the doctrine of the inferiority of the negro becomes a school boys' tale. They are simply an undeveloped people. In school, ghosts made themselves manifest and cracked-brain theories constantly arose, but the "have gone a-glimmering into the dreams of things that were." Now living men appear; and real and existing conditions demand careful thought, wise speech and cautious actions. If my time were not limited I could write a volume about the present conditions and the demands of the hour.

Somehow I can not [sic] become very enthusiastic over industrial education as it is understood by our northern friends. I am pleading for an education which [sic] will take an undeveloped soul and make, not a carpenter or a blacksmith, but a MAN. Give me this as the first product and you may make anything you wish out of the MAN.

But a discussion of my thoughts and opinions can be of little interest to you who are so far removed from the people under discussion.

I spoke of the progress and advance of a few negroes that I met; do not get the impression that all are so fortunately situated. The bright side appeals especially to me because so many are hunting the dark side.

Yours very truly,
S.H. Archer[142]

Archer's speeches at Colgate, and his letter to his classmates after graduation, provide a shadowy view of the thought process of the man who would later become the fifth president of Morehouse College. Morehouse was, and is, the preeminent HBCU and has educated some of the best minds in the country. Archer was unafraid to speak publicly to his White counterparts about the injustices and disparate treatment of his Black brethren. He was a man who observed history as it was happening and recognized the significance of the disenfranchisement of Black people by Jim Crow laws and racial terrorism. He was resolute in his beliefs, as reflected in his speeches that the Black man should not be deterred, because nothing that is sustaining happens quickly. He urged Black people to refocus their energy on economic freedom. As a man of religion, his speech, "The Ethical Ideal of American Life" speech stressed the need of man to rise to a higher power to correct the ills that befall the poor and downtrodden. He eloquently urged the wealthy to not focus on what they own, but what they owe. He criticized those who had become wealthy 'not of their own means' as a direct attack against the southern hierarchy that created and sustained the slavery oligarchy. In his letter to his classmates, he was resolute in educating his White classmates to not fall prey to the false narrative that existed about the plight of southern Blacks. Archer believed that academic education was essential in the pedagogy for the advancement of Black communities in the South and that it was necessary to educate Black men and women to empower Black people politically and economically. This viewpoint was in opposition of the pedagogy advanced by Booker T. Washington who advocated teaching Black men and women practical skills designed to keep the Black communities economically and politically subservient to White society.

Archer's commitment to educate Black people landed him at Roger Williams College, teaching mathematics. Roger Williams College, founded in 1864 as an elementary school, was one of four HBCUs in Nashville, Tennessee. Its founder was a White Baptist missionary who intended to prepare students to become Baptist preachers. It became a Baptist college in 1866, and its name was changed to Nashville Normal and Theological Institute and in 1883, it was incorporated as Roger Williams College.

Roger Williams College was committed to not only educating Blacks but also employed Blacks as professors and several served as trustees. In January and May of 1905, mysterious fires destroyed most of the buildings forcing the school to close. Students transferred to Atlanta Baptist College (to be renamed Morehouse College). Archer also went to Atlanta Baptist College and in Atlanta, Archer had a long and illustrious career as a scholar, administrator, pastor, and leader.

Archer's influence at Morehouse was instant and lasting and he was affectionately nicknamed "Big Boy."[143] He coached football from 1905-1915, compiling records that stood for years and was instrumental in the formation of the Southern Intercollegiate Athletic Conference (SIAC). Off the field he served as a dorm proctor, mathematics professor, dean and vice-president. His tenure at Morehouse spanned a total of 36 years and his presidency ran from 1931-1937. He resigned due to ill health and died in 1941.

Morehouse and Colgate were both founded on the principles of Baptist theology, and both prepared men to enter the ministry which would prove to be crucial to the future of the Civil Rights Movement and the emergence of Morehouse educated Baptist ministers such as the Rev. Dr. Martin Luther King, Jr.

King enrolled at Morehouse in 1944 at the tender age of fifteen. His formal training at the institution represents a conspicuous linkage between the early Black men at Colgate and their tradition of striving for academic excellence and service to the Black community. It was Archer who planted seeds that motivated the desire to transform the moral conscience of a nation which would eventually inspire Dr. King. The Archer thought process, and his legacy, undoubtedly had a direct influence on Martin Luther King, Jr., the student, as it did for countless other Black students enrolled at Morehouse. Dr. King stands in a long line of Baptist ministers that runs through Archer, Raiford, Brewer, Hazel, Hippolyte,

Gilbert, Vassar, Jones, Gardner, Simmons, Simpson, Townsend, and the other early Black men at Colgate.

The fear Rev. Jones expressed in his letter to Rev. Corey, for supporting Richmond Institute's reorganization into Virginia Union, was that it might trigger a brain drain of some of the gifted Black students and citizens to the North. His fear was not misplaced. The catalyst for the Great Migration was to seek a reprieve and a better quality of life from the suffocating and demoralizing White terrorism that was persuasive in the South. These factors attempted to stunt the growth southern Blacks needed to erase the vestiges of slavery. Black people of all walks of life would leave in search of a better life for themselves and their children. Unfortunately, moving North did not insulate Black people from racism; it merely manifested it differently.

Archer became president of Morehouse during this critical period of the school's development, but also the shifting times of the South when the education of men seeking to become leaders was critical to the continued fight for the economic, social, and civil rights of all Black people in America. Despite the migration, southern Blacks worked tirelessly to create sustainable communities and improve their quality of life. Archer's philosophy and work ethic was the imprimatur that galvanized and catapulted Morehouse into the premier institution for educating Black men. White institutions were still, if at all, admitting very few Black people at a time when the need and demand were great. Morehouse graduates became politicians, civil rights leaders, preachers, business leaders, doctors, scientists, and cultural icons. (Martin Luther King, Jr.'s father and grandfather were Morehouse men and King, Sr. graduated in 1931 during the era of Archer.)

Archer's philosophy which is echoed in the Morehouse overview book of 1933 continues today.

> The purpose of education should be to enable a man to think constructively, to work effectively, to live abundantly and in harmony with his neighbors, and to work together with him in making the world a better place in which to live.[144]

Archer's move to Atlanta came during a time when the leading Black educators and leaders, Booker T. Washington and W.E.B. Dubois, were in a public debate over how best to educate Black people in order to transition them into the White mainstream. Archer's philosophy, in many respects echoed that of Du Bois and his postulate that the path to transformation included the need to educate the 'Talented Tenth.' His lifelong philosophy of the education of Black men to be leaders was consistent with Du Bois' philosophy of educating Black people to enter all professions. His relationship with Du Bois had an impact on the struggle for civil rights that rivaled the influence he asserted over Rev. Martin Luther King, Sr. and Rev. Martin Luther King, Jr.

Archer was president during the Great Depression and faced the challenges presented by this era. His leadership propelled Morehouse as a leading institution and kept it financially healthy. Understanding that funding was crucial to the longevity of an institution, Archer was a prolific fundraiser. His campaign to increase the endowment resulted in a successful campaign that raised one million dollars in 1931 during the Great Depression.[145]

Little is known of his experiences as a Black man at Colgate, but he did not forget his alma mater and contributed financially to Colgate throughout the years. Perhaps as a testament to his memories of his education and experiences at Colgate as a scholar-athlete, Archer gave Morehouse the same colors as Colgate's maroon and white as well as the block M which mimics Colgate's block C. Perhaps it was his prowess on and off the field as a letterman at Colgate and as a football coach at Morehouse (still unmatched with the most wins on record), that prompted him to honor his past (Colgate) and his present (Morehouse).

Martin Luther King, Sr. was an honorary pall bearer at his funeral in 1941[146] and a sample of the many condolences[147] of his passing illustrate the character and legacy of Archer:

He was one of the three great teachers of Morehouse... To us, he always 'walked with the King'.

We will miss him, his council, and the import of his influence which was a tower in Zion to help men and women to think and act aright.

As one of the men of Morehouse...he helped in his lifetime to shape the character of, what many of us think, is the finest group of Negro men in America.

We know of his efficient leadership and the untiring efforts which he put forth to promote a program of higher education for Negro Youth of Atlanta and of the nation. For years I have known of his great contribution to Negro and American education.

Those he served memorialized him in the naming of one of the Morehouse academic buildings "Samuel H. Archer Hall" and a primary school was also named after him. His legacy has not been forgotten at Morehouse.

Considered the godfather of the Civil Rights movement, Howard Thurman was a Morehouse man who graduated in 1923 and knew and admired Archer. In his autobiography, "With Head & Heart: The Autobiography of Howard Thurman," he writes of the "two men of extraordinary leadership" at Morehouse; President Dr. John Hope and Dean Samuel Howard Archer (Archer would become the president many years after Thurman graduated.)[148] Thurman characterized "Hope as the guiding mentor and Archer as the wise, supportive father."[149] He stated that whenever Morehouse men gathered they each had a "special story to tell about 'Big Boy,' as Archer was called." He called Archer a "great teacher" who "helped us define the meaning of the personal pilgrimage on which we were all embarked."[150]

Thurman wrote:

> Hope and Archer-what a team!- were pioneers in education: they undergirded the will to manhood for generations of young Black men, tapping out the timeless rhythm of "Yes," which countered all the negatives beating in upon us from the hostile environment by which we were surrounded.[151]

Colgate recognized Archer with an Honorary Divinity Degree in 1932. The local Hamilton paper mentioned all the honorary degree recipients. Mysteriously, the legacy of Archer at Colgate has been forgotten for decades. His association with the University and contributions to the civil rights campaign through his associations with Rev. King, Du Bois, Thurman, and others remain invisible. Sadly, his story, and the stories of the other distinguished Black men of Colgate was uncovered only as a by-product of the research and preparation for the Colgate bicentennial celebration in 2019. This exposes a common theme in the history of Colgate and begs the question of why the University elected to ignore this part of its history which includes Townsend's expulsion, the work of many early Black men in academia and in the pulpit who each in their way sought to transform this country and elevate a race. The commentary on the topic of eugenics and the Cutten presidency at Colgate on the pages to follow makes this inquiry decidedly less mysterious.

✦ CHAPTER XI ✦
Gordon Blaine Hancock

Upon my arrival at Harvard I served notice on them that I did not want to pursue theological or philosophical studies farther, but instead wanted to enter the field of economics and sociology which would be of far greater help to me in my endeavors to help my stricken people of the south among whom I had decided to live and serve the remainder of my life.

Gordon Blaine Hancock'1919, B.D.'1920

Colgate kept its Baptist roots until the 1920s. Several Black men were among the last to obtain a Bachelor of Divinity Degree.

George Blaine Hancock, Class of 1919; 1920, Honorary Degree, 1969

George Blaine Hancock was born in 1884 in South Carolina. He received two degrees from Benedict College in South Carolina (a historically Black Baptist college) before he was encouraged to apply to Colgate. At the age of 34, he entered Colgate as a junior and moved to Hamilton with his wife. This was the first time in his life that he was in a situation where he had to interact with Whites, and he found himself as one of only four Blacks in the Town of Hamilton. He credited the experience at Colgate on his racial attitudes. In the book by Raymond Gavins, "The Perils and Prospects of Southern Black Leadership Gordon Blaine Hancock 1884-1970," Gavins writes:

Experience in South Carolina, not to mention Northern race riots in 1919, taught Hancock to beware of white people. Nevertheless, it is probable that the kindness and unprejudiced behavior exemplified by some whites did soften his suspicions. "Some of my high opinion of white men and my indisposition to curse out the whole lot because a few are lynchers is based largely on the fact of the fine men I met at Colgate," he testified. "I have outlived hatreds. I am free to respect and love all men."[152]

Hancock graduated in 1919 with his Bachelor of Arts (A.B.) and was one of two Blacks to obtain his Bachelor of Divinity (B.D.) from Colgate in 1920. In the seminary he had a Smith Scholarship, was class vice-president and gave the valedictory speech at graduation. His B.D. thesis was prophetically entitled "Christian Education and the Negro Problem."[153] It was noted he gave an "unusually beautiful address" at graduation as noted in the publication, "Colgate University: The One Hundred and First Anniversary of the Theological Seminary." He continued his education after Colgate and earned degrees from Harvard (M.A.), Cambridge, and Oxford.

Hancock returned to the South like many of his Colgate predecessors and led a career as both a minister and an educator. In letters, he made it clear that while he had choices to go elsewhere it was his calling to return to the South to help the 'Negro' race. He taught economics, religion, and sociology at Virginia Union College from 1925-1963 and served as the pastor of Moore St. Baptist Church. Like many of his Colgate predecessors, Hancock used his education toward the improvement of the Black community. He advocated for self-determination, pride, and economic sustainability for Black people, which encompassed both the philosophies of Washington and Du Bois.

Black men heeded the call to duty and enlisted and fought in World War I. Despite segregated armed forces, and their participation in the fight for freedom in Europe, they returned home to the same discrimination they faced before they left: sanctioned discrimination, White violence, lynchings, false incarcerations, substandard housing, poor education, voter suppression, and a lack of sustainable employment. As World War II (WWII) approached and Black men rose to the challenge to fight for the freedom of others, Hancock and many others were concerned about the treatment of the soldiers and what quality of life they would have once they returned. They knew that the World War I (WWI) veterans who returned were met with the same racial animus as before they left and the hope was to work toward changing the racial environment for the returning veterans as well as the southern Black community. Hancock saw the need to address the hardship and blatant discrimination of his brethren. He believed that the dialogue between the 'Negro' and White citizens to work towards cooperation between them would result in an increased quality of life. Hancock credited his time at Colgate as a basis to work with Whites towards better race relations.

His willingness to forgo a career elsewhere and to return to the South to work and live did not go unnoticed. In a 1944 article on Hancock in the Richmond, Virginia "Times-Dispatch," the newspaper acknowledged his extensive travels and educational background. It reported that Hancock could work anywhere, but chose to return to the South and devote his time and energy to improving race relations.

Hancock believed that racial injustice was the most pressing issue facing the South and he felt it was imperative that legal segregation be immediately ended. Hancock with others met to discuss the pressing issue of Jim Crow and racial discrimination and organized what became known as the all Negro Durham Conference in 1942.[154] It was hailed as the most significant gathering of its kind and Hancock served as the key note speaker at the conference. As a result of the meeting, the organizers felt it was important to document and publish their findings.

The Durham Manifesto was created in 1943.[155] The conference issued the "Durham Manifesto" which articulated what Blacks expected from the post war South and nation in the areas of political, civil rights, employment, education, agriculture, military service, and social welfare. It was met with wide approval and the Manifesto was the catalyst for several subsequent Black conferences and the first interracial conference with White southerners. Hancock was one of the leaders that established the Southern Regional Council which had the objective of justice for Black people throughout the South.[156] Hancock thought it was important for the conference to be a southern Black conference and did not invite any northern Blacks. He felt that southern Blacks were speaking for themselves and he wanted to challenge White southerners who wanted to work for a New South that included equality for all people.

The Durham Conference focused on seven issues that were critical to the Negro community: political and civil rights, industry and labor, service occupations, education, agriculture, armed forces, and social welfare and health. The published Manifesto addresses all seven issues and strongly condemned Jim Crow and sought dialogue with White southerners. When opening the conference, Hancock delivered the 'Statement of Purpose' which included the inception, and purpose:

It has been said, there are some hours of more than sixty minutes and some minutes of more than sixty seconds, surely we have come upon such a great moment in the history of our race and nation. It is a moment of great possibilities and not a little surcharged with drama. Many things have been spoken for him and against him, to him about him; but the Southern Negro is today speaking for himself. His laudable attempt should be a source of pride to the Negro and white South, and to the Negro and white North, East, and West....

The inception of this conference hinges about the tragedy that took place at the close of World War I, when returning Negro soldiers were met not with expressions and evidences of the democracy for which they had fought and for which thousands of their fellow race-men died. Instead there was a sweeping surge of bitterness and rebuff that in retrospect constitutes one of the ugliest scars on the fair face of our nation. Interracial matters were left adrift and tragic was our experience and distressing was our disillusionment.... Today the nations are locked in mortal combat...but this we know, that the Negro is again taking the filed in defense of his nation. Quite significant also is the fact that whereas the pronounced anti-Negro movement followed the last war, it is getting under way even before the issues of war have been decided. In an hour of national peril, efforts are being made to defeat the Negro first and the Axis powers later. Already the dire threat to throw again the Negro question into the politics of the South is becoming more and more dangerous.

The Purpose of The Conference

...is to try to do something about this developing situation. We are proposing to set forth in certain "Articles of Cooperation" just what the Negro wants and is expecting of the post-war South and nation. Instead of letting the demagogues guess what we want, we are proposing to make our wants and aspirations a matter of record, so clear that he who runs may read. We are hoping in this way to challenge the constructive cooperation of that element of the white South who express themselves as desirous of a New Deal for the Negroes of the South.

...to be sure, our task is a delicate one, but delicate tasks are never impossible, if performed by men who are not themselves delicate in spirit. More often the firm handling of delicate issues proves the wiser course. The matter handled in Panuel Hall was delicate, but it was firmly handled and the world thereby was blessed. So in this historic meeting today, whatever advance step we may make in race relations will rebound to the advantage of the South and nation no less than to the advancement of the Negro race. Let us bear ever in mind that the soul of the South and nation are at stake no less than the fortunes of the Negro race.

The document continued with a 'Statement by Southern Negroes':

The war has sharpened the issue of Negro white [sic] relations in the United States, and particularly in the South. A result has been increased racial tensions, fears, and aggressions, and an opening up of the basic questions of racial segregation and discrimination, Negro minority rights, and democratic freedom, as they apply practically in Negro-white relations in the South. These are acute and threaten to become even more serious as they increasingly block, through the deeper fears aroused, common sense consideration for even elementary improvements in Negro status, and the welfare of the country as a whole.

...We are fundamentally opposed to the principle and practice of compulsory segregation in our American society, whether of races or classes or creeds, however, we regard it as both sensible and timely to address ourselves now to the current problems of racial discrimination and neglect and to ways in which we may cooperate in the advancement of programs aimed at the sound improvement of race relations within the democratic framework. "...We regard it as unfortunate that the simple efforts to correct obvious social and economic injustices continue, with such considerable popular support, to be interpreted as the predatory ambition of irresponsible Negroes to invade the privacy of family life."

Addressing the seven issues:

Political and civil rights:
...We regard the ballot as a safeguard of democracy. Any

discrimination against citizens in the exercise of the voting privilege, on account of race or poverty, is detrimental to the freedom of these citizens and to the integrity of the State and urge: The abolition of the poll tax; of the white primary; all forms discriminatory practices, evasions of the law, and intimidations of citizens seeking to exercise their right of franchise; exclusion of Negroes from jury service; personal security against abuses of police power by white officers of the law...which include wanton killings,...routine beatings,... not only out of regard for the safety of Negroes, but of common respect for the dignity and fundamental purpose of the law...employment of Negro police will enlist the full support of Negro citizens in control of lawless elements of their own group. In the public carriers and terminals, where segregation of the races is currently made mandatory...it is the duty of Negro and white citizens to insist that these provisions be equal in kind and quality and in character of maintenance.

. . .although...a decline in lynching, the practice is still current in some areas of the South....defended by resistance to Federal legislation designed to discourage the practice... effective enforcement of present or new laws against this crime by apprehending and punishing parties participating in this lawlessness...urge support of all American citizens... securing Federal legislation against lynching.

Industry and Labor:
...economic survival and development for Negroes is inclusion in unskilled, semi-skilled and skilled branches of work in the industries or occupations of the region to the extent that they are equally capable...the President's Fair Employment Practices Committee are regarded by us as sound and economically essential...same pay for same work... opportunities for collective bargaining and security through

membership in labor organizations...labor unions of white workers should seek the organization of Negro workers... only labor unions that admit Negroes to membership and participation on a fair and democratic basis should be eligible for the benefits of the national labor Relations Board, Railway Labor Act, State Labor Relations Acts and other protective labor legislation...Negroes should have equal opportunity in training programs carried on by industries and by labor organizations...Negro representation on regional organizations concerned with the welfare of workers...we regard the wage and job freezing order of the War Manpower Commission as...distinct disadvantage to Negroes and other marginal workers...most of these workers are now employed in the lowest-income job brackets...the freeze order can remove the opportunity for economic advancement... the South's economic and cultural development can be accelerated by increasing the purchasing power and skills of Negro workers.

Service Occupations:
Any realistic estimate of the occupational situation of Negroes...will be employed in greatest proportions for a long time in service occupations...more training should be provided workers who plan to enter the service field,...reward and treatment on the job should be such as to make the workers feel that their training is justified. Opportunity...to advance through the opening up of additional opportunities...a wholesome environment, living accommodations, food, uniforms, and rest rooms, all of an approved standard, should be provided...opportunity to live, after stipulated hours of work, as an individual undisturbed in his private life by the whims and caprices of his employers...service workers should be organized into unions with recognized affiliations...provisions for old age insurance, unemployment compensation, workmen's compensation, the wage and hour

act, and other benefits of Social Security legally provided to workers of other categories.

Education:

...equal opportunity for all citizens is the very foundation of the democratic faith, and...Christian ethic which gave birth to the ideal of democratic living, it is imperative that every measure possible be taken to insure an equality of education to Negroes...improvement in Negro education is better schools, expenditures by States of considerably more funds for the Negro schools...equalization of salaries of white and Negro teachers on the basis of equal preparation and experience...expanded school building program for Negro schools designed to overcome the present racial disparity in physical facilities...revision of the school program in terms of the social setting, vocational needs and marginal cultural characteristics of the Negro children...same length of school term for all children...our growing knowledge of the effect of environment upon the intelligence and social adjustment of children... to insure equality of educational opportunity it is not enough to provide for the under-privileged child...the same opportunities provided for those on superior levels of familial, social, and economic life...a function of Government to assure equalization far beyond the mere expenditure of equivalent funds for salaries...increased demand for graduate and professional training...made available equally for white and Negro eligible students in terms defined by the United States Supreme Court in the decision on the case of Gaines versus the University of Missouri...Federal funds should be made available to overcome the differentials between white and Negro facilities and between southern and national standards...demands for intelligent and sympathetic representation...on school boards by qualified persons of the Negro race...education of the Negro youth can be measurably aided by the use of Negro enforcement officers of truancy and compulsory education laws...

Agriculture:

The South is the most rural section of the nation, and Negroes, who constitute 33 per cent of its population, are responsible for an important share of the agricultural production on southern farms...the South is economically handicapped and...deeply rooted in agricultural maladjustments...Negroes are a large part of the sharecropped and tenant group...establishment of sufficient safeguards in the system of tenancy to promote the development of land and home ownership and more security on the land, by written contracts, longer lease terms, higher farm wages for day laborers, balanced farm programs, including food and feed crops for present tenant and day laborers, adequate Federal assistance to Negro farmers should be provided on an equitable basis...equitable distribution of funds for teaching agriculture in the Negro land grant colleges to provide agricultural research and experimentation for Negro farmers...appointment of qualified Negroes to governmental planning and policy making bodies concerned with the common farmer...membership of Negro farmers in general farmers' organizations and economic cooperatives, to provide appropriate representation...

Military Service:

Negro soldiers, in line of military duty and in training in the South, encounter particularly acute racial problems in transportation and in recreation and leave areas. They are frequently mistreated by the police...these problems... unnecessary and destructive to morale.

Social Welfare and Health:

...acute problems of Negro health, family and personal disorganization are reflection of deficiencies in economic opportunity...mandatory provisions that a proportion of the facilities in all public hospitals be available for Negro patients...Negro doctors be either included on the staff for services to Negro patients, permitted as practitioners the same privilege and courtesy as other practitioners in the public hospitals...Negro public health nurses and social workers be more extensively used in both public and private organizations...slum clearance and erection of low-cost housing...Federal government has set an excellent precedent.

The report concluded:

...the wicked notion that the struggle of the Negro for citizenship is a struggle against the best interests of the Nation...to urge such a doctrine...is to preach disunity and to deny the most elementary principles of American life and government....The effect of the war has been to make the Negro, in a sense, the symbol and protagonist of every other minority in America and in the world at large. Local issues in the South...must be met wisely and courageously if this Nation is to become a significant political entity in a new international world....The correction of these problems is not only a moral matter, but a practical necessity in winning the war and in winning the peace. Herein rests the chance to reveal our greatest weakness or our greatest strength.[157]

The conference articulated the effects of the racialized South and outlined a blueprint to reverse the effects of racism and provide equal opportunities to balance the inequities. Several of the points espoused at the Conference directly rebuked President Franklin Delano Roosevelt's (FDR) "New Deal," which many Blacks called the "Raw Deal." To ensure southern support for the New Deal, FDR excluded domestic workers and farmers in the creation of social security. These were occupations specifically held by southern Blacks and the decision has had repercussions to this day. The Durham Manifesto articulated the cause and effect and need for change within the racialized southern environment and Hancock furthered his vision of racial equality in the classroom.

At Virginia Union, Hancock taught that the Black race was not inferior or more prone to commit crimes. He is credited with developing and teaching the first course on race relations in the country. He understood the need for the Black community to hold jobs, be laborers, and obtain an education in order to move into all professions and civic engagement. He proposed the "Double Duty Dollar" to encourage Black people to keep jobs, land, and money and to spend in their own communities. He also started a 'keep your job" campaign in the Black community. This same strategy would be used during the civil rights movement of the 1950s and beyond.

Hancock used his pen to advocate for equality and wrote regularly for various newspapers advocating economic, political, and social equality for the Black community. He published a weekly syndicated column for the Associated Negro Press from 1928-1965 which appeared in over one hundred Black newspapers across the nation. Topics included focused on politics, desegregation, economics, and Black leadership. He also authored several books such as, "Christian Education and the Negro Problem," "The Interrelationship of the Immigrant and the Negro Problem," and "Three Elements of African Culture."

Although known as a 'conservative' Hancock believed that Black people should learn vocational skills, buy land, have good relations with Whites (Washingtonian view), and that there should be a 'talented tenth' to become leaders of the community (Du Bois view).[158] He wrote fondly of Du Bois in one of his weekly columns in the Associated Negro Press that "There is a shout in the heart of Negroes everywhere, for Du Bois has long been our symbol of manhood and integrity."

Hancock understood and appreciated the educational philosophy of Tuskegee and Hampton and the "once deplored...inclination of those schools to desert the field of their specialty for pursuits in the arts and sciences of a more academic endeavor"... making it clear that he "always advocated more emphasis on the practical arts." In 1949 he wrote to the Board Secretary at Colgate, Reed Alford, regarding his representing Colgate University at the inauguration of Dr. Moran of Hampton Institute. Hampton Institute believed in the Booker T. Washington educational philosophy of attaining vocational trades for Black men and women.

He expressed gratitude regarding the offer to represent Colgate in the inauguration of a new President at Hampton and he believed the new president would return to the roots of the founders. This, of course, put him squarely in the camp of Booker T. Washington who believed that the best route for Blacks was to learn a trade in order to pull themselves out of the ravages of centuries of enslavement. Hancock also believed that one should not seek to continue to pit the pedagogy of Washington and Du Bois at odds. (See Appendix for the text of the letter).

As with Archer, Booker Jones, and other Colgate men, Hancock recognized the significant work needed to bring educational, economic, political, and social parity in line with White southerners. There was much work to be done in order to overcome the racial divide, and Hancock dedicated his life to this mission.

Having the benefit of a Colgate education, Hancock was sensitive to the need for Blacks to continue to attend the University. He would, like other Black alums who attended Colgate, recognized the obvious shift in admissions to exclude Black students during the Cutten years and he was not shy in writing the institution about the obvious omission of Black students. He remarked to a fellow alum of Colgate in 1944, that he "deplored," but was not "surprised," that there were no 'Negroes' at Colgate as he knew about President Cutten's attitude toward 'Negroes'. [159]

One of the few times Colgate recognized the achievements of a Black graduate was bestowing the honorary Doctor of Law degree in 1969 to Hancock, shortly before his death. (See Appendix for the text).

In 2017, Colgate furthered recognized the transformative work of Hancock and named one of its four residential commons after George Blaine Hancock.

William Tucker Parker, Class of 1920, Bachelor of Divinity; M.A., 1923

William Tucker Parker was born in 1886 in rural Georgia. His father and grandfather before him had been enslaved. From a humble beginning, he worked to put himself through primary school and then Georgia State College where he graduated with an Associate Degree in 1917. He received his Doctorate of Divinity (D.D.) from Virginia Theological Seminary College before traveling with his wife Daisy to attend Colgate. He received his Bachelor of Divinity (B.D.) in 1920.

His 1918 draft card illustrated his work ethic and his occupation was listed as a Pullman Porter at Grand Central Station and that he resided with his wife in the Bronx.[160] His WWII draft card (although he was 56 at the time) has him listed as the pastor of the First Baptist Church in Princeton, New Jersey.

After Colgate, he devoted his life to the ministry and he was the 7th pastor at Second Baptist Church in Mumford and LeRoy, New York from 1920-1927. He later became the pastor of the First Baptist Church in Princeton from 1932 until his retirement in 1964. He died in 1968, and like his fellow Black alums, he was credited with rebuilding his parish and tripling its membership. Parker was mentioned in "The Crisis" in 1939 when he delivered opening and closing prayers at the Interracial Good Will Hour held at First Baptist Church. In 1950, "Town Topics," a local newspaper in Princeton, New Jersey nominated Rev. Parker as "Princeton's Man of the Week."

Town Topics
WE NOMINATE

William Tucker Parker, dean of Princeton's active clergymen and one of the community's best known citizens, who this week, in accordance with the wishes of a grateful parish, is celebrating his 20th anniversary as pastor of the First Baptist Church. The grandson of a slave, the son of a Georgia farmer born into slavery, Parker-as well as any living Princetonian-personifies the advance of democracy down through the years and provides what can be accomplished in the face of dismaying odds. His is an American story, a story that could only be lived, and written, in these United States.

Now in his 22d year as Director of Religious Education under the Afro-American Baptist and the New Jersey Baptist Conventions, he was a youngster of "eight or nine," when at a religious meeting near his native Thomaston, Georgia, he made up his mind that "some day I will be educated." He kept his hopes and plans to himself, saved every penny he managed to earn and at age 20, with $21 to his name and in the face of parental opposition took the initial long step forward by enrolling in the first grade at Butler, Ga.

"Working one's way through school" connotes self-sacrifice, but seldom does it mean combining studies with six hours of wood-cutting in the Georgia Pines, and with noon-day meals consisting of a roll and a glass of water. "Without receiving a dime from anyone" until he qualified for a scholarship at Colgate University in 1917, Parker found his academic bearings at the Central City College of Macon, Ga., and earned his B.A. at Georgia State College. His off-term employment during those undergraduate years ranged from deck-duties on a dredge to the first of 11 summers in Pullman service.

Parker, who holds four degrees, including a Master of Arts from Colgate and a Doctor of Divinity from Virginia Theological Seminary and College was called here after he had divided a decade between Baptist churches in New York and elsewhere in New Jersey. Since establishing his home in Princeton, he has literally 'rebuilt' his parish, and has tripled its membership, in addition to devoting 10 years to directing the Baptist Young People's State Convention and to giving of himself to so many organizations and committees that he can rightfully say, "I do everything I can for Princeton."

For being, in the words of one of his own parishioners, not only a Minister of the Gospel but a true friend, always ready to help; for exemplifying the guiding principle of his life, "Seek God first and everything else will come in order," for meriting the esteem of all of Princeton; he is TOWN TOPICS' nominee for PRINCETON'S MAN OF THE WEEK.

Howard Franklyn Lewis, Class of 1920

Little has been uncovered about Lewis's life. He was mentioned in "The Crisis" upon graduating from Colgate in 1920 with a Bachelor of Divinity degree.

Black men, like Lewis, who received their Divinity degrees from Colgate continued to demonstrate the power of their faith, intellect, and commitment through their life's work. They provided substance to their communities with the hope of transforming the nation.

⤚ CHAPTER XII ⤙
The Men of the New Century 1900-1920

How fine it would be if every white college boy in the United States could meet a colored school mate like this!

Comment from classmate on the passing of
N.Lloyd. Gilbert, Class of 1915

At the dawn of a new century, the racial divide was widening and becoming more entrenched. In his seminal work, "Souls of Black Folk," Du Bois articulated that the problem of the 20th century was the problem of the 'color line'. A 'problem' that has consumed this country for the 20th and now the 21st centuries.

The first generations post-slavery worked tirelessly to uplift Black communities. They continuously faced overt obstacles in the South and covert obstacles in the North. The South had embedded in its economy, politics, culture, housing, health care, and education two separate societies; one Black, the other White. They were not equal and in 1896, the United States Supreme Court in its landmark decision, **Plessy v. Ferguson** 163 U.S. 537 held that segregated laws and services were constitutional. It would take over fifty years to overturn the decision and declare segregated laws and facilities unconstitutional in the landmark decision, **Brown v. The Board of Education of Topeka, Kansas,** 347 U.S. 483.

Many Black people frustrated with the tyrannical grip of White supremacy in the South and keeping Blacks as second-class citizens, began to leave the South for the West and North in what would become known as the "Great Migration." The "Great Migration" was one of the largest movements of a people in America outside the forced migration of the Native Americans. Blacks left the agricultural South for northern and western cities in search of higher paying jobs, better housing, and education. However, not all Blacks who came North stayed, and as the following Colgate men demonstrate, they were born in the South, educated in the North, and returned South to uplift a new generation.

Peter Neal Carter*
George Lewis Hayes- 1903
John Brown Watson*
Everett Booker Jones- 1905
Newton Lloyd Gilbert- 1915
Burwell Townsend Harvey- 1916
Ira David Pinson- 1918
Garnet Langton Hegemen- 1919
*transferred after a year

George Lewis Hayes- Class of 1903

Hayes was born in Virginia and attended Wayland Institute before attending Colgate. It appears he was a classmate of Archer's at both Wayland and Colgate. At Colgate, Hayes was a Kingsford Speaker and played both football and baseball. After Colgate he became a teacher, assistant principal, and principal in the public-school system in Indianapolis. He did graduate work in education at Harvard, the University of Chicago, the University of Michigan, the University of Wisconsin, and Butler University. He taught summer school at Tuskegee Institute for six summers and was associated with Dr. Booker T. Washington and Dr. George Washington Carver. He served as the director of Summer School at Morehouse College for four summers and he worked with Archer at Morehouse. He also taught during certain summers in Kentucky and in North Carolina. He joined the faculty of Atlanta University in 1930.[161] His Colgate yearbook in his senior year states as follows:

Leo is a youth of large expectations. ...where he passed his childhood days in eating, sleeping, and dreaming of future greatness. Later, he wandered off to Wayland Seminary... Much might be accomplished by him if only his activity equaled his confidence. His conversational powers (a la Sphinx) are worthy of mention. A wearied expression now and then beclouds his manly brow, as if life were a burden and all forms of activity a hardship.

The description of Hayes' "wearied expression now and then beclouds his manly brow, as if life were a burden and all forms of activity a hardship" reveals the detachment Colgate community had with respect to its Black students. The weight of the world was pressing against Hayes and others who were barely a generation beyond bondage. Still steeped in the hotbed of racist Jim Crow, Hayes' "wearied expression" bemoaned the burden of life because this was his reality. This serves as yet another example of the White Colgate haze and their inability to conjure empathy and see beyond their racism.

Everett Booker Jones, Class of 1905

Everett Booker Jones was born in Tallahassee, Florida in 1876. He graduated from Florida Agricultural and Mechanical University (FAMU) before attending Colgate. At Colgate he played baseball and joined the German Club and Chemistry Society and graduated in 1905.[162] Jones obtained a Master of Science degree in 1907 from the University of Iowa and returned to FAMU as a science professor where he spent the majority of his career. His tenure at FAMU, an HBCU, ran from 1906-1924. He taught chemistry and biology there until his wife became Dean of Women at Lincoln University in Missouri. The family moved to Missouri and Jones began teaching chemistry at Lincoln University.[163]

Jones' decision to form a literary society at FAMU is an indication that he understood the value of the 'Talented Tenth' and, as Archer was fond of saying, "[educating] a MAN and not a carpenter or a blacksmith." The Du Bois view, of course, aligns with the idea of the liberal arts education, but more importantly it was critical of the development of the economic, social, and political development of the Negro community. Jones died in 1929 and like Archer and others before him, he taught and prepared some of the greatest minds (both men and women) for medical careers. His dedication to teaching at FAMU was not forgotten. The school honored his contributions and legacy by naming one of the dormitories on campus - Jones Hall. [164]

Additionally, in honoring Jones in 1962, the FAMU Hall of Fame Series wrote:

EVERETT BOOKER JONES-Dr. Jones; a native of Tallahassee, graduated from Florida A. and M. University in 1895. After teaching several years, he entered Colgate University from which he graduated with a Bachelor of Science degree in 1904. It was at this time that he earned the Phi Beta Kappa key. He earned the Master's degree in Science in 1926, and did further study toward the Ph.D. degree. Prior to his death, he was serving as Professor of Chemistry at Lincoln University in Missouri.

Many science students and medical doctors in Florida and elsewhere claim that they were fortunate to receive science training under Jones. His devotion to teaching young men and women in the sciences was reflected in his tireless efforts and success in building the science department at FAMU.[165] Jones was also the organizer and first President of the FAMU Alumni Association and organized the "College Witts," the first literary society for college men in the institution.[166] He is remembered by those with whom he came in contact as one who inspired his associates through his example and devotion to duty.

As with Archer, Jones elected to teach the 'Talented Tenth' to become future Black scientists and doctors who would enter the American mainstream and serve their communities. Jones had a fondness for his alma mater and returned for several of his class reunions over the years.

Through the years, many of the HBCUs have not survived and many have closed due to a lack of funding or shrinking student enrollment. The Colgate men who gave their intellect, energy, and dedication to HBCUs such as Morehouse, FAMU, and Virginia Union University have all thrived and are still educating Black people to this day.

Newton Lloyd Gilbert, Class of 1915

Gilbert is the first known Black legacy student. His father was Matthew Gilbert, Class of 1887 and 1890, and president of Selma University in Selma, Alabama. Newton died before his senior year, but he was well regarded by his community and peers. The Colgate Student Body issued a Resolution in the Madisonensis:

> Whereas, the Omniscient Creator has seen fit to remove from this earth the soul of our beloved friend and fellow-student Newton Lloyd Gilbert. Be it Hereby Resolved That we, the Students' Association of Colgate University, extend to his family our sincere sympathy, and Be it further Resolved, That a copy of these resolutions be sent to the stricken family and also published in the Madisonensis.[167]

In addition, his classmates, as recorded in "The Crisis," stated: "How fine it would be if every white college boy in the United States come to meet a colored school mate like this!"

This statement was made at a time African American men, women, and children were lynched with regularity in the South, subject to domestic terrorism from the KKK and other White hate groups, in a country with constitutionally segregated unequal schooling.[168]

In its July 1915 publication, "The Crisis" published the Dean of Colgate's remarks on Gilbert's passing; "A very fine student indeed… was with us for three years and would have been graduated with honor if he had lived."

Burwell Townsend Harvey, Class of 1916

Harvey ran track at Colgate and, as team captain he competed with the team at the Penn Relays. In 1916, Harvey became a physics and chemistry professor at Morehouse College and remained at Morehouse as a professor for 42 years.[169] Harvey has been credited as the most successful athletic coach in Morehouse College history, and the Morehouse football stadium (B.T. Harvey Stadium) was named in his honor. He was the first commissioner of the Southern Intercollegiate Athletic Conference (SIAC) and continued as commissioner for 25 years (1941-1965). He coached basketball, baseball, and football and had the highest winning percentage in the entire history of Morehouse College basketball coaches. Harvey was inducted into the hall of fame at SIAC, National Association of Collegiate Directors of Athletics, and Atlanta University. He also founded and published a weekly newsletter, "Bench Talk Heard," on Black college sports and professional athletics.[170]

Ira David Pinson, Class of 1918

Prior to his coming to Colgate, Pinson obtained a B.A. from Benedict College. At Colgate, Pinson was a member of the glee club earning an M.A. After Colgate, Pinson graduated from Yale with a Bachelor of Divinity (B.D.). He taught German and philosophy at Morris College, a historically Black Baptist college in South Carolina that was incorporated in 1911. After the departure of the second president, the college was failing financially and was forced to transition into a junior college. Pinson became the third president of Morris from 1930-1939 and during his tenure, he was able to restore the junior and senior programs. He died in a car crash in 1939.

John Brown Watson, Class of 1904

Watson transferred and graduated from Brown University. He would go on to become the president of Leland College, and the University of Arkansas at Pine Bluffs.

P. Carter Neal

Neal graduated from Wayland Seminary, and Lincoln University before coming to Hamilton Theological Seminary for one year. He was mentioned in the "Who Who's of Colored Baptist in the United States" in 1913 "as a public speaker among the best... as a sermonizer, clear and pointed, and his lectures are models of elegance, and drive home to the hearts...."

⤞ CHAPTER XIII ⤝
Jim Crow Comes to Colgate

The problem of the twentieth century is the problem of the color-line—the relation of the darker to the lighter races of men in Asia and Africa, in America and the islands of the sea.

W.E.B. Du Bois, "The Souls of Black Folk"

Raymond Vaughn, 1929

Raymond Vaughn was a star football player and the first in his hometown of Oil City, Pennsylvania, to play football and study at Colgate. However, it was the 1920s, Jim Crow was alive and thriving, and George Cutten was president of Colgate. It was a time in the history of the United States when it was clear that Black life was still as disposable as it had been prior to the Civil War. The resurgence of the southern economy was fueled in large part by Black bodies through forced imprisonment, stealing of land, and sharecropping. The rise of the KKK's unchallenged terrorism, the suppression of the Black political and economic voice, Jim Crow laws, and the denial of the right to vote bore an even deeper hole in the resilience of the Black collective. Lynchings were a common occurrence in the South and many Black families joined the Great Migration in search of a better life and an opportunity to breathe, support your family, educate your children, find decent housing, and in general have a better quality of life than the one they faced in the South. However, the 'color line' did not end with the migration from the South, its tentacles reached far and wide, and Colgate was not immune nor did little to avoid its grip.

In 1925, Raymond "Ray" Vaughn was recruited to study and play football at Colgate. Colgate had a proud tradition on the football field, and Cutten, who had played football, was known to be at every game cheering for the team in all kinds of weather. Alice Smith, Cutten's longtime secretary, confirmed Cutten's interest in sports by publishing one of her journal entries in the 1924 *Salmagundi* (Colgate yearbook) under the caption, "The Man In The Stands." The article recounts the events in a game of particular importance:

> Several thousands of enthusiasts undaunted by the forecast of rain from a clouded and darkened sky had come to welcome the new president of the university and also to cheer the team on to victory. The game began, the players fought, the students cheered, little heeding the pouring rain that drenched the players and the crowd. ...the alumni began to forsake the bleachers for a place of shelter.... When the final whistle blew the alumni bleachers contained but a handful of spectators.... The game was over... The players departed from the field; the students stood in the pouring rain to pay homage to their Alma Mater.... As the words of the Alma Mater floated across the field, the eyes of the singers were caught by a scene so significant and characteristic of real leadership,... For there in the opposite bleachers, stood a man, alone, for his friends and guest had departed, but there he stood, with his hat in his hands... with rain dropping from his broad forehead and running down his smiling face stood the man of the hour and new leader of Colgate men.[171]

Alice wrote that Dr. Cutten was very interested in sports and recounted:

> He had played football at Yale and at Colgate is credited with assisting Andy Kerr in the development of the deceptive

lateral pass. He said 'Many things make football attractive to college men. Its inspiring spirit, its co-operative effort, its healthful exercise, its moral equivalents, its educational advantages, its sacrificial demands, all coupled with a tinge of daring which brings forth a fine brand of courage.'[172]

Little did Vaughn realize that when he chose to attend Colgate, his football prowess would take a back seat to Jim Crow. Vaughn was a star running back and became the starting running back after his freshmen year. He lettered in '26, '27, and '28. He also was a member of the track and gym teams. Vaughn's prowess which helped secure a victory over Michigan State, and a 60 yard march against Syracuse for a 30-6 win, were both legendary. Off the field, Vaughn was a scholar and a member of the sociology club and the Maroon Key. Nonetheless, the 1926 and 1928 seasons garnered national attention not for success on the field but for decisions made off the field. Colgate succumbed to pressure and left Vaughn, and later both Vaughn and Crosby, at home against teams that refused or made it clear they would not play a team that had a 'Negro' player on the field.

In 1926, Vaughn was benched and did not travel with the team to play Navy or the University of Pittsburgh. Colgate was scheduled to play Navy at Annapolis; however, Navy made it clear, but denied it publicly, that their midshipmen would not take the field if a 'Negro' was on the field. The Naval Academy athletic director denied to the *Boston Daily Globe* that Vaughn was left at home at the request of Navy.[173] However, in a letter received by the *Pittsburgh Courier* on Oct. 29, 1926, Vaughn stated that he had been benched against the University of Pittsburgh, on Pitts's protest. Vaughn also stated that he had been kept out of the Navy game by a similar protest. Vaughn wrote that the Colgate coach told him they had received a letter from Navy prohibiting him from playing and was told it was the same reason that he didn't go to Navy and Pitt. The paper recorded that Vaughn had played every game since his freshmen year until the Pitt and Navy games. The press reported that many of his friends and family from Oil City had traveled to see him play against Pitt.[174] The *Baltimore Afro-American* press reported on Nov. 6, 1926, that Navy denied the accusation that they would not play with Vaughn on the field. It was further reported that Vaughn sent a telegram to the NAACP, saying that while Navy had not officially requested that he not play, some of the athletic officials at Colgate talked it over and they (Vaughn included) decided it was best not to go to Navy. This contradicted a previous statement by Vaughn that he had been shown a letter from Navy indicating their opposition, suggesting Vaughn may have been pressured to recuse himself. The article further reported and suggested that Navy had sought to draw the 'color line' through unofficial channels. Despite the Navy athletic director's denial, it was reported that members of the Navy team were aware that Vaughn was Black, and there was always some excuse for why Navy never played a game with a Negro on the field.[175] Colgate lost both games. With a 5-2-2 record for the 1926 season, Colgate lost to Navy 7 to 13, and lost to the University of Pittsburgh 16 to 13. In 1928, with a season record of 6-3, Colgate lost to Vanderbilt 12 to 7, and beat Virginia Polytech 35 to 14. Vanderbilt and Virginia Polytech were the other schools who refused to play if Vaughn and Crosby took the field.

Written documentation of Cutten's involvement in the Colgate decision to bow to racist demands has not surfaced. However, it is unimaginable that a decision of this magnitude and attention would not have been discussed with President Cutten. Cutten, a man heavily involved with the athletics program and an avowed racist, certainly did not overrule the decision to bench Vaughn and Crosby.

After graduation Vaughn taught anthropology and coached football at Morehouse College during Archer's tenure. One might imagine that, perhaps, Archer interceded in the hiring of Vaughn, but there is no evidence of this in the records. Vaughn was an assistant principal and physical education teacher at Harlem High School in Brooklyn, New York, and during World War II, he was the USO director for the state of Washington at Tacoma and later in San Francisco, California. He also served as a probation officer with the

Brooklyn, Queens, and Manhattan Family Courts.[176]

When asked by a classmate 50 years later about that "less than pleasant experience of the past," Vaughn responded, "That's water over the dam."

Vaughn is the forgotten Colgate gridiron legend. He lettered all three years playing varsity football, and was credited with the wins against Michigan and Syracuse. Nonetheless, he was forced to sit out three games due to Colgate's willingness to acquiesce to racism. After Vaughn, there would be no other Black Colgate athletes during the remainder of Cutten's tenure.

← CHAPTER XIV →
Cutten

Say what you wish but be careful what you write. People forget what you have said, but what you have written rises up and stabs you in the back years after you have forgotten what you have written.

Dr. George Barton Cutten's advice to young men[177]

By the end of the Civil War, there had been a steady trickle of Black men who attended Colgate. However, despite that lofty statistic of an 8th ranking in 1900 (see Chapter 5), the doors and access to a Colgate education were slammed shut in 1927. There would not be a Black student on campus again until the late 1940s and early 1950s. Sadly, the steady reemergence of Blacks in more than single numbers would not take place until the mid-1960s.

There existed, and still exists, a false narrative among many that the Jim Crow era that enforced subjugation of the Black mind and body through legislation, terror, economics, culture, and the criminal justice system, was confined to the South; however, nothing was further from the truth. In northern states, Black people were generally concentrated in urban areas that contained inferior housing, education, services, and jobs. Redlining, the system of excluding Black families from White neighborhoods, was commonplace. Banks refused mortgages, realtors steered prospective buyers to segregated Black neighborhoods, and the White community enforced restrictive covenants that contractually prohibited Whites from selling their homes to Blacks. The quality of schools paralleled (and still does) to the wealth and Whiteness of the neighborhood and ensures the prevalence of inferior schools in predominately Black neighborhoods. This, coupled with substandard housing, underemployment, and unemployment plaguing the Black communities, was the covert Jim Crow that was as destructive to Black communities in the North as the overt Jim Crow in the South. There were race riots, where White mobs burned and destroyed sustainable and thriving Black communities in all regions of the country. There were also communities that sprung up as a result of White privilege and its exclusion of the Black community from participating fully in mainstream American society.

With the shift away from its Baptist roots, Colgate's students entering the 20th century were not necessarily pursuing careers in the ministry. As the 20th century progressed, Black men who attended Colgate used their Colgate degrees to further the cause for equality, social justice, quality healthcare, voter rights, and opening the doors for others to follow in their chosen professions and lifestyles.

There is indisputable evidence that the position taken by Eaton and his colleagues in the early 1800s on the question of slavery had a chilling effect on White student activism. The attitudes of the administration and faculty may have influenced the expulsion of Townsend and the public debate between Eaton and Smith may have been a factor in the admission of Colgate's first Black graduate, Henry Livingston Simpson. Henry Livingston Simpson was also one of the earliest Black men to receive a degree from an American college. One may theorize that the admission of formerly enslaved men after the Civil War may have been an attempt by the University to assuage its guilt with respect to its position on slavery. Or perhaps it may have been an attempt to ensure that Baptist theology would be at the forefront at a critical moment in history as the education of Black men and women expanded in America; however, we will never know for certain.

Admittedly, history is always seen through the lens of the person, people, or community that shape the focus, narrative, and memory through their dominant experiences. Whether conscious or unconscious, marginalized people and communities are often left out of the historical narrative. The historical narrative will also minimize a narrative when that narrative, viewed through the historical lens, ends up on the 'wrong side of history.' The Colgate historical narrative is not immune to this gaze. Looking back at this history, enables us to look forward during the University's bicentennial year of 2019.

In 1922 Colgate installed its eighth president, George Barton Cutten. Over the course of his 20-year presidency, Cutten transformed Colgate. He expanded the land holdings from 275 acres to approximately 1,000. He balanced the budget during the Great Depression; doubled the faculty and increased the student body. He instituted the "Colgate Plan" to wide national admiration, which was described as having three advantages: cultural, vocational, and psychological. The Plan would give the Colgate men a broader outlook of the world of knowledge. With the survey courses, a Colgate man would be better prepared to choose his life's work and psychologically, the survey courses would stimulate curiosity that would last a lifetime. The modern iteration of the "Colgate Plan" is today's "Core Curriculum." Cutten's legacy extended beyond improvements to the educational, fiscal, and physical landscape of the University.[178] His inauguration also marks the beginning of a controversial race policy at Colgate during his tenure from 1922 to 1942. On the occasion of his inaugural ceremony, *The Colgate Maroon* wrote:

> Dr. Cutten will lead Colgate University through a golden age and towards the goal of the institution, the development of strong **Christian** manhood (bold added).[179]

The glowing tribute to Cutten neglected to mention that he was a eugenicist, and his views were not private. He openly expressed his disdain for the "feebleminded," "low intelligent," and "immigrants." Cutten was not alone and many American educators, politicians, and scientists embraced eugenics in the early 20th century. Their model became the bedrock for the rise of Hitler's master race philosophy. The Germans were quick to point to the Americans who embraced

INTO the LIGHT

eugenics as the basis for their belief in the superiority of the White race and the justification for slaughtering millions of Jews, Catholics, and Gypsies during the lead up to and during World War II.

The merchants who trafficked in this poison came to Colgate and reviewed the athletic program and facilities, which at that moment in time was devoid of a Black presence. Cutten, seemingly embraced the Nazis and welcomed top ranking Nazis to the Colgate campus in 1933. Moreover, two German 1936 Olympic Committee officials touring the United States went to Colgate to observe the athletic program.[180] From 1935 to 1939, Colgate admitted one foreign exchange student yearly from a German University.[181]

In less than ten years, Cutten had succeeded in dismantling the fragile, but decades old diversity at Colgate. Non-White men studied at Colgate as early as the 1820s, with the first Americans Indians, as well as Asian students, and a Black in the 1840s. The trend continued and Colgate educated formerly enslaved and free Blacks after the Civil War up until the time of Cutten's presidency. Colgate had 'tolerated' the (few) Black bodies, yet under Cutten's leadership it became clear that the Black body was no longer welcomed at Colgate.

The first obvious manifestation was the University's sanctioned benching of its star Black football player to appease schools that refused to play with a Black man on the field. Navy, the University of Pittsburgh, and Virginia Poly Tech made their racialized policies clear by refusing to participate in any games with a Black opponent and Colgate, of course, acquiesced.

The second manifestation was an admission policy under Cutten in (circa) 1926 that blocked the enrollment of Black men. As a result, Colgate saw the last Black graduates in 1930 and not a single Black student appeared on the campus after 1930, for the duration of his tenure. This policy of 'racial cleansing' appeared to resonate with the overtones of 'ethnic cleansing' practiced by the Nazis, and indeed it did. In addition to the color ban, Cutten imposed and enforced a strict quota on the enrollment of Jewish students.

The third manifestation was the "Cutten Plan." The nationally lauded educational model embedded Cutten's philosophy and pedagogy. The Core Curriculum was, and is, the current bedrock of the Colgate educational model. Today's Core Curriculum has its foundational principals in the "Colgate Plan," a plan that sought to educate men and ignore the history, culture, philosophy, and religion of people from non-European areas unless presented in a dismissive or derogatory manner. (See the Appendix for courses offered during Cutten's tenure)

Unlike the Black Colgate men whose personal narratives were in the shadows, Cutten's views were carefully articulated and clearly preserved in bright light. Two particular speeches, his Inaugural Address in 1922, entitled the "Reconstruction of Democracy,"[182] and his convocation address given at Colgate in 1935, entitled "Natural Checks or Higher Controls Which?"[183] defined Cutten and his philosophy, and exposed his policy to eradicate the precarious ethnic and religious diversity the University had crafted for a century. In his inaugural address, Cutten clearly articulates his views on democracy, who should be the leaders, and how to ensure continued leadership by the chosen ones:

> The idea of democracy is not only founded upon the mistaken theory that all men are born free and equal... Of course, it was the height of folly to permit people of mental subnormality [sic] to vote simply because they were males, or to deny highly intelligent people the privilege simply because they were females; but we have not ameliorated conditions by extending the suffrage to more people of the same mentality.[184]

The Cutten "solution" to this perceived problem, this "indiscretion," was to create an aristocracy that was "fitted by intellectual ability."

> ...inevitably be the most intelligent, but it must also be well trained, benevolently inclined, and willing to admit any others to its membership who are fitted to belong. Democracy then

comes to be a government of the people, for the people, by all those of their number fitted by intellectual ability, moral ideas, and careful training.[185]

Cutten believed it was the task of the colleges and the universities to train this aristocracy. By limiting the number of Jewish students and eliminating all Blacks from attending the University. It is clear that he did not believe that men of the Jewish faith or of African descent possessed the intellect to be trained as 'the aristocracy' that would lead democracy. The question for scholars is whether Cutten's brand of extremism represented genuinely held beliefs or was merely a pretext for the evils of 'ethnic and racial cleansing' practiced by the Nazis and others.

Cutten accepted the premise that the intelligence quotient and capability of a child rarely changed. His belief was supported by a faction of the scientific and academic communities who believed a simple test could determine one's intelligence.

Therefore, it can be determined in early life the class of vocation, he is best fitted, and, to certain extent, destined. Those of high intelligence will be directed into lines of occupations which [sic] call for leadership... each person will then be directed on a scale of intelligence down to those whose work is of the most routine character of which an imbecile is capable....It must inevitably destroy universal adult suffrage, by cutting off at least 25% of the adults, those whose intelligence is so low as to be impossible of comprehending the significance of the ballot. On the other hand, it will throw the burden and responsibility of government where it belongs, on those of high intelligence... [186]

Cutten further believed that this system would not be challenged by the "low mentality;"

[A] portion of the population of lower mentality would be

engaged in occupations for which they would be perfectly fitted and consequently they would be contented-contented people do not rebel... it has been shown... people of low mentality do not object to being governed by others provided the government is benevolent. [187]

He advocated against those he considered 'mentally unfit' in society;

...at the same time if the mentally unfit and those of low mentality would be prevented from propagating their kind, for in such a scheme only is there hope for the race.[188]

This ideology by Cutten and other Americans who believed in eliminating the reproductive capabilities of those deemed of "low mentality," provided the seeds of the Nazi "master race" and the foundation for the elimination of those who were not part of the master race. Cutten believed that education should provide both general training and moral training, and that the University was responsible for "training the intellectual aristocracy."

[The] system is strong on the receptive side, and weak on the creative, and this although we realize that when our sons and daughters leave the college or the university, we expect them to produce results in initiative and creation.... In some way, more attention must be given to this requirement, and the college which accepts the responsibility for training the intellectual aristocracy must furnish a curriculum which contains the possibility of training along active, constructive, and creative lines.[189]

In his address, we also see the blueprint of what would become the "Colgate Plan":

...the training which must be given those of highest mentality in order to make its greatest contribution to society is that which will enable them to meet a unique situation. This has been the value of the broad Arts course, where the student is enabled to come in contact with all kinds of subjects and to solve all kinds of problems. The situation which [sic] is incomprehensible to those who have not had the broad training may not seem absolutely unique to the man of wide knowledge. Problem work is the contribution we try to make to creative training, but in most of our colleges this is neglected in favor of purely receptive work. Ability to meet a unique situation, which the Arts course is supposed to develop, is the contribution which the trained man makes to society, but in addition to this is the value of such a course to the man himself.[190]

Cutten was not alone in his thinking of controlling and eliminating the spread of those he deemed of 'low mentality' or 'feeble-minded.' Margaret Sanger, the advocate for birth control and pioneer of Planned Parenthood, believed it was important to limit reproduction of the unfit. President Theodore Roosevelt also believed the 'feeble minded' should not have offspring. Books and articles were written by physicians, educators, and politicians for the need to control the 'feeble-minded' by controlling their reproduction, at the same time that Congress enacted immigration policies to limit those who were considered to be of low intelligence, which included Jews, Italians, and others. The United States Supreme Court in, Buck v. Bell, 274 U.S. 200, written by Justice Oliver Wendell Holmes, found that the Virginia statute that mandated sterilizing the mentally unfit was constitutional. It is of little surprise that Cutten would continue to support the policies of eugenics in his 1935 convocation address entitled: "Natural Checks or Higher Controls Which?"

In this address, Cutten first makes clear his belief that people coming from certain parts of the world are naturally inferior:

The anthropologists point us to such experiences as the glacial periods-for there were four of them-and express the opinion that these periods, with their severe and merciless climate, did more for the progress of the race than several times the same length of time of monotonous climatic conditions.[191]

This theory justified the racialized perceptions that Africans, West Indians, Asians, and southern Europeans are inferior. Cutten also argued that even nature itself was not "content" with "unfit breeding stock":

Nature's methods whether we like it or not, and though it may be severe it is very effective. She is never content to let well enough alone. She selects the best to propagate the race in hopes that the race may be still better. She has nothing against the weak individually, but the only way she can be sure that they do not pollute the blood stream is to get rid of them. He argued that the achievements of philanthropy and modern medicine made his views justifiable and inescapable: "...the injury is not in prolonging the lives of the unfit in itself, for the end of the generation would be the end of the menace but prolonging the lives of the unfit to become the breeding stock of the nation is suicidal." He asked whether "...we not conserve the fine things philanthropy and medicine have given us and continue to improve the race?... We are sure of one thing, however, there must be checks. The danger is in removing natural checks and substituting nothing else. We are experimenting...which we hope will be successful, ... the first in higher control is intelligence... our most serious problems today is that of feeblemindedness. Nature would solve this very quickly...but what is ours? Intelligence says sterilization...not the whole solution, to be sure, but the most effective one of which we know. Birth control among the borderline cases would aid.... A civilization which removes natural checks before it fosters higher controls is committing suicide."

Cutten saw World War I as a tragic loss to the "master race":

"the tragedy of the war was not that millions of men lost their lives, as horrible as that is to contemplate, but that the finest breeding stock of all the nation involved was destroyed- and can never be replaced."

In retrospect and to its credit, Colgate has acknowledged its position on the 'wrong side of history' when in 2017, after two internal investigations, including a thorough review of Cutten's legacy in its entirety, the Board of Trustees, and University President Brian Casey, ordered the removal of Cutten's name from its residence halls. The era of eugenics and, ethnic and racial cleansing at Colgate had finally come to a close. The effect of erasing a generation of Black students at Colgate and their contribution to the Colgate community and nation is unknown but given the past is a loss.

✦ CHAPTER XV ✦
The Last Generation

The 1920s saw little change in the lives of Black Americans. Black communities were still under the burden of Jim Crow in the South, and an influx of southern Blacks in northern cities who were still looking for a dream that had not materialized. Poverty, discrimination, substandard and crowded housing, poor health and educational access were facing the majority of the Black communities in all regions of the country. Colgate continued to be a school that attracted Black men seeking an education. These men were different than many of their predecessors, they were pursuing careers other than education or the ministry.

Following graduation, the Black Colgate men of the 20th century became educators, morticians, ministers, lawyers, politicians, corporate executives, and doctors. They were the first generation of Colgate men to aspire to careers outside of the ministry and education. These men saw opportunities beyond the pulpit and classroom, as active participants in the struggle to transform this nation. They shared the ambition that all men and women would one day be treated equally, and have equal access to quality health care, education, housing, a just criminal justice system, and enjoy the ability to work, vote, and live in peace. Some of the men served their country at war abroad fighting for the rights of Europeans when, ironically, these same rights were denied to them at home. As the Colgate men before them, they rose to the challenge in working to transform the imperfect nation into a nation that would live up to the platitudes of equal justice for all of their fellow citizens.

The last Blacks to attend Colgate before Cutten succeeded in imposing a color line all but eliminating Black enrollment which are as follows from 1921-1930:

Leon Bogigian, aka Frankie Quill, 1921
William Henry Arthur Booke, 1922
Herbert Morrison Smith, 1922
James Robert Bess, 1923
William Ravenell, 1923
Granville Hamilton Martin, 1925
Enoch Abel Gousse, 1926
William Maynard Allen, 1926
Henry Shields Robinson, 1926
George Edward Allen, 1926
Pierre Gousse, 1927
Merton Blair Anderson, 1927
Raymond "Ray" Vaughn, 1929
John Edward Enoch, 1930
Adam Clayton Powell, 1930
Daniel "Major" Crosby, 1930

Leon Bogigian, aka Frankie Quill, Class of 1921

Bogigian hailed from Massachusetts and played football and baseball at Colgate. After Colgate, he became a professional boxer taking Frankie Quill as his professional boxing name. Quill was described as a better than average student who fought for money. Outside the ring, he had jobs that others felt, as a Colgate graduate, were beneath his station.[192]

In the spring of 1922, prior to the installation of Dr. Cutten as the 8th president, six Black students formed the Besmanbomara Literary Society. The purpose as described in the *Crisis Magazine* was to gain a deeper knowledge and appreciation of the achievements of the Negro in all the higher pursuits of life. The society met weekly and filled an important aspect of life for Negro students at Colgate, giving them a real understanding of the great past, and the even greater future of the Negro race.[193] It is not known whether the society fulfilled its mission and the need for cultural sustenance for the Black students at the primary White institution. However, it is evident that it was a prescience of the changing climate that would prevail during the Cutten years.

The men who formed the Besmanbomara Literary Society were: William Henry Arthur Booker, Class of 1922, Herbert Morrison Smith, Class of 1922, James Robert Bess, Class of 1923*, William Ravenell, Class of 1923, Merton Anderson, Class of 1927 and Granville Hamilton Martin, Class of 1925.

Booker, Ravenell, and Martin were also registered in the theological seminary that combines college and seminary work and leads to a Bachelor of Theology Degree.[194]

William Henry Arthur Booker, Class of 1922

Booker received his Bachelor of Theology from Colgate and he was a member of the Besmanbomara Literary Society. He taught at various colleges around the country and was the fifth pastor, following his father, at St. Paul's Baptist Church in Harlem from 1949-1960. He wrote book reviews, stories, articles, poems, and one act plays.

Herbert Morrison Smith, Class of 1922

Smith completed his course work in three years and was the president of the Besmanbomara Literary Society. Fluent in German he wrote to Du Bois and offered to translate for him.[195]

William Ravenell, Class of 1923

Ravenell was born in South Carolina and was a transfer student from Lincoln University (an HBCU) in Pennsylvania. He was the secretary-treasurer of the Besmanbomara Literary Society and penned the letter to the *Crisis Magazine*. He received a Bachelor of Arts and a Master's of Arts from Colgate, and his Bachelors of Divinity from Rochester Divinity School. He also studied at Harvard and Andover-Newton Theological School. He was pastor of Ebenezer Baptist Church in Boston for 23 years. His family endowed the William S. Ravenell Memorial Prize at Lincoln University to be awarded annually for academic excellence in the fields of religion or philosophy.[196]

Granville Hamilton Martin, Class of 1925
A member of the Besmanbomara Literary Society and debate club at Colgate.

William Maynard Allen, Class of 1926
There was no information found on Allen.

Enoch Gousse, Class of 1926
Enoch and his brother, Pierre were born in Haiti and did preparatory work at Mt. Hermon in Massachusetts before enrolling at Colgate. Enoch followed in his father's footsteps and became a doctor. At Colgate, he was a member of the Biological Society and the Mt. Hermon Club. After graduating from Colgate, Enoch was routinely rejected by several medical schools solely on the basis of race. He finally secured admission and did his residency at Harlem Hospital before returning to Haiti where he devoted his life to providing health care to the poor. Enoch received an honorary degree of Doctor of Science from Colgate in 1988. The tribute read as follows:

Enoch Abel Gousse- Missionary and Physician
Colgate alumnus of the Class of 1926, resident of the island of Haiti, you spent your life in service to the poor and sick of your native land. Tireless physician and preacher, for more than 55 years you have given faith and comfort to the people of southern Haiti- treating them in the tiny clinic in your home, pastoring in the Tabernacle Baptist Church, or traveling on horseback, on foot and by boat-to mountain villages in the interior to heal and to pray where you are needed. The love for you by your patients is legendary. Through many

years those whom you served in turn protected you from the retribution of the Duvalier regimes. Colgate is distinguished by your life.[197]

Henry (Robbie) S. Robinson, Jr., Class of 1926

Robinson was born and raised in Washington, D.C. A fellow classmate of Enoch Gousse, he went on to Howard Medical School. He began his medical career in Maryland before returning to Washington, D.C. where he combined medicine and health care with politics. He opened his medical office in D.C. in 1942. Robinson was an active member of various local and national organizations, such as the Urban league, NAACP, Boys Club, and medical and fraternal organizations. Robinson was elected to the city council when home rule was established in Washington, D.C. During his tenure on the city council, he advocated for minorities to receive health services, including birth control information. He also fought to improve standards for nursing home administration, liberalize abortion laws, screen for sickle cell anemia, and establish Spanish-speaking health services for the Spanish community. His advocacy went beyond health care services and included reduced penalties for marijuana, better pollution controls, free day care for low-income parents, and improvement of land use planning.[198] As a Republican in a town overwhelmingly Black and Democratic, he was appointed by President Nixon as mayor until the home rule charter took effect, for which he was criticized as an 'Uncle Tom'[199] by many in the Black community.

William M. Allen, Class of 1926

Class notes indicate that he taught at Straight College in New Orleans and later in his hometown high school in Durham, North Carolina. He was listed as a high school principal and took advance study at Cornell University. In the Up to Now 1926 class notes, Allen reports that he is teaching in his home town high school and trying to build a cultural background in people who for the most part lacked it. He often confessed a need to fall back on his old

Colgate fight to carry him through the day when he was almost too tired to think.

George Edward Allen, Class of 1926

Allen was a transfer student from Lincoln University.

Merton Blair Anderson, Class of 1927

Anderson was also a member of the Besmanbomara Literary Society and was the corresponding secretary. He was a member of the biology and cosmopolitan clubs at Colgate. In his senior year, he held himself out as the mentor of the incoming Black men who were all athletes, except one, Adam Clayton Powell, Jr. Although it was the practice that the Blacks either roomed with each other or alone, Powell used his fair skin and did not acknowledge his ethnicity until it was discovered when his father came to campus to speak. Anderson and the other Blacks were angered. Anderson also fair skinned felt it a matter of racial pride not to pass.[200] Anderson, a biology major, received a Master's of Art in bacteriogly and his medical degree from Meharry Medical College (an HBCU). He taught at various colleges including Howard University and belonged to numerous associations. The Dr. Merton B. Anderson Award in Pathology was set up at Howard Medical School in his honor.

Pierre Gousse, Class of 1927

Pierre followed his brother to Herndon and Colgate.

John Edward Enoch, Class of 1930

An athlete, Enoch played baseball, basketball, and was on the swimming and cross-country teams. After Colgate he was a YMCA executive secretary.

Adam Clayton Powell, Jr., Class of 1930

Adam Clayton Powell, Jr. was born in 1908 in New Haven, Connecticut. Powell was one of the most controversial alums in all of Colgate's history. Powell transferred to Colgate from New York

City College. It was not until his father, Reverend Adam Clayton Powell, Sr., came to campus to lecture that his White classmates discovered he was Black; a fact that angered many of his Black classmates. After graduation, Powell worked at his home church, Abyssinian Baptist Church, as an assistant minister to his father. Powell received a Master's of Art from Columbia University in 1932 and a Doctorate in Divinity from Shaw University in 1935. He took over as pastor of Abyssinian Baptist Church in Harlem in 1937.

Powell became an activist in the New York City area for equal rights and access for the Black community. He was elected to the New York City council in 1942 and as a congressman representing Harlem in 1944. He served for 12 terms as a congressman, and before his downfall was the ranking member of the Education and Labor Committee. While chair, the Committee approved over fifty pieces of legislation, authorizing the increases in the minimum wage, education and training for the deaf, school lunch, student loans, standards for wages and work hours, and aid for public schools and libraries.[201] Both Presidents Kennedy and Johnson credited Powell's committee with helping to shape the social policy of both administrations.[202] However, Powell was not without controversy.

The Powell Amendment, the brainchild of Powell himself, was an anti-discrimination rider Powell sought to attach to any legislation that was considered discriminatory. As Powell wrote in his autobiography:

> In January of 1945, in an address at Charlotte, North Carolina, I had pleaded for real democracy, saying, 'This nation can never return to pre-Pearl Harbor days of pseudo-democracy'.... I decided to create the Powell Amendment, forbidding Federal funds to those who sought to preserve segregation,.... 'No funds under this Act shall be made available to or paid to any State or school...'...I was to use this important weapon with success, to bring about opportunities for the good of man and to stop those efforts that would harm democracy's forward progress. Sometimes I used it only as a

deterrent against the undemocratic practices that would have resulted if that amendment had not been offered."[203]

The Powell Amendment had its critics. In 1956, Eisenhower sought to fund school construction, but representatives from the South did not want this funding and were resistant to the Powell Amendment added to the bill. Although the bill found support among northern representatives, the bill ultimately died. It has been debated for years whether the Powell Amendment was the cause of his downfall or other issues.[204] The controversies surrounding Powell would be his downfall and in 1971, he lost his congressional seat to Charles Rangel.

Powell stayed somewhat connected to his alma mater over the years. He sent in regular reports for class notes, and he openly questioned admission policies. He was already a rising star according to his fifth reunion class notes and not the least bit modest about mentioning his accomplishments. Powell was listed as follows:

Clergyman, Director of Abyssinia Church in Harlem, a member of the Columbia University faculty from 1933-1935 teaching; 1 year at Union theological Seminary MA in religious education and had traveled extensively through 12 countries in Europe, Asia Minor, and Africa.[205]

In the 25th class reunion notes, the editor remarks:

Adam sent in a long list of achievements attains since graduation from Colgate and space will not permit mention of all the honors accorded him down through the years. [206]

The notes mention the following:

Congress since 1945, V.P. World Assn. Of Parliamentarians for World Government. First negro to be elected Delegate-at-large to the Democratic National Convention in 1952.[207]

It was common knowledge among at least the Black alum that no Blacks had been accepted to Colgate after 1927 and the remainder of Cutten's tenure and beyond. Powell in his letter to President Case (the president who succeeded President Cutten) of April 30, 1947 questioned the obvious exclusion of Blacks and what steps could be taken to ensure that Blacks would again be admitted. Powell wrote asking to "find out if the policy of exclusion of Negro men still obtains at Colgate, if not, what steps should be taken for the right type to apply for admission."[208] Correspondence between Powell's classmate, Robert Bruce, and President Case made it clear that there was discussion of Powell's letter and perhaps Powell's motivation in writing the letter as well as Bruce's opinion on the question of Blacks at Colgate during his time.[209]

Bruce wrote to Case about a prior correspondence he had with Powell the previous year. In the correspondence for support of the 1947 Colgate Annual Fund Drive, Powell told Bruce "he would be happy to contribute if he receives the 'right answer' to a 'letter addressed to you'"[210] Bruce in his letter to President Case wrote:

> Powell contributed to last year's fund without raising this question. Consequently, I am curious to know whether he raised it because some Negro or Negroes have been unable to obtain admission this year, or whether he merely seeks assurance of the University's policy.[211]

Bruce also adds his personal opinion on the issue of Negroes attending Colgate:

> During my years at Colgate there were at least three negro **boys** of outstanding character and ability, including Adam. It had never occurred to me that Colgate tradition or its objectives contemplated any discrimination other than on the basis of character and ability. I would be surprised and disappointed to learn that there was any foundation for the question put by Powell.[212]

He concluded in his letter to Case:

On a number of occasions I have been genuinely moved by your careful and stimulating statement of Colgate's problems, opportunities and objectives. As I understand them, there is no room for discrimination of a racial or religious character.[213]

In his letter of May 11, 1947, President Case responds to Powell's letter of April 30th. (See Appendix). Case wrote that he spoke to the Director of Admission and responded that he and the director found Powell's question "puzzling, if not actually disingenuous."[214] Case goes on to defend the University and deny any exclusion and mentions the lack of civilian White or 'Negro' men on campus during the war and the few 'Negro trainees' on campus during the war were welcomed. Case defends the lack of 'Negroes' applicants in part by writing:

…is not strange considering our remoteness from more cosmopolitan centers of population and the limited opportunity for intercourse with other educated negroes afforded by the community of which College is a part…the caliber of the relatively few who have applied has, generally speaking, afforded no assurance that the candidate would, if admitted, do successful college work or be a representative of his people as you and we would want him to be.

He concluded his letter by advising that as an alum,

…you have every right to propose men, white or colored, Christian or Jewish who are, in your judgment, qualified for admission. Obviously, we cannot admit all who Alumni recommend, especially when the recommendation is the result of social, business, or political pressures. When Alumni address themselves to the question objectively, however, their recommendations and appraisals are not only welcome but genuinely helpful, and any such recommendations as you may make as an Alumnus, irrespective of the applicant's race, creed, or color, will have the Committee's most careful consideration. I hope this answers both your questions.

It is unknown whether Powell's letter had an effect on the school reexamining the absence of Black men on campus after a legacy of Black men over the previous one hundred years. However, what is known is that Black men did not reappear on campus until the late 1940s.

However dismissive and disingenuous President Case was to Powell's inquiry, the fact remained, and was well known, that after 1930 Black men were not admitted, and there was a strict quota on the number of Jewish men admitted to Colgate. This was part of the Cutten legacy.

Daniel B. (Major) Crosby, Class of 1930

After Powell's ethnicity was revealed, Crosby became his roommate. Crosby was also benched with Ray Vaughn in 1928 and banned from traveling with the football team to Vanderbilt and Virginia Polytechnic. He worked in public housing, was a delegate member of the National Association of Housing Officials, auditor for Union Baptist Church, board member North End Community Center, Greater Hartford Council of Churches, and co-chairman of the men's division of United College Fund.

These men showed the breadth and depth of the men who attended the University in the 1920s. As opportunities opened for Black men, they were quick to step in and help to transform the nation by their presence in all walks of life. These men proved what should have been known all along; that Black men were beyond capable of contributing value to society, despite the clamor of White privilege to disrupt their rise.

The early Black men at Colgate committed their lives to the promise of education. Their intentions and motivations within an institution such as Colgate are inspirational, as evidenced everywhere in the pages of this book. We see the glory of the human intellect unfurled and on display in their life stories, even in forlorn times of legal and social upheaval, and trouble. From the first appearance of Black men on campus, during the Cutten presidency, and across a nation once racially divided by the slave oligarchy and the burden of its legacy, we review the lives of these men and remark at their resilience and perseverance. If we are to draw any lesson from their Colgate experiences, let it be that there is no greater struggle and no sweeter victory than to ensure that their light continues to shine for future generations.

Listen, I tell you a mystery: We will not all sleep, but we will be changed – in a flash, in the twinkling of an eye, at the last trumpet. For the trumpet will sound, the dead will be raised imperishable, and we will be changed. 1 Corinthians 15:51-52

EPILOGUE

Researching and writing this book has been an arduous yet exhilarating journey to uncover forgotten terrain. Often the history has been painful, but it was a backdrop to the incredible lives of these men, who in living their lives helped transform a nation. Yet, the story is incomplete. The book was purposeful in limiting the time period of 1840-1930, to chronicle the first Black man entering Colgate to the last Black men to graduate, before the Cutten legacy.

However, there were other men of color who also attended Colgate in the early years; American Indians as early as the 1820s, as well as Asian students beginning in the 1800s. It is my hope that their stories will also be told, celebrated, and remembered for future generations of Colgate students, faculty, and alumni.

The 1960s changed American culture and society and Colgate changed with the times. The range of men and women of color broadened and so did their stories and impact on Colgate, America, and the world. Let us never forget their stories.

ACKNOWLEDGEMENTS

The quest to resurrect African American legacies can be challenging. First, it is a challenge to find primary source material. Second, when primary source documents are sparse, are there reliable second source material? Can we find photos, diaries, or stories told by, or about African Americans? Often, some material is in plain sight, if you know where to look or whom to ask. This book involved extensive research, and it could not and was not done alone. I have been fortunate to have help from many and without it this book would not be possible.

Two people who provided invaluable support with their research skills, sharing their research, and talking together about what we learned, and always trying to find more- Dr. Jason Petrulis, Lecturer in the History Department at the University of Hong Kong and former visiting assistant professor of history and bicentennial research fellow; and Leigh Eckmair, Archivist at the Gilbertsville Library, Gilbertsville New York.

Jason did extensive research on the early men of color who attended Colgate, including early African Americans. He graciously shared his research with me saving hundreds of hours of research. He complied what we believe is a fairly accurate list of African American men who attended Colgate before the 1960s. As with any list, this list is as accurate as the tools available to identify racially marginalized men. More often than not, ethnicity was not labeled making the process more difficult. Jason however, is credited in identifying the first two known Black men to attend Colgate University: Jonas Holland Townsend and Henry Livingston Simpson. It was sheer determination and the desire to find them that led to the piecing together of clues and connecting the dots that have provided us all with these men, not only for their place in Colgate history, but in American History. Additionally, Jason and I would bounce ideas and sources off each other to help flush out a picture of what life was like for these early men and their contribution to this nation.

Leigh and I have been digging into Central New York Black History for decades. We first met when I was searching for my

Black ancestors. So, when I decided to take on this project, I knew she would be all in, and she was. She worked with Jason to help fill in the missing pieces of his exhaustive research, and she helped me flush out timelines and piece together the stories of the two early men, Townsend and Simpson. Often, there are gaps in their narratives, and we would try to surmise as best we could the missing pieces. Her love and knowledge of American history put their lives into context of the bigger narrative. Leigh helped focus and sharpen the inquiry to be able to find material from other libraries, archives, and researchers. She developed relationships with others who do this work and they shared with her and thus with me what they uncovered on the lives of Townsend and Simpson. She also took time to do fact checking, organizing, and editing the chapters on Townsend and Simpson.

I met Selicia Gregory Allen, archivist from Virginia Union University via email. Several men attended Virginia Union University before attending Colgate. The Virginia Union University archives had several letters from these men. The letters provided a rare glimpse of the lives of these men during their Colgate years and after. Not only did she share these letters, but she also provided links to other materials in their collection that was not only useful in understanding these men, but also the role the school had in educating Black men and women after the Civil War. Several of the men who first attended Virginia Union University, returned there to teach after getting their degrees from Colgate.

To the collectors, archivists, professors, and researchers, who have made it their mission to preserve documents and stories that were available so this story could be told, thank you. To those who provided information directly or helped me find information:

Jazmine Smith, Chester Co. Historical Society, West Chester, PA, Ryan Conroy, Chester County Historical Society, West Chester, PA, J.R. Ertell, Chairman, HSPA Archives Committee, Johnny Smith, Assistant Grand Secretary, Most Worshipful Grand Hall Lodge of California, David Johnson, Asst. Historian, Prince Hall Masons, San Francisco, CA, Pete Rivera-Bey, Grand Secretary,

Prince Hall (formerly Boyer) Grand Lodges, Larry Mitchell, the Most Worshipful, Tami Suzuki, Librarian and Municipal Records Archivist, San Francisco History Center and Public Library, Jo-Ann Wong, Librarian, The Chancellor Robert R Livingston Masonic Library, Masonic Service Association of North America, Gayle W. Hanson, Texas State Historical Association, Herbert Price, Jr., Past Historian, Prince Hall Grand Lodge of California, San Francisco, CA, Perry Travis, Prince Hall Grand Lodge of California, Los Angeles, Most Worshipful Prince Hall Grand Lodge of Texas, 3433, Rosenberg Library, Galveston, TX, David Johnson, Most Worshipful Prince Hall Grand Lodge, Assistant Historian, Michael Mery, Schomburg Center for Research in Black Culture, Sean McConnell, Rosenberg Library, Galveston, TX, Jami Durham, Cultural History Historian, Galveston, TX, Elise Thornley, Research Archivist, Glenn G. Bartle Library, Binghamton University, Catherine C. Quillman, Historian/Journalist, West Chester, PA, Dr. Clifford Muse, Archivist, Howard University, Washington, DC, Christopher Harter, Deputy Director, Amistad Research Center, Tulane University, New Orleans, LA, Samantha Meredith, Executive Director-Curator Chatham-Kent Historical Ctr., Jessie Reich, The Seward House Museum, Auburn, NY, Jennifer Haines, The Seward House Museum, Auburn, NY, and Michael Malloney, Schenectady County Historical Society.

Thank you.

To the Colgate community. The bicentennial provided the inspiration to ensure these legacies are celebrated as part of the Colgate narrative. First, to Sarah Keene and her staff in Special Collections. There was never a question that she and her team were not able to track down the answer or a path to finding an answer. The Special Collections department has over the years collected material on as many alumni as possible. The archives prepare a file on each man (and now women) and collects as much material as they can on their lives. The material comes from a myriad of sources. These bios were a goldmine in learning about these early men's lives during and after Colgate. Special Collections have collected newspaper clippings, excerpts from books, and photos of alumni at different stages of their lives. The bios were a great tool, but information was also found in faculty minutes, year books, student files, class notes, presidential papers, and student newspapers to name a few. Sarah and her staff often were able to direct me to the less than obvious files where information could be found on these men. Emily Jefferies, the digital archivist for the Bicentennial provided digital images from the archives of many early African American men.

The larger Colgate community was instrumental in helping me. I had research help from Max Longoria, a student and Imani Ballard, a recent graduate, who both did incredible research for me and worked with the Special Collections department when I was unable to travel to Colgate. They also organized and prepared material for me. Elizabeth Wonka, a fellow alumnae, who spent time in the archives gathering material on President Cutten. She was able to help me shape the narrative on his impact both positively and negatively at Colgate.

It was a great source of comfort to have folks that I could talk about my work with and were always encouraging, Jim Smith, Leroy Cody, Veronica McFall, many Alumni of Color, Jill Harsin and Laura Jack co-chairs of the bicentennial committee, Professor Harvey Sindima, and Dean Tracy Hucks to name a few. I am grateful to Professor Graham Hodges for his review and Professor Sindima for his praise of the book.

To the ladies of my book club who listened and encouraged me through this process.

To my editorial team, my brother James whose insight helped to sharpen my focus in telling the larger story, Leigh Eckmair who did exhaustive fact checking, and Jane Malloy. I knew Jane from our time as trustees at the Trenton Museum Society Board. Her razor-sharp pen in crafting documents made me realize she would be perfect for this project and she has been. It was important to me that those who edited my book knew me and knew my passion and voice. Jane made sure that the story was clear while retaining my voice. They did and I am grateful.

Lastly, to my family. My brother, James who wanted to make sure his sister could tell this story. My daughter, Kali who always encouraged me to keep going and who read the very first draft. And to my husband, Daryl. Daryl has always been the man who gave me space. Space to pursue my passions, understanding the days that I traveled to search for documents, the hours I spent on my computer, and the times when this book was the only thing I was thinking about. Thank you.

Diane Ciccone

2019

NOTES:

Chapter III Appendix

1. United States Passport for Jonas Holland Townsend
2. "An Address to the Slaves of the United States of America," Buffalo, N.Y., 1843, by Henry Highland Garnet
3. Roster of Elected Lodge Officials, Boyer Grand Lodge

1. United States Passport for Jonas Holland Townsend

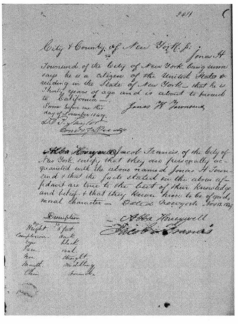

2. TO THE SLAVES OF THE UNITED STATES OF AMERICA (REJECTED BY THE NATIONAL CONVENTION, 1843.)

An Address to the Slaves of the United States of America, Buffalo, N.Y., 1843

BY HENRY HIGHLAND GARNET.

Brethren and Fellow-Citizens:—Your brethren of the North, East, and West have been accustomed to meet together in National

Conventions, to sympathize with each other, and to weep over your unhappy condition. In these meetings we have addressed all classes of the free, but we have never, until this time, sent a word of consolation and advice to you. We have been contented in sitting still and mourning over your sorrows, earnestly hoping that before this day your sacred liberties would have been restored. But, we have hoped in vain. Years have rolled on, and tens of thousands have been borne on streams of blood and tears, to the shores of eternity. While you have been oppressed, we have also been partakers with you; nor can we be free while you are enslaved. We, therefore, write to you as being bound with you.

PREFACE.

The following Address was first read at the National Convention held at Buffalo, N.Y., in 1843. Since that time it has been slightly modified, retaining, however, all of its original doctrine. The document elicited more discussion than any other paper that was ever brought before that, or any other deliberative body of colored persons, and their friends. Gentlemen who opposed the Address, based their objections on these grounds. 1. That the document was warlike, and encouraged insurrection; and 2. That if the Convention should adopt it, that those delegates who lived near the borders of the slave states, would not dare to return to their homes. The Address was rejected by a small majority; and now in compliance with the earnest request of many who heard it, and in conformity to the wishes of numerous friends who are anxious to see it, the author now gives it to the public, praying God that this little book may be borne on the four winds of heaven, until the principles it contains shall be understood and adopted by every slave in the Union.

Many of you are bound to us, not only by the ties of a common humanity, but we are connected by the more tender relations of parents, wives, husbands, children, brothers, and sisters, and friends. As such we most affectionately address you.

H.H.G.

HENRY HIGHLAND GARNET
ADDRESS TO THE SLAVES OF THE UNITED STATES

Two hundred and twenty-seven years ago, the first of our injured race were brought to the shores of America. They came not with glad spirits to select their homes in the New World. They came not with their own consent, to find an unmolested enjoyment of the blessings of this fruitful soil. The first dealings they had with men calling themselves Christians, exhibited to them the worst features of corrupt. and sordid hearts: and convinced them that no cruelty is too great, no villainy and no robbery too abhorrent for even enlightened men to perform, when influenced by avarice and lust. Neither did they come flying upon the wings of Liberty, to a land of freedom. But they came with broken hearts, from their beloved native land, and were doomed to unrequited toil and deep degradation. Nor did the evil of their bondage end at their emancipation by death. Succeeding generations inherited their chains, and millions have come from eternity into time, and have returned again to the world of spirits, cursed and ruined by American slavery.

The oppressors themselves have become involved in the ruin. They have become weak, sensual, and rapacious—they have cursed you—they have cursed themselves—they have cursed the earth which they have trod.

The propagators of the system, or their immediate ancestors, very soon discovered its growing evil, and its tremendous wickedness, and secret promises were made to destroy it. The gross inconsistency of a people holding slaves, who had themselves "ferried o'er the wave" for freedom's sake, was too apparent to be entirely over- looked. The voice of Freedom cried, "Emancipate your slaves." Humanity supplicated with tears for the deliverance of the children of Africa. Wisdom urged her solemn plea. The bleeding captive pleaded his innocence, and pointed to Christianity who stood weeping at the cross. Jehovah frowned upon the nefarious institution, and thunderbolts, red with vengeance, struggled to leap forth to blast the guilty wretches who maintained it. But all was vain. Slavery had stretched its dark wings of death over the land, the Church stood silently by—the priests prophesied falsely, and the people loved to have it so. Its throne is established, and now it reigns triumphant.

The colonists threw the blame upon England.. They said that the mother country entailed the evil upon them, and that they would rid themselves of it if they could. The world thought they were sincere, and the philanthropic pitied them. But time soon tested their sincerity. In a few years the colonists grew strong, and severed themselves from the British Government. Their independence was declared, and they took their station among the sovereign powers of the earth. The declaration was a glorious document. Sages admired it, and the patriotic of every nation reverenced the God-like sentiments which it contained. When the power of Government returned to their hands, did they emancipate the slaves? No; they rather added new links to our chains. Were they ignorant of the principles of Liberty? Certainly they were not. The sentiments of their revolutionary orators fell in burning eloquence upon their hearts, and with one voice they cried, Liberty or Death. Oh what a sentence was that! It ran from soul to soul like electric fire, and nerved the arm of thousands to fight in the holy cause of Freedom. Among the diversity of opinions that are entertained in regard to physical resistance, there are but a few found to gainsay that stern declaration. We are among those who do not.

Nearly three millions of your fellow-citizens are prohibited by law and public opinion (which in this country is stronger than law) from reading the Book of Life. Your intellect has been destroyed as much as possible, and every ray of light they have attempted to Slavery! How much misery is comprehended in that single word. What mind is there that does not shrink from its direful effects? Unless the image of God be obliterated from the soul, all men cherish the love of Liberty. The nice discerning political economist does not regard the sacred right more than the untutored African who roams in the wilds of Congo. Nor has the one more right to the full enjoyment of his freedom than the other. In every man's mind the good seeds of liberty are planted, and he who brings his fellow down so low, as to make him contented with a condition of slavery, commits the highest crime against God and man. Brethren, your oppressors aim to do this. They endeavor to make you as much like brutes as possible. When they have blinded the eyes of your mind—

HENRY HIGHLAND GARNET
ADDRESS TO THE SLAVES OF THE UNITED STATES

When they have embittered the sweet waters of life—when they have shut out the light which shines from the word of God—then, and not till then, has American slavery done its perfect work.
bloody footprints of the first remorseless soul-thief was placed upon the shores of our fatherland. The humblest peasant is as free in the sight of God as the proudest monarch that ever swayed a sceptre. Liberty is a spirit sent out from God, and like its great Author, is no respecter of persons.

To such Degradation it is sinful in the Extreme for you to make voluntary Submission. The divine commandments you are in duty bound to reverence and obey. If you do not obey them, you will surely meet with the displeasure of the Almighty. He requires you to love him supremely, and your neighbor as yourself—to keep the Sabbath day holy—to search the Scriptures—and bring up your children with respect for his laws, and to worship no other God but him. But slavery sets all these at nought, and hurls defiance in the face of Jehovah. The forlorn condition in which you are placed, does not destroy your moral obligation to God. You are not certain of heaven, because you suffer yourselves to remain in a state of slavery, where you cannot obey the commandments of the Sovereign of the universe. If the ignorance of slavery is a passport to heaven, then it is a blessing, and no curse, and you should rather desire its perpetuity than its abolition. God will not receive slavery, nor ignorance, nor any other state of mind, for love and obedience to him. Your condition does not absolve you from your moral obligation. The diabolical injustice by which your liberties are cloven down, neither God; nor angels, or just men, command you to suffer for a single moment. Therefore it is your solemn and imperative duty to use every means, both moral; intellectual and physical that promises success. If a band of heathen men should attempt to enslave a race of Christians, and to place their children under the influence of some false religion, surely, Heaven would frown upon the men who would not resist such aggression, even to death. If, on the other hand, a band of Christians should attempt to enslave a race of heathen men, and to entail slavery upon them, and to keep them in heathenism in the midst of Christianity, the God of heaven would smile upon every effort which the injured might make to disenthrall themselves.

Brethren, the time has come when you must act for yourselves. It is an old and true saying that, "if hereditary bondmen would be free, they must themselves strike the blow." You can plead your own cause, and do the work of emancipation better than any others. The nations of the old world are moving in the great cause of universal freedom, and some of them at least will, ere long, do you justice. The combined powers of Europe have placed their broad seal of disapprobation upon the African slave-trade. But in the slave- holding parts of the United States, the trade is as brisk as ever. They buy and sell you as though you were brute beasts. The North has done much—her opinion of slavery in the abstract is known. But in regard to the South, we adopt the opinion of the New York Evangelist—"We have advanced so far, that the cause apparently waits for a more effectual door to be thrown open than has been yet." We are about to point you to that more effectual door. Look around you, and behold the bosoms of your loving wives heaving with untold agonies! Hear the cries of your poor children! Remember the stripes your fathers bore. Think of the torture and disgrace of your noble mothers. Think of your wretched sisters, loving virtue and purity, as they are driven into concubinage and are exposed to the unbridled lusts of incarnate devils. Think of the undying glory that hangs around the ancient name of Africa:—and forget not that you are native-born American citizens, and as such, you are justly entitled to all the rights that are granted to the freest. Think how many tears you have poured out. upon the soil which you have cultivated with unrequited toil and enriched with your blood; and then go to your lordly enslavers and tell them plainly, that you are determined to be free. Appeal to their sense of justice, and tell them that they have no more right to oppress you, than you have to enslave them. Entreat them to remove the grievous burdens which they have imposed upon you, and to remunerate you for your labor.

Brethren, it is as wrong for your lordly oppressors to keep you in slavery, as it was for the man thief to steal our ancestors from the coast of Africa. You should therefore now use the same manner of resistance, as would have been just in our ancestors....

HENRY HIGHLAND GARNET
ADDRESS TO THE SLAVES OF THE UNITED STATES

...them renewed diligence in the cultivation of the soil, if they will render to you an equivalent for your services. Point them to the increase of happiness and prosperity in the British West Indies since the Act of Emancipation. Tell them in language which they cannot misunderstand, of the exceeding sinfulness of slavery, and of a future judgment, and of the righteous retributions of an indignant God. Inform them that all you desire is freedom, and that nothing else will suffice. Do this, and for ever after cease to toil for the heartless tyrants, who give you no other reward but stripes and abuse. If they then commence the work of death, they, and not you, will be responsible for the consequences. You had far better all die—die immediately, than live slaves, and entail your wretchedness upon your posterity. If you would be free in this generation, here is your only hope. However much you and all of us may desire it, there is not much hope of redemption without the shedding of blood. If you must bleed, let it all come at once—rather die freemen, than live to be the slaves. It is impossible, like the children of Israel, to make a grand exodus from the land of bondage. The Pharaohs are on both sides of the blood-red waters! You cannot move en masse, to the dominions of the British Queen—nor can you pass through Florida and overrun Texas, and at last find peace in Mexico. The propagators of American slavery are spending their blood and treasure, that they may plant the black flag in the heart of Mexico and riot in the halls of the Montezuma's. In the language of the Rev. Robert Hall, when addressing the volunteers of Bristol, who were rushing forth to repel the invasion of Napoleon, who threatened to lay waste the fair homes of England, "Religion is too much interested in your behalf, not to shed over you her most gracious influences."

...has done this, to make you subservient to its own purposes; but it has done more than this, it has prepared you for any emergency. If you receive good treatment, it is what you could hardly expect; if you meet with pain, sorrow, and even death, these are the common lot of the slaves.

You will not be compelled to spend much time in order to become inured to hardships. From the first moment that you breathed the air of heaven, you have been accustomed to nothing else but hardships. The heroes of the American Revolution were never put upon harder fare than a peck of corn and a few herrings per week. You have not become enervated by the luxuries of life. Your sternest energies have been beaten out upon the anvil of severe trial....

The patriotic Nathaniel Turner followed Denmark Veazie. He was goaded to desperation by wrong and injustice. By despotism, his name has been recorded on the list of infamy; and future generations will remember him among the noble and brave.

Fellow-men! Patient sufferers! Behold your dearest rights crushed to the earth! See your sons murdered, and your wives, mothers and sisters doomed to prostitution. In the name of the merciful God, and by all that life is worth, let it no longer be a debatable question, whether it is better to choose Liberty or death.

In 1822, Denmark Veazie, of South Carolina, formed a plan for the liberation of his fellow-men. In the whole history of human efforts to overthrow slavery, a more complicated and tremendous plan was never formed. He was betrayed by the treachery of his own people, and died a martyr to freedom. Many a brave hero fell, but history, faithful to her high trust, will transcribe his name on the same monument with Moses, Hampden, Tell, Bruce and Wallace, Toussaint L'Ouverture, Lafayette and Washington. That tremendous movement shook the whole empire of slavery. The guilty soul- thieves were overwhelmed with fear. It is a matter of fact, that at that time, and in consequence of the threatened revolution, the slave States talked strongly of emancipation. But they blew but one blast of the trumpet of freedom, and then laid it aside. As these men be- came quiet, the slaveholders ceased to talk about emancipation: and now behold your condition today! Angels sigh over it, and humanity has long since exhausted her tears in weeping on your account!

Next arose the immortal Joseph Cinque, the hero of the Amistad. He was a native African, and by the help of God he emancipated a whole ship-load of his fellow-men on the high seas. And he now sings of liberty on the sunny hills of Africa and beneath his native palm-trees, where he hears the lion roar and feels himself as free as that king of the forest.

HENRY HIGHLAND GARNET
ADDRESS TO THE SLAVES OF THE UNITED STATES

Next arose Madison Washington, that bright star of freedom, and took his station in the constellation of true heroism. He was a slave on board the brig Creole, of Richmond, bound to New Orleans, that great slave mart, with a hundred and four others. Nineteen struck for liberty or death. But one life was taken, and the whole were emancipated, and the vessel was carried into Nassau, New Providence.

Noble men! Those who have fallen in freedom's conflict, their memories will be cherished by the true-hearted and the God-fearing in all future generations; those who are living, their names are surrounded by a halo of glory.

Delivered before the National Convention of Colored Citizens, Buffalo, New York, August 16, 1843. Published in Henry Highland Garnet, Walker's Appeal, with a Brief Sketch of His Life. And also Garnet's Address to the Slaves of the United States of America. New York, Printed by J. H. Tobitt, 1848, pages 89–97.

Brethren, arise, arise! Strike for your lives and liberties. Now is the day and the hour. Let every slave throughout the land do this, and the days of slavery are numbered. You cannot be more oppressed than you have been—you cannot suffer greater cruelties than you have already. Rather die freemen than live to be slaves. Remember that you are four millions!

It is in your power so to torment the God-cursed slaveholders, that they will be glad to let you go free. If the scale was turned, and Black men were the masters and white men the slaves, every destructive agent and element would be employed to lay the oppressor low. Danger and death would hang over their heads day and night. Yes, the tyrants would meet with plagues more terrible than those of Pharaoh. But you are a patient people. You act as though you were made for the special use of these devils. You act as though your daughters were born to pamper the lusts of your masters and overseers. And worse than all, you tamely submit while your lords tear your wives from your embraces and defile them before your eyes. In the name of God, we ask, are you men? Where is the blood of your fathers? Has it all run out of your veins? Awake, awake; millions of voices are calling you! Your dead fathers speak to you from their graves. Heaven, as with a voice of thunder, calls on you to arise from the dust.

Let your motto be resistance! resistance! resistance! No oppressed people have ever secured their liberty without resistance. What kind of resistance you had better make, you must decide by the circumstances that surround you, and according to the suggestion of expediency. Brethren, adieu! Trust in the living God. Labor for the peace of the human race, and remember that you are four millions.

The Minutes of the (1855) convention recorded some of this thoughts on the issue of colored being called as witnesses in Court proceedings.

I deny that the pitiful support which the law offers can be called a protection. Are we heard before the bar of justice? Are we recognized as having souls, and comprehending the nature and responsibility of an oath? "'Tis but a few months since a negro was stabbed in the streets of San Francisco, in the presence of twenty witnesses. The murderer was a Spanish man, he was arrested, and discharged on bail. On the day of his trial his counsel ridiculed the idea of his being punished, and said he had 'only killed a nigger who attempted to strike him down" What was the result? The murderer was cleared, and in a few hours he was walking the streets openly. There is indeed a semblance of protection, but it is not real."

Townsend wrote of his impressions of California and they have survived.

"I have become so much of a Californian, that the refinement of the Eastern States would almost present a novelty to me. San Francisco has arisen from a miserable village of a few huts to become a great city, covering areas of some six square miles; and it is now the fourth among the great commercial emporiums of the Union, all within the short space of six years, showing a spirit of energy that is unsurpassed in the world's history.

California, to use a vulgar phrase, has in a great measure, ('caved in,') become like the older States; her palmy days are numbered! The poor man's chance is like the money on the Monti Bank, very uncertain. We are overrun with hordes of Chinamen and Spaniards, who have reduced wages to almost New York prices. The country is full of speculators the hirelings of the rich in the Eastern States, who monopolize all the avenues that open with any favorable prospects for the poor man.

As to the colored people who are always poor, they are scarcely recognized among the human family in this country. We have no vote, no oath against a white person, no protection against the insults and brutal barbarity of the common street loafers and vagabonds, of which numbers there is not a few; yet there is a good state of public sentiment in our behalf in this city. We are subject, it is true, to most degrading laws; but here we meet with but few insults from the better class of the community.

The colored people here are very active and energetic. They are in almost every class of business, from the highest to the lowest. Some are doing a good business, while others are getting along very poorly. It is the height of my ambition to see colored men take a bold and decided position before the world a stand upon the platform of truth and justice, and act like men. It will command respect from our most inveterate enemies, and eventually obtain our rights."

3. ROSTER OF ELECTED LODGE OFFICERS BOYER GRAND LODGE

Year   Grand Master   Deputy Grand Master   Senior Grand Warden   Junior Grand Warden   Grand Treasurer/Grand Secretary

UNITED GRAND LODGE

Year	Grand Master	Deputy Grand Master	Senior Grand Warden	Junior Grand Warden	Grand Treasurer/Grand Secretary
1845	Paul Drayton		James Barnett	Alexander Elston	C.C.Boyer, Sr.
1845	Paul Drayton		James Barnett		
1845	Paul Drayton		James Barnett		
1845	James Barnett	Jacob R. Gibbs	Alexander Elston	Arnold R. Ricks	Charles Horton
1845	James Barnett	Jacob R.Gibbs	Alexander Elston	Arnold R.Ricks	Charles Horton
1845	James Barnett	Jacob R. Gibbs	Alexander Elston	Arnold R.Ricks	Charles Horton
1845	James Barnett	JacobR.Gibbs	Alexander Elston	Arnold R. Ricks	Charles Horton
1852	William Clark	Jacob R. Gibbs	Alexander Elston	Arnold R.Ricks	Charles Horton
1853	Charles Horton	Jacob R. Gibbs	Alexander Elston	Arnold R. Ricks	C.A. Hooten
1854	James Barnett	Jacob R.Gibbs	Alexander Elston	W.C.H.Curtis	CA Hooten
1855	James Barnett	Jacob R. Gibbs	Alexander Elston	W.C.H.Curtis	CA Hooten
1856	James Barnett	Jacob R. Gibbs	Alexander Elston	John R. Porter	C.A. Hooten
1857	Alexander Elston	Felix Dorsey	John R. Porter	Jeffrey Van Clef	C.A. Hooten
1858	Alexander Elston	Jeffrey Van Clef	John R. Porter	William Clark	C.A. Hooten
1859	Ransom F. Wake	John R. Porter	William Clark	William A. Mare	CA Hooten
1860	Ransom F. Wake	John R.Porter	William A.Mars	Peter W. Rey	John Peterson
1861	Patrick H.Reason	Jonas H.Townsend	Peter W. Ray		John Peterson
1862	Patrick H. Reason	Jonas H.Townsend	Peter W. Ray	John M.Thomas	John Peterson
1863	Patrick H. Reason	Peter W. Ray	John M.Thomas	William R.Conner	John Peterson
1884	Patrick H.Reason	Peter W.Ray	Moses B.Coss	Wm.H. Anthony	John Peterson
1865	Pamck. H. Reason	Peter W. Ray	Wm. H. Anthony	John R. Porter	John Peterson
1866	Patrick H.Reason	Peter W.Ray	Wm.H.Anthony	Wm. A. Elston	John Peterson
1867	Parrick H.Reason	Peter W.Ray	Wm. H. Anthony	Arnold R.Ricks	John Peterson
1868	Peter w.Ray	Moses B.Coss	Stephen A. West	Arnold R.Ricks	John Peterson
1869	J.H.Townsend	Wm. H.Anthony	Wm.H.Elston	Samuel Manning	John Peterson
1870	W.C.H.Curtis	John R. Porter	Samuel Manning	Geo.A Manning	Wm.F.Randall
1871	W.C.H.Curtis	John R. Porter	Geo. Manning	Peter T. Jewell	Wm. F.Randall
1872	W.C.H.Curtis	John R. Porter	R.H.MacOougall	Charles W. Lane	Wm.F.Randall
1873	W.C. H.Curtis	Wm. H.Anthony	Peter T.Jewell	Arnold R.Ricks	Wm.F. Randall
1874	W.C.H.Curtis	Wm. H.Anthony	Alexander Corpew	Charles Rogeis, Jr.	Wm.F.Randall
1875	R.H.MacDougall	Peter T. Jewell	Alfred J. Aldridge	Richard H.Sampson	William A. Mars
1876	Alfred J. Aldridge	Alexander Corpew	Elijah J. Wormsley	James E.States	William A. Mars
1877	Alfred J. Aldridge	Peter T. Jewell	James E. States	Thomas Mann	William A. Mars

Lewis Hayden
Ransom F. Wake
John Peterson

Patrick H. Reason
John R. Porter
Jonas H. Townsend
W.A. Elston
Albert Wilson
J.M. Butler

Chapter IV Appendix

1. New York Central College
2. Background on Fugitive Slave Law
3. WILBERFORCE: Newspaper Comments on Simpson's
Graduation Speech

1. New York Central College, McGRAWVILLE

Central New York's white and Black abolitionists actively pressed for the emancipation of enslaved people. In 1845, the Southern Baptists had withdrawn from the National Baptist Society over the issue of slavery. A large number were conscientious objectors to slavery. Colgate University, showing a lack of vision and perhaps foreseeing financial constraints from this threat, stayed neutral in the debate in the church over the question.

In 1848, New York Central College came into existence at McGrawville in the neighborhood of Colgate and Hamilton. The school's mission was the education of all regardless of sex, color, or religious belief, incorporated in 1851. Financial support came from prominent liberals and philanthropists who publicly supported abolition such as William Lloyd Garrison, Wendell Phillips, Henry Ward Beecher, Horace Greeley, Gerrit Smith of Peterboro, New York, and Senator John P. Hale of New Hampshire. Fredrick Douglass threw all his weight as an orator to raise funds for the school.

Despite the energy of many, the school did not survive financially and closed in 1859, but before it closed it was reported to be the first institution of higher learning to employ Negroes to its faculty.

William G. Allen, Professor of Greek at New York Central College was the second colored staff member. Gerrit Smith was William G. Allen's benefactor when he studied at Oneida Institute. He also studied law in Boston Allen wrote:

"The college was founded by a few noble-minded men whose object was to combat the vulgar American prejudices, which can see no difference between a man and his skin. They sought to illustrate the doctrine of Human Equality, or brotherhood of races; to elevate the nation's morals, and give it more elevated views of the aims and objects of Christianity. Such a college, in the midst of corrupt public sentiment, could not fail to meet with the greatest opposition. It was persecuted on all sides, and by all parties, showing how deep-seated and virulent is prejudice against color. The legislature countenanced the college so far as to grant it a charter, and empowered it to confer degrees but would not, seemingly on no earthly consideration give it the slightly pecuniary patronage. The debates took place in the State House at Albany, when the bill relating to the college came up for consideration, in vulgar flings at 'negroes,' 'cries of amalgamation' and such like, would have disgraced a very assemblage of pagans. However the college held on, though its efficiency is of course greatly marred. All the other professors were white; so also were the majority of the students."

The first president of the school was Leonard G. Calkins, a member of the class of 1851 at Madison University. P.15

The founding of the New York Central College at McGraw derived from the activities of "left-wing" Baptists who withdrew from the national denominational organization before that group split on the question of slavery. In 1846, the "ultraists," as they were known to their more conservative brethren, incorporated in Maine as the American Baptist Free Mission Society. Among their leaders was Cyrus P. Grosvenor, editor of the Free Missionary (later Christian Reflector and Free Missionary), a newspaper he published for a period in Utica and later at McGraw.

Grosevenor and his associates, dissatisfied with the conservative policies of the Madison (Colgate) University faculty-especially on the issue of slavery, decided in 1847 to establish their own school. The principles to be followed at the institution were announced as:
1. Anti-slavery
2. "Equality of the sexes"
3. Manual labor

4. Christian education, with the Bible as the textbook in morals
5. Temperance p.45

Grosvenor was president of the faculty and associated with him were three former Colgate students, one who graduated with the Class of 1839. A few others who had been supporters of the Hamilton Institution gave allegiance to 71 the New York Central College as well.

2. Fugitive Slave Law
With the passage of the Fugitive Slave Law, of 1793, Blacks who were free or formerly enslaved were rightfully concerned for their safety. With the growth of the abolition movement, southerners pressured the federal government and a second Fugitive Slave law was enacted in 1850. The new law provided for the use of U.S. Marshals to arrest, detain, and return freedom seekers to their enslavers and fees were paid to anyone assisting in this effort. People who assisted in hiding or helping the freedom seekers faced criminal prosecution. In 12 Years a Slave, Samuel Northup, a free Black, recounted his tale of being forced into slavery by slave catchers who kidnapped him from the streets of a town in Upstate New York. He was a free man, and it took twelve years before he regained his freedom and was reunited with his family. Regional white and Black abolitionists were aggressive in opposing the new Fugitive Slave Law, holding anti-slavery conventions, condemning the law, helping freedom seekers hide, and eventually assisting in their journey to Canada. It was against this backdrop, Simpson attended and completed his course of study at the Colgate.

3.WILBERFORCE: Newspaper Comments on Simpson's Graduation Speech
The news article reads:
We cannot from year to year go into an analysis of several exercises of Commencements. We shall particularly allude to only one of the young men. There was great applause at the announcement

of the name of Henry L. Simpson. The reason was obvious when he appeared. He is of African descent. His physiognomy and entire personal appearance are good...The rareness of such occurrences led us thus to notice this address, and we do it without insinuating that it was in advance of others, or even equal to several of them in ability.

("Editorial Correspondence: Madison University Commencement") As reported in the New York Chronicle, The author of the piece 'Wilberforce' was very warmly applauded, partly because he is a colored young man, whose character and conduct have won him high esteem and partly because his performance was replete with just and noble sentiments.

Still another report appeared in a separate newspaper:
Henry L. Simpson, the speaker, is a young man of Africa descent.... His subject was "Wilberforce" and a...theme he could not have chosen...we were subsequently informed that he is quite a favorite with the professors and students and with the community generally, having won their confidence and esteem by the modesty of his demeanor and the purity and propriety of his life.

William Wells Brown, "Colored People of Canada"
    -Fall 1861, William Wells Brown, "The Colored People of Canada," in Abolitionist papers. During HLS's time in Chatham, Canada

"Taking a seat in a front pew last Sunday, I listened to a well-conceived and eloquently delivered sermon from the Rev. H.L. Simpson, at the Baptist Church. Born in Columbia County, N.Y., a faithful student, and finely educated, Mr. Simpson is an honor to his profession, as well as to his race. His well-turned periods, faultless dramatic gestures, short, but forcible sentences, and his overpowering earnestness, reminded me of the best efforts of Henry Melville, the master of the English pulpit. In his younger days I should judge that the Rev. Gentleman often looked upon the boards, and took delight in the sock and buskin, for certain am I that no man ever became such a master of the art of the tremble of the uplifted hand, without gazing upon Macready's Hamlet, or Forrest's Gladiator. I think him the most polished preacher, colored or white, that I have heard for years."

•William Charles Macready and Edwin Forrest (plays Spartacus)

1. Letter from Sterling Gardner, dated March 13, 1871

Sterling Gardner

Hamilton N.Y.
March 13. 1871

Dear Sir

Your letter was received this afternoon. It arrived here last Saturday, 11th inst, but one of the students took it from the Post Office and forgot to give it to me. I have thought that the class wished to abolish the honors because I was in it and I have told some, in a way to avoid an appearance of pride, that I thought thine, but they deny that was the thing which moved them and they think that no one was moved by such a motive. There is no outward appearance of such a thing just now, but I am afraid that it is in some. Some of the other classes speak of doing the same thing, but my class was

Vassar, but I think I would feel about the same way as I do now. You are going to close school very early this year. I hope you will come here at the Commencement if possible.

My regard to all.

Please reply soon.

Yours humbly,
Sterling Gardner

continued next page

the first. The reason why this is it
is, to promote the good feeling and
friendship of the classmates, so that
when we graduate we will not
despise one another on account of
honors, as it usually is.
But the thing is settled in my class
now. The honors are given up.
I did not vote either way and
another one voted against. I gave
reasons for not voting.
But I think I can study without
reward as well as any one, and
I will sign the resolution, provided
that the motive is pure.
I have not had an opportunity of
ascertaining my standing from the
professors since I rec'd your letter,
but some of the class members say
that I stood a chance for the valedict. I stand among the best
scholars in every thing, except speaking.

I would be glad to see Jones and
Vassar in some northern college;
it would be a great advantage
for them.
They couldn't well enter the lowest
class in the preparatory department
next time, for that class will
have reviewed the common english
branches and studied Greek two
terms. Jones and Vassar know more
about Latin than the class and
therefore might be able to make
up; they would also have the Summer
vacation for class.
If they come, I have no doubt but
that they will be disappointed in respect to some things, but I don't
know where they can get a better
preparation for college.
I would not like to remain here
another year, but it is not as I
please.
I would like to see Jones and

Chapter VIII Appendix

1. The Madisonian- Beet-hoven Society program, Special Collections and Archives, Colgate University Libraries

56   THE MADISONIAN.

Beet-hoven Society.

QUANTITAS NON QUALITAS.

NATHAN DIMON,   -   -   Boss of the Baton

WE SUSTAIN THE SOLOS.

"Hark! I hear an Angel Sing,"   -   -   LEWIS, Soprano
"Are you Silent for Admiration?"   -   MacCLYMONT, Alto
"I was Seeing Nellie Home,"   -   -   MUNRO, Tenor
(Heavy on the low tones),   -   -   -   JONES, Bass

CHORUS,

"Mother would Comfort Me if she were Here," - MacLALLEN
"Ragged, Sassy, Fat and Tall,"   "   "   - ROBINSON
"I wish I was a Married Man,"   "   "   - EASTON
"Strike the Liar,"   -   -   "   - BOSTWICK
"Free and Easy, Fat and Greasy,"   "   "   GORDON
"Kiss Me Quick and Let Me Go,"   -   "   - MAXIM
"Floating on the Wind,"   -   -   : BRONSON
"The Soap-fat-man,"   -   -   "   COPELAND
"Go on, Go on, Go on?"   -   -   : STOCKWIN
"I'm the Blackest Nigger that ever you did See," - LEFTWICH
"How could they do Without Me,"   "   "   TUPPER
     N. B.—No rehearsals necessary.

Chapter X Appendix

1. Wayland Seminary Letters
2. Colgate University, Department of Rhetoric
   And Public Speaking Letter

1. Wayland Seminary and College.

George Rice Hovey,
President Washington D.C.
October 18, 1898

Dear Mr. Archer,

It gives me pleasure to testify to any who may be interested, to your character and scholarly ability and attainment. In order that you may have such testimony in convenient shape to use. I put it on another sheet of paper and enclose it to you. I hope you will succeed in making the sophomore class and will have a profitable and pleasant year.

We have some twelve or fifteen more students than we had at this time last year. Our college class is much more even in ability than last year: Barco Wad and Curtis are all good scholars, and B.F. White is taking some studies with the class as well as medical work at Howard.

Yours truly
George Rice Hovey

- Samuel Howard Archer collection. Archives Division, Auburn Avenue Research Library on African-American Culture and History, Atlanta-Fulton Public Library System Wayland Seminary and College.

George Rice Hovey,
President Washington, D.C.
Oct. 18, 1898

To whosoever it may concern:

It gives me pleasure to testify to the character and scholarly ability and attainment of Mr. S.H. Archer, who has been a student in Wayland Seminary and College for several years. He was one of our most faithful and trustworthy students, as well as one of the most gifted intellectually. He completed the work of the Freshman class in college, and has such ability that in my opinion, he would be able to over-take a class that had advanced some distance beyond him. I am confident that he will do very satisfactory work wherever his is placed.

George Rice Hovey

- Samuel Howard Archer collection. Archives Division, Auburn Avenue Research Library on African-American Culture and History, Atlanta-Fulton Public Library System Colgate University Department of Rhetoric and Public Speaking

2. Colgate University, Department of Rhetoric And Public Speaking Letter.

Ralph Wilmer Thomas
Hamilton, New York
26 July 1902

Mr. Samuel Howard Archer was a student in Colgate University for four years, graduating in June 1, 1902 with the degree of Bachelor of Arts. During his college course, Mr. Archer maintained a good general standing in all his studies and made good use of his opportunities.

He did especially good work in English and Public Speaking; he was careful and painstaking in the class-room work, and very successful in the various prize competitions of the course. In the Junior and Senior years, he was awarded first prizes in Oratory and Debate. I regard Mr. Archer as admirably equipped, intellectually, to teach the subjects of this department.

During the four years that I have known Mr. Archer, he has maintained an excellent character. I believe in him, and in his future. His work is not to be confined to the class-room, but his power over men will become an influence for good. I cordially commend his to any one who may have need of his services.

Ralph Wilmer Thomas
Professor of Rhetoric and Public Speaking, Colgate University.

Chapter XIV Appendix
1. The Colgate Plan with selected course offerings

1. The Colgate Plan

Cutten transformed the Colgate education with his Colgate Plan. The structure of the Plan survives in the current Core curriculum. The Colgate Plan restructured the liberal arts approach to education, and provided three groupings from which students could elect to study:

1. Language, Literature, Arts
2. Math and Natural Science
3. Mental and Social Science

Students in a particular grouping had to choose from a menu of courses to satisfy the requirements of the grouping. For grouping (1) a student needed 27 hours which included six in either English or English literature and 12 hours of language with six hours in either Greek or Latin. For grouping (2) the 27 hours of grouping (1) were divided by 18 hours in more than one subject area and nine hours in one of the natural sciences. For grouping (3) nine of the 27 hours had to be in a single subject.

All sophomore students, in addition to the above, had to take a minimum of six hours in the third grouping. The available courses to satisfy the requirement were psychology, history, economic, or sociology.

The listed courses reflect the attitude of Cutten and the faculty, which memorialized Cutten's belief in the superiority of the White European, Christian ethos.

In 1928: The Modern World Since 1763:

This course aims to show how the new political ideas of the eighteenth century, the industrial revolution, and the development of the scientific method and knowledge have produced the problems of the present day. Their effect upon the institutional life of Europe is first shown, and their effect upon the secondary European civilizations of the United States, Latin America, and the British

Dominions. A brief study of the Oriental civilizations and the customs of the backward races is made, and the mutual reactions among these civilizations from the development of imperialism are shown. Special emphasis will be placed on the international relations leading to the World War and study of contemporary institutions.

In the 1930-1932 course book:
American History
A general course in the development of institutions within the United States, emphasizing political and constitutional aspects, but in relation to the economic and social changes. Included are European background and influences, rise of different customs in the colonies, significance of separation, development of nationalism and democracy, attitude towards business and social problems, and foreign policies.

In the 1932-1933 course book:
History Courses:
European History from 1763 to 1871:
This seminar continues the study of England along with France, Italy, Germany, and Russia, and to a lesser degree the minor countries of Europe. It includes an analysis of the philosophical, economic, social, and political factors of the eighteenth century; the French revolution and Napoleonic era and their consequences; the Industrial Revolution and the rise of democracy and nationalism.

In the 1933-1934 course book:
Sociology Courses:
Seminar 6: Population
Past, present, and predicted rates of nature increase in relation to social and economic conditions; pre-Malthusian, Malthusian,* and post-Malthusian theories of population with a special stress on contributions of contemporary thinkers here and abroad; demographic influences on international relations; problems of quality including differential birth rate, control of the socially inadequate classes and a critical examination of Eugenics.

In the 1934-1935 course book:

History Course:

Modern World Since 1871 introduced the liberal tendencies in Europe; the growth of imperialism, and effects throughout the world; the pre-war diplomacy and the World War; institutional changes and international relations since the World War.

Sociology Courses:

Welfare Administration

A critical examination of the problems, agencies, legal background, and techniques of the administration of public welfare under municipal, county, state, and federal governments. Also a study of the private and semi-public welfare agencies, and the effects of recent social changes and social disorganization upon the general problems and relations to private and public agencies. A considerable amount of field work and investigation will be required. The general program and the outside trips for the filed work will be planned, as far as possible, to meet the needs and interests of the individual students.

Race and Social Biology

The classification of races; questions of superiority and inferiority. Race conflict, genesis, extent, methods of controlling, biological, and social aspects of race mixture. Human genetics especially as related to the genesis of the "social problem" group. A consideration of the extent to which mental and physical characteristics are correlated with social status. Eugenics, or the possibility of race improvement.

In the 1935-1936 course book:

American History, Before 1850

Consideration of certain topics in the early history of the United States, particularly colonial development in the eighteenth century, the American Revolution, the formation of the Federal Constitution, westward expansion, the growth of democracy, and the rise of the common man.

American History, Since 1850

An intensive study of the outstanding problems in the emergence of modern America, such as the slavery controversy, the Civil War, Reconstruction, the rise of big business, overseas expansion, the Progressive Movement and the World War.

In the 1937-1938 course book:
The Modern World

An intensive study of contemporary European civilization with major emphasis on the period since 1890. Considerations of the diplomacy of Bismarck, pre-war diplomacy, Imperialism, intellectual currents, the growth of socialism, the World War, the Versailles Conference, the Russian Revolution, post-war Germany, Fascist Italy, the League of Nations, and present day international relations. Biographical studies of Bismarck, William II, Clemenceau, Poincare, Edward VII, Grey, Lenin, Stalin, Mussolini, and Hitler.

Course Catalogues, various years, Special Collections and Archives, Colgate University Libraries

*The theory of T.R. Malthus, which state that population tends to increase faster, at a geometrical ration, than the means of subsistence, which increases at an arithmetical ration, and that this will result in an inadequate supply of goods supporting life unless war, famine, or disease reduces the population or the increase of population is checked.

1. Adam Clayton Powell, Jr. Letters

ADAM CLAYTON POWELL, JR.
22ND DISTRICT, NEW YORK

NEW YORK ADDRESS:
132 WEST 138TH STREET

COMMITTEE ON EDUCATION
AND LABOR

Congress of the United States
House of Representatives
Washington, D. C.

MAY 2 1947

April 30, 1947

Dr. Everett Case
Colgate University
Hamilton, N. Y.

My dear Dr. Case:

I'm writing to find out if the policy of the exclusion of Negro men still obtains at Colgate, if not, what steps should be taken for the right type to apply for admission?

Very sincerely yours,

Adam Clayton Powell, Jr.

ACP:lmd

McLanahan, Merritt & Ingraham   ABRAM I. ELKUS
                                                            COUNSEL
40 WALL STREET

WALTER GORDON MERRITT
HENRY A. INGRAHAM
SAMUEL C. WORTHEN
BURGESS OSTERHOUT
JOSEPH B. MILLER   NEW YORK 5, N.Y.
H. GEORGE CARROLL
ROBERT H. BRUCE
HENRY CLIFTON, JR.
E. ALLEN MAC DUFFIE
MYLER CONNELL   May 2nd, 1947.
VINCENT W. QUINN
RICHARD SWAN BUELL

Dr. Everett Case, President,
Colgate University,
Hamilton, New York.

Dear Dr. Case:

        In answer to a recent letter from me to my classmate,
Congressman Adam Clayton Powell, Jr., requesting his financial
support of the 1947 Colgate Alumni Fund Drive, Powell indicates
that he will be happy to contribute if he receives the "right
answer" to a letter addressed to you under date of April 30th.
That letter reads:

        "I'm writing to find out if the policy of the exclusion
        of Negro men still obtains at Colgate. If not, what
        steps should be taken for the right type to apply for
        admission?"

        Powell contributed to last year's fund without raising
this question. Consequently, I am curious to know whether he
raised it because some Negro or Negroes have been unable to obtain
admission this year, or whether he merely seeks assurance of the
University's policy.

        During my years at Colgate there were at least three
Negro boys of outstanding character and ability, including Adam.
It had never occurred to me that Colgate tradition or its objectives
contemplated any discrimination other than on the basis of character
and ability. I would be surprised and disappointed to learn that
there was any foundation for the question put by Powell.

        On a number of occasions I have been genuinely moved by
your careful and stimulating statement of Colgate's problems,
opportunities and objectives. As I understand them, there is
no room for discrimination of a racial or religious character.

                                Sincerely yours,

                                Bob Bruce

11:rm

3 May 1947

My dear Mr. Powell:

　　　　In Mr. Case's absence
I wish to acknowledge your
letter of 30 April concerning
Colgate's admission policies.
I will bring it to Mr. Case's
attention immediately upon his
return to the office Monday.

　　　　　　Yours very truly,

　　　　　　Gordon Boyce
　　　　　　Assistant to Mr. Case

The Honorable Adam Clayton Powell, Jr.
House of Representatives
Congress of the United States
Washington, D. C.

3 May 1947

Dear Mr. Bruce:

In Mr. Case's absence
I wish to acknowledge your
letter of 2 May in reference
to Congressman Adam Clayton
Powell's inquiry about Colgate's
admission policies. I will
bring it to Mr. Case's attention immediately upon his
return to the office Monday.

Yours very truly,

Gordon Boyce
Assistant to Mr. Case

Mr. Robert R. Bruce
McLanahan, Merritt & Ingraham
40 Wall Street
New York 5, New York

11 May 1947

Dear Mr. Powell:

I have discussed with Mr. Werntz, Director of Admissions, your inquiry of 30 April. Both of us feel that such a question coming from you is rather puzzling, if not actually disingenuous.

I have, of course, been responsible for Colgate's policies only since assuming my present office in September 1942, and Mr. Werntz's official responsibility, dating as it does from his release by the Navy slightly more than a year ago, is even shorter. During the war there were no Negroes and very few white students enrolled as civilians, but while the number was not large, I recall that Negroes were included in the various complements of trainees assigned to Colgate by the Navy. I think these men would assure you that the University on its part extended the same welcome to them as to others. Certainly I felt honored by their presence at the receptions in our home which Mrs. Case and I held for the trainees from time to time.

It is true that so far our post-war enrolment includes no Negro students, but as you ought to know from correspondence with Mr. Werntz that is not the result of any policy of exclusion. On the one hand, we have had very few Negro applicants, which is not strange considering our remoteness from the more cosmopolitan centers of population and the limited opportunity for intercourse with other educated Negroes afforded by the community of which the College is a part. On the other hand, the caliber of the relatively few who have applied has, generally speaking, afforded no assurance that the candidate would, if admitted, do successful college work or be as representative of his people as you and we would want him to be. These, you may remember, were the points which Mr. Werntz raised in the inquiries he addressed to you before the present freshman class was admitted. He told me at the time that you had been most helpful in appraising the chances of two or three applicants, and we had hoped that we could count on your future assistance.

Although pressures for admission next fall are more intense than ever, I, for one, would welcome the opportunity to find a place for Negro applicants who clearly qualify for admission in open competition with the field. All Alumni have been advised of the broad criteria governing admissions which include character and promise, as well as the applicant's total performance in school, academic and extracurricular. Some weeks ago Mr. Werntz advised me that among the 2,000 applications completed for September, there were one or two from Negroes, which, on the face of it, warranted the Admission Committee's serious consideration. While I would hope that these men might finally qualify, I would feel more comfortable if the number were not so small. Should one or two men only qualify, however, our policy would be to admit them, and leave to each individual the decision as to whether he would be happier here or elsewhere.

As an alumnus of this College, of course you have every right to

-2-   11 May 1947

propose men, white or colored, Christian or Jewish who are, in your judgment,
qualified for admission. Obviously, we cannot admit all whom Alumni recommend, especially when the recommendation is the result of social, business,
or political pressures. When Alumni address themselves to the question objectively, however, their recommendations and appraisals are not only welcome but genuinely helpful, and any such recommendations as you may make as
an Alumnus, irrespective of the applicant's race, creed, or color, will have
the Committee's most careful consideration. I hope this answers both your
questions.

                            Faithfully yours,

                            Everett Case

The Honorable Adam Clayton Powell, Jr.
House Office Building
Washington, D. C.

11 May 1947

Personal

Dear Mr. Bruce:

Perhaps the best way I
can reply to your letter of 2 May
is to enclose a copy of my reply
to Mr. Powell. You will, I trust,
find it reassuring. I am glad to
know that in your own words you
'would be surprised and disappointed'.
I would be, too, and I suspect that
Mr. Powell himself knows better.

Faithfully yours,

Everett Case

Mr. Robert Bruce
McManahan, Merritt & Ingraham
40 Wall Street
New York, New York

Selected Sermons From:

Rev. Wm. J. Simmons
Rev. G.W. Raiford
Rev. M.W. Gilbert

The Colored Baptist Ministers in 1890 published a collection of sermons and papers:
"The Negro Baptist Pulpit." A collection of Sermons and Papers on Baptist Doctrine and Missionary and Educational Work, edited by E.M. Brawley, D.D.

In the preface,

A QUARTER of a century has passed away since the colored Baptist began to live under their new and changed conditions...The present, and for many years to come the great work of our ministry must be that of development, particularly along the line of Baptist doctrine and work. Much has been done by living voice to rain and lead the people, but the time has come when the pen must also be employed. Our trained leaders must write.

This book, therefore, makes no apology for coming into existence. It is needed. The various parts have all been prepared by men of culture and experience, many of them being products of Baptist institutions ranking among the foremost in the North. Madison and Bucknell and Morgan Park and Kalamazoo and Denison, and others, are all represented here, while all the writers are loyal men and true.

Colgate in 1890 was still named Madison, following are three sermons of men who attended Colgate.

THE LORD'S SUPPER.
WM. J. SIMMONS, D.D., L.L.D.
District Secretary of the American Baptist Home Mission Society for the South.

"For I have received of the Lord that which also I delivered unto you, that the Lord Jesus the same night in which he was betrayed took bread: and when he had given thanks, he brake it, and said, Take, eat; this is my body, which is broken for you: this do in remembrance of me. After the same manner also he took the cup, when he had supped, saying, This cup is the new testament in my blood: this do ye, as oft as ye drink it, in remembrance of me. For as often as ye eat this bread, and drink this cup, ye do shew the Lord's death till he come." -1 Cor. 11:23-26.

LIKE all good Jesus, Christ was observing the Passover which they had been ordered to keep as a memorial (Exod. 12:21-29.) The table was supplied with unleavened bread, wine, the bitter herbs, and the paschal lamb. The bread was unleavened as a symbol of their afflictions in Egypt. (Deut. 12:3.) And also because it commemorated their speedy exit from the land of the Pharaohs, as it is remarked in Exod. 12:39, that "the dough was not leavened, because they were thrust out of Egypt, and could not tarry." For this same reason the feast was eaten standing, to typify the fact that they were in a hurry to depart, and had no time to sit.

The wine was an emblem of rejoicing, and was mingled with water, which was drunk after the following thanks: "Blessed be thou, O Lord, who has created the fruit of the vine; blessed be thou for this good day, and this holy convocation, which thou hast given us for joy and rejoicing. Blessed be thou, O Lord, who hast sanctified Israel." Herbs were to symbolize to the Jews the bitterness of their lives as well as to indicate that in their haste they had no time to select better seasoning; to this they afterward added a sauce of dates, raisins, and other ingredients, mixed to the consistency of mustard, to indicate the clay in which they labored. The lamb was to be a male without blemish; it was to be roasted, to avoid eating raw or boiling, as was the manner of the heathen. This mode of cooking the lamb indicated the fires of persecution. It should be eaten without breaking a bone, in private, each family having a lamb, and all must be eaten. This was an offset to the great public feasts of the Egyptians and Syrians, who carried around the sacrificial victims with great show and pomp, and then devoured them, carrying away some portions as relics. These preparations for the feast of the Passover being made from year to year, kept in the Jewish mind the great passing over by the angel, when he saw the blood on the lintels of the doorposts.

Christ observed the Passover, and at the end thereof instituted "The Lord's Supper." The one ceremony was a fitting introduction to the other. The one was the symbol of the fading shadow of Christ as foreseen in the slain lamb, while the other is the new feast of saints in a new dispensation, and Christ himself the Paschal Lamb. Hence, we read that Paul calls Christ our Passover. (1 Cor. 5:7.) In examining the conditions, and the figures, it will be seen that there are many points of agreement between the Jewish Passover, and "The Lord's Supper"; between the emblems of the one and the other; the lessons to be taught by the former and the latter. Yes, remarkably true is it that the "Person of Christ," "the suffering and death of Christ," "the fruits of Christ's death," and the manner in which we are to be made partakers of the rich and glorious fruits of his sacrifice are boldly, vividly, and strongly typified in the Jewish Passover, and the Lord's Supper. The former is of the old dispensation, the latter of the new.

Yet another thing to be impressed upon us is this, that "Blood is the price of liberty." "Born in iniquity and in sin," there is no escape from the thralldom thereof till "the blood of Christ cleanseth [sic] us from all sine." (1 John 1:7.) "For if the blood of bulls and of goats, and the ashes of an heifer sprinkling the unclean, sanctifieth [sic] to the purifying of the flesh, how much more shall the blood of Christ, who through the eternal Spirit offered himself without spot to God, purge your conscience from dead works to serve the living God. And for this cause he is the mediator of the new testament, that by the means of death, for the redemption of the transgressions that were under the first testament, they which are called might receive the promise of eternal inheritance. For where a testament is, there must also of a necessity be the death of the testator. For a testament is of force after men are dead; otherwise it is of no strength at all while the testator liveth [sic]." (Heb. 9:13-17.) Now Matt. 26:26-29; Mark 14:22-25; Luke 22:19, 20; and 1 Cor. 11:23-26, all give accounts of the introduction of this the second ordinance of Christ, baptism being the first. John is silent on this subject. Paul alone tells us that it is to be observed "till he come," even as the Passover was to be kept till Christ came the first time.

I. The elements.

We have briefly spoken of the elements used for this Supper, and desire now to speak more specifically. There are two, elements, bread and wine, which were in olden times brought by the members of the church, each bringing some. What was necessary was used in the administration of the ordinance, and the balance was gathered and appropriated for the benefit of the poor. How deep an interest the members must have had when in this way they prepared these offerings! No doubt it is from this beautiful custom of individual contributions that a collection is generally taken for the poor saints at the Lord's Table. For the most part now the elements are provided by the deacons. It should be recalled here that Christ sent his disciples to prepare the Passover wherein also offerings for the Supper were also prepared. There were no deacons to prepare the "Lord's Supper," but they were afterward appointed, apparently to attend to the poor in the distribution of what was left after eating. It was because of this apostles declared: "It is not reason that we should leave the word of God, and serve tables."

The reasons for using bread are perhaps as follows: 1. To harmonize with its uses in the Passover. He took the loaf and broke it. So he was broken. 2. To symbolize Christ as the great food for the spiritual system. (John 6:51.) 3. Because it is easy to get, and is commonly understood as containing the results of the divine energy in nature, being produced from the earth by the rain and the sum. 4. To remind them that he had given the Jews manna in an unaccountable way; and as it came down from heaven, so did Christ himself. 5. As no one can tell how bread enters the system and produces life, strengthens bones and muscles, etc., so there is a mystery in that Christ becomes our strength and life. Bread produces strength in the body, so does Christ in the soul.

Baptists believe the matter of little moment whether the bread be leavened or unleavened, and hence both are used. Now as regards wine. It is well to notice that word "wine" is not used by the master, but the "fruit of the vine." When this idea is of itself brought in contact with the word itself in the original, it is evidence that no violence is done by using the word wine. Much controversy has obtained as to fermented and unfermented wine, but no one disputes that the "fruit of the vine" is wine; and indeed scholars tell us that the word generally used is the one for unfermented wine. (Matt. 9:17; John 2:3-10; Rom. 14:21; 1 Tim. 3:8; Titus 2:3.) Wine is used: 1. To call to mind the fact that the Lamb was slain. That he gave his life for us. "The life is the blood." (Gen. 9:4.) This his blood caused God to pass over us as the blood of the lamb did on the Jewish doorposts. 2. It is a reminder of Jesus' pains and sufferings, and that he was wounded for our transgressions; yet it is an emblem of joy. 3. As the fruit of the grape is crushed to secure wine, so was he bruised to secure grace for transgressors. Other analogies might be suggested, but these will suffice.

II. The Name

The most common and most acceptable term for this ordinance known to intelligent Baptist is the Lord's Supper. Other terms are applied to it, as "the Sacrament," "the Communion," "the Eucharist"; but the term "Lord's Supper" seems the most appropriate, and as in every way meeting the demands of the case. It is the term which the Apostle Paul in 1 Cor. 11:20 uses to designate the ordinance. It is the term, moreover, which most fully recognizes our Lord's relation to that which is pre-eminently his in its institution and symbolism. It is the term which most generally, if not always, should be used. It was on Thursday night that the Lord's Supper was instituted, but to emphasize the relation of the Christian Sabbath to the resurrection of our Lord, the early Christians celebrated the ordinance on that day. (Acts 20:7.)

Says Rev. J. Newton Brown, in his "Encyclopedia of Religious Knowledge," "Much has been said respecting the time of administering the Lord's Supper. Some plead for the morning, others for the afternoon, and some for the evening; which latter indeed was the time of the first celebration of it, and is most suitable to a supper. How often it is to be observed has been a matter of different opinion. Some have been for keeping it every day in the week, others four times a week, some every Lord's Day, which many think nearest the apostolic practice, a practice which was long kept up, and only deviated from when the love of Christians began to wax cold. Others have kept it three times a year, and some once a year; but the most common custom for its observance is once a month. It appears, however, both from Scripture and from the nature of the ordinance, that its observance ought to be frequent."

One word more as to the posture in taking the Supper. The Passover was first taken standing, but after the Israelites had entered Canaan they took it in the position which Christ and his disciples assumed in the upper room. This custom of reclining showed signs of equality and strict union. For is not Christ "our Elder Brother"? His Father our Father? We see many Pedobaptists kneeling at the Lord's Supper. This method was introduced by the Roman Catholic Church. It was intended to be an act of worship. The Roman Catholics believe the elements to be the body and blood of Christ; hence in kneeling they are worshiping him, as recognized in the bread and wine.

III. The significance of the ordinance

Let us somewhat in detail, though briefly, notice the significance of the Lord's Supper:

1. It is commemorative of the blessed Saviour [sic]. He commands his disciples thus: "This do ye, as often as ye drink it, in remembrance of me." What glorious memories! How grand!

2. It is emblematic, teaching his will and an acknowledgment thereof. A sign of acceptance of his doctrines. "This cup is the

new testament in my blood." The old testament replaced by a new one.

3. It is a type of that which is to come. Recalling the past and suggesting the great future. "But I say unto you, I will not drink henceforth of this fruit of the vine, until that day when I drink it new with you in my Father's kingdom."

4. It is demonstrative, showing that his disciples are to meet to vindicate their belief in the Lord and the Lord's death, and to testify to his second coming, as well as to exhibit faith in his having come. The Jews reject Christ.

5. It exhibits the love of his disciples, not only for the Master but for each other; establishing the fact that all can unite in Christ and form one family. Remember the Jewish Passover was a family institution, and was confined to one family or two small families united. In the time of Josephus not less than ten nor more than twenty persons were allowed. Here we see Christ and his twelve disciples, though it is commonly believed that Judas ate the Passover, but not the Lord's Supper. This was Christ's family. Is not he the Bridegroom of the church? He had no other family. His was a household of faith. This gives splendid evidence of the social character of his church. With one accord around his table they met, and lovingly they meet to-day. Accepting the rendering of Dr. A.N. Arnold: "Because there is one loaf, we the many are one body; for we all partake of the one loaf." Is not this a union of blessed import, Christ's body food for all?

6. It is a bond that holds us together. While it was not probably the Master's intention to hold the church together by this ceremony, yet it is a bond that tightens around his disciples. Indeed, to the soul that loves Christ, this is a precious season. It crystallizes our sentiment and openly publishes the fact that this rallying time is a season for cementing us together. One has only to recall his feelings when he has changed his relations from one church to another. How gladly you can sit down with entire strangers and feel that indeed you are drawn

by invisible yet irresistible bonds to "love the brethren."

7. It advertises to the world that we are keeping intact, faithfully and surely, the very simple, plain ordinance he gave us through his disciples. It portrays truly that the ministry are faithful and that through all these ages there have been those who have delivered it just as he gave it; and that there are myriads who are willing to still do so. Aye, more; when we consider as Baptists what opposition we encounter to be able to deliver it as we received it, we grow proud of our position. But none of these things move us. Not a single heresy is traceable to Baptists. It is our pleasure to keep from the table all whom we believe are not disciples, or who, if they are, do not live free from following after "strange doctrines." Yes, Lord, we will, aided by thee, deliver this glorious Supper, just as thou gavest [sic] it to us! It never grows old.

IV. The prerequisites.

This leads us naturally to consider the prerequisites to this table of the Lord. Mind our language; not our table, but the Lord's table. Not our supper, but the Lord's Supper. We must surely find the conditions in his teaching or that of the teachings and practices of the apostles.

The three requisites admitted by the creeds and most of the members of all denominations are repentance, baptism, and church membership. Christ ate with disciples. Do not forget this; for "Jesus took bread, and brake it, and gave it to his disciples." Christ drank with disciples. Do not forget this; "And he took the cup and gave thanks, and gave to them, saying, Drink ye all of it." They had repented, been baptized and united with Christ. Yet we see a host of people, who profess to repent and will not be baptized. How can they justly claim that we thrust them from the table when we believe that baptism is immersion. This is the Lord's Supper, not ours. Does any man work for another and act according to his own will? If the master of the house bids his servant invite certain guests who fulfill certain conditions, how dare he invite others, who not only fall short of these conditions, but who, on the contrary, have violated these very conditions? Nor does it make a difference how much one may claim to have fulfilled these conditions; it is my duty and yours to satisfy ourselves, as the Master's servants, that the person bidden has observed the conditions. No one doubts the fact that "repentance, baptism, and church membership" are prerequisites to the Lord's Supper. The Lord Jesus, when he gave the great commission, plainly showed this; "Go ye, therefore, and disciple all nations, baptizing them in the name of the Father, and of the Son, and of the Holy Ghost, teaching them to observe all things whatsoever I commanded you." Here we have:

1. Discipling. 2. Baptism 3. Observing commands. Now read in connection with the great commission, Acts 2:38-41; 8:12, 35-38; 9:17, 18; 22:16; 10:47-48; 16:14, 15; 16:29-33; 18:8. From the above, baptism is seen to be a grand essential.

Someone congratulates himself that John and the apostles were not baptized. While the Scripture is silent on that point, it is a more just inference that they were baptized than that they were not. Even if they were not, to them was given the charge to baptize; and it came from high authority [sic] and was of the nature of those things to which Paul refers in the test, when he says: "For I have received of the Lord that which also I have delivered unto you."

But lest some one may accuse me of teaching Baptist doctrine, forgetting in the charge that all Bible doctrine is Baptist doctrine, or that I may be charged with wresting the Scriptures, I will put here the convictions of a few Pedobaptists. But I will state it plainly. Baptists reject from the Lord's Supper such as have not been baptized. They do not believe any one baptized except he is immersed. Should one be immersed and unite with a Pedobaptist church, then we reject him, as by his course teaching error, and thereby failing to practice and teach the truth.

We are not keepers of the consciences of such, but our own. The coming to the table depends on repentance, baptism, and union with a church. If we do not acknowledge a man's baptism, he cannot get to our Lord's table. Pedobaptists are consistent in inviting us, for they believe we are baptized, while we do not believe they are.

We have a baptism accepted throughout the world, by even those who practice sprinkling and pouring, while these last-names are rejected by millions. This is all there is to what is called "close communion." It is a question of baptism and holy life. I pass over the question of "church," as to whether these great Pedobaptist organizations are a "church," etc., as it is not material to this present argument. Suffice it to say, that Baptists and Pedobaptists disagree as to what is a church, but do not disagree on the fact that a man must be baptized and join a church, no matter how widely they may differ as to what that baptism is.

I take these extracts from a pamphlet by Rev. Henry F. Colby; Dr. Pendleton's "Doctrines," and Hiscox's "Baptist Short Method."

Dr. Wall, in his "History of Infant Baptism," p. 2, chap. IX., says: "No church ever gave the communion to any persons before they were baptized. Among all the absurdities that ever were held, none ever maintain that any person should partake of the communion before he was baptized."

Dr. Dick, in his "Theology," says: "None have the right to the holy table but those who have been previously purified by the washing of water and the word."

Justin Martyr says: "This food is called by us the Eucharist, of which it is not lawful for any to partake but such as believe the things taught by us to be true, and have been baptized."

Dr. Cave says: "The communicants in the primitive church were those who had embraced the doctrines of the gospel, and had been baptized into the faith of Christ. For, looking upon the Lord's Supper as the highest and most solemn act of religion, they thought they could not take care enough in the dispensing of it."

Baxter says: "What man dare go in a way which hath neither precept nor example to warrant it, from a way that hath a full current of both? Yet they that will admit members into the visible church without baptism do this."

Doddridge says: "It is certain that as far as our knowledge of antiquity reaches, no unbaptized person received the Lord's Supper.

How excellent soever [sic] a man's character is, he must be baptized before he can be looked upon as completely a member of the Church of Christ."

Dr. Dwight, a Congregationalist, says: "It is an indispensable qualification for the ordinance that the candidate for communion be a member of the visible Church of Christ in full standing. By this I intend that he should be a person of piety; that he should have made a public profession of religion; and that he should have been baptized."

Dr. Hibbard, a Methodist, says: "Both Baptist and Pedobaptist churches agree in rejecting from communion at the table of the Lord, and denying the rights of church membership to all who have not been baptized. Valid baptism they consider essential to visible church membership. This also we hold. The only question then that divides us is, What is essential to valid baptism?"

Dr. Hodge, the Presbyterian, says: "The Christian Church requires of those whom it receives to membership in visible communion nothing more than a credible profession of faith, the promise of obedience to Christ and submission to baptism as the initiatory ordinance."

V. The benefit of the ordinance.

I wish to ask now what benefit is bestowed by the observance of this ordinance upon the individual himself, and what really is the character of the elements when partaken of? There are four views held touching this mater.

1. Transubstantiation. This is a big word that explains the Roman Catholic belief, and means that the substances, bread and wine, are changed to the actual body and blood of Christ.
2. Consubstantiation, a word to represent the views of the Lutherans, and means that the actual body and blood is really mingled with the bread and wine.
3. The Calvinists believe that through the bread and wine, by some mysterious spiritual power Christ's life is made common to us, and that we feed upon him as spiritual food.

4. Baptist believe with Zwingli, that these elements are only emblems, and this view is sufficient to call to remembrance the word and works of the Lord Jesus.

Let us consider a few practical lessons:

In eating the Lords' Supper, we are commanded to examine ourselves, for many become worthless, benumbed, useless, sleepy Christians from eating unworthily, and are not approved of God. (1 Cor. 5:1-8; 1 Cor. 2:27-32.) "Ye are my disciples if ye do whatsoever I command you." He has commanded us to love one another; also, to do this in remembrance of him. As often, therefore, as we do so, we show our love for our brethren, and obey the Lord's command.

We owe to our Master to make this constant protest against the evils of sprinkling, pouring, and the like, for God needs us to preserve that which has been committed to us. It makes us stronger and stronger as often as we please Christ by a ready compliance with his will. It tests our title to discipleship.

Again this is a church ordinance, given to a church, for a church, and should be kept in the church. So long as the church stands, just so long will we lovingly remember Jesus around the table. The scenes of the cross will grow brighter and brighter, and our duty to preach our distinctive views grows none the less obligatory. As we practice so shall we preach; and the great God who made us prosper the word! In the language of Dr. Thomas Armitage, in his "History of the Baptist":

"When men are willing to return to the gospel order of regeneration and baptism, their obedience to Christ will remove all controversy on these subjects by restoring things to the gospel status, and then there must of necessity be again one Lord, one faith, one baptism, and one table. Until then there never can be, and what is more, there never ought to be, except on this apostolic church principle."

"REPENT YE, AND BELIEVE THE GOSPEL." MARK 1:15
REV. G. W. RAIFORD
Pastor of the Bethesda Baptist Church, Georgetown S.C.

REPENTANCE and faith when considered in their connection with each other, with man's need of them, in order to pardon of sin and peace with God, and their invariable effect upon the heart and life of those who live in the continual exercise of them, may be considered as second to none among the doctrines of Christianity. If man had continued in his original state of innocence, there would be no need of salvation through our Lord Jesus Christ; but sin has made a terrible wound, with which must be healed; and must be laid bare as a preface to tis healing. "I wound, and I heal, saith [sic] the Lord." Therefore, the painful ordeal through which each believing soul must pass.

Gospel repentance looks toward a change of life both inwardly and outwardly. This is especially true, when taken in connection with faith. When Jesus began to preach in Galilee the gospel of the kingdom of God, and that it was at hand (Mark 1:15,) the Jews fondly expected the Messiah to appear in external pomp, not alone to free the Jewish nation from the Roman yoke, but to give it power over all its neighbors. They therefore thought that they must prepare for war and victory; but Christ told them they must repent and believe the gospel. They had broken the moral law, and could not be saved under the old covenant, for both Jews and Gentiles had come far short of its obligations. They must therefore have the benefit of a covenant of grace, submit to the remedy proposed by it, vis.: Repentance toward God, and faith toward our Lord Jesus Christ. (Acts 20:21.) Peer, on the day of Pentecost, stood up in the midst of the people, and arraigned the Jews for the cruel and malignant murder of Jesus Christ. His stern, accusing words did not fail to produce a good result, for the Jews were both startled and convinced-startled because they had committed so ruthless a crime against the Messiah; convinced that they had need of immediate action. Thus aroused, their cry was "What shall we do?" Peter told them what to do. Then Peter said unto them: "Repent, and be baptized every one of you in the name of Jesus Christ for the remission of sins." (Acts 2:38.) Repent! this was the same duty that John the Baptist and Jesus Christ had preached. Be baptized every one of you in the name of Jesus Christ; that is, they must firmly believe in Jesus Christ as a Saviour, [sic] and in baptism make a solemn and open profession of him, and come under an obligation or agreement to live a new life. "For godly sorrow worketh repentance to salvation, not to be repented of, but the sorrow of the world worketh death." (2 Cor. 7:10.)

In order that there may be a full and genuine repentance there must be:

1. A deep and genuine sense both of sin and God's infinite love and righteousness. This is true on the one hand, because but for sin there would be no need of repentance; and, on the other hand, but for a knowledge of God, his will, his just and equitable law, there could be no holy concern for his honor, will, or law.

2. Repentance must be attended both with sorrow and shame. Holy shame is a necessary as holy sorrow. The more definite our knowledge of sin, and our sense of God's love and justice, the more genuine will be our sorrow for sin, and the more keen our shame.

3. There must be a hatred of sin. This intense sorrowing for sin quite naturally leads to a hatred of it. Sin must be hated in all of its forms. It strikes at the authority of God, and its blighting influence may be felt in the palace of the noble, as in the most despicable hovel of the most lowly. We must loathe and hate sin. We must loathe ourselves too as sinners in the sight of a holy God. If sin be truly an abomination to us, sin in ourselves will especially be so-the nearer the more loathsome; and if sin lurk at the bottom of love for self, then there can be no repentance without an abhorrence of self. Our self-abhorrence and abandonment of sin will be in proportion to our knowledge of the direful effects of sin, as

seen in ourselves, and of the mercy and goodness of God as manifested toward us.

Here is the dividing line between every soul and Jesus Christ. If crossed, it means life; if uncrossed, it means [sic] death. Here, to change the figure, is the battleground of every individual; the scene of conflict for the emancipation of the soul, or where its bondage is made more secure. Here we begin to come nearer to God, or to be driven farther from him. How important, then, in view of these facts, that each one should look at repentance and faith in their true light, and estimate them at their true worth!

4. In true repentance there must be a fixed purpose to forsake our sins. Our hatred of sin should be so deep, our contrition so sincere, as to form within us this fixedness of purpose. The very nature of repentance implies this, and the genuineness of our repentance may be determined by its existence. For to form and carry out this purpose carries with it all of the real results of repentance, since change in our life is due to the faithful performance of this purpose. The carrying out of this purpose alone sets forth the change. In this matter of repentance and faith we want to bear in mind that there is no atoning efficacy in them for sins of the past. There is that in the work of Jesus Christ and in that alone. And it is made effective to us by means of repentance and faith. "For by grace are ye saved through faith, and that not of yourselves, it is the gift of God." (Eph. 2:8.) Not only is the being saved by faith the gift of God, but the faith also through which we are saved. The presence of faith in us is the evidence rather than the reason of our being saved. If I should be asked why am I saved, the answer would be, because the Lord chose to save me; but if I should be asked why I know that I am save, it would because I believe on the Lord Jesus Christ. The fact that I believed is evidence to me that I am saved.

Spiritual life in man is the immediate result of union with Christ; if to be united with him is to hear him, come to him to touch him, to have one's life hid with Christ in God. Faith is in no wise the procuring cause of this life; but faith joined with repentance makes that life operative at once. Nor is it faith which a dead soul exercises, but faith which "is the gift of God," bestowed in response to the imploring need of the convicted soul, whereby Jesus Christ is made its own. Faith must unconditionally and unreservedly look to the Lord Jesus Christ; must trust him for his promises. Faith therefore accepts Christ as the promised Messiah, believes in him as the victim that bears away the sins of the world, trustingly accepts his death as satisfactory to Divine justice. Christ alone could do this, and at the same time restore man to the favor of the Father, because in him alone were united the qualities requisite to so mighty and mysterious a task. Christ alone was truly human and divine, and his power to save lies in the fact that he possessed both the divine and human nature. Divine and human, Jesus assumed the mighty task. Clad in human form, he came to earth, and by his obedience unto death vindicated the divine law, and made it possible for man to be saved. We walk the earth now with rays of divine light and mercy shining upon our pathway. The terrible clouds of darkness and woe which should justly have gathered and broken with fury upon our heads, broke and spent their fury upon Christ's devoted head, when he stood between guilty man and God, against whom man had sinned. For man's sake he alone bore the penalty. In that moment hope sprang up for the world. Through the mist and darkness of human sin and the thunderings [sic] of divine wrath light shines forth from the cross of Christ.

"In the cross of Christ I glory,
Towering o'er the wrecks of time;
All the light of sacred story
Gathers round its head sublime."

Faith evermore looks to that cross; and the soul exclaims meanwhile, as it looks to the past: "I live because he died!" And as it looks to the future: "I live because he lives."

REPENT, THEN, AND BELIEVE. LET ALL HEED THE CALL; FOR IN HEEDING IS EVERLASTING LIFE.
REV. M. W. GILBERT, A.M.
Pastor of the First Colored Baptist Church, Nashville, Tenn.

"And Jesus came and spake [sic] unto them, saying, All power is given unto me in heaven and in earth. Go ye therefore, and teach all nations, baptizing them in the name of the Father, and of the Son, and of the Holy Ghost."- Matthew 28:18,19.

ALL the precepts of Jesus rest upon his power to command. He is King. We owe him allegiance and obedience because he is God manifested in the flesh. His authority is derived from the Father. His rule is spiritual; and his power to command is beyond question.

"All power is given unto me in heaven and in earth." Does this absolute authority of Jesus mean anything to the redeemed church? Does it signify anything to humanity at large? The great commission and the foundation of the Christian Church rest upon the authority of Jesus as our Supreme Lawgiver. All missionary enterprises are undertaken because Jesus commands it. We preach his commandments, we follow his precepts, we obey his mandates, because he so bids us. The Lord says in our text: "Inasmuch as all authority is given unto me in the heaven and in earth, by reason of this authority, I, your Master, your Lord, and your Redeemer, bid you make disciples of all nations, baptizing them in the name of the Father, and of the Son, and of the Holy Ghost." Our Lord, by his own words, commands us to make disciples of all nations, and to baptize those thus made disciples.

Observing the order of the text, we are-

I. To make disciples of all nations.

Our text places the discipling of the nations before their baptism. It first says: "Go and teach, or make disciples, of all nations." First convert the nations of the earth, turn them to God, persuade the people everywhere to accept Christ as a crucified, risen, ascended, and living Saviour; [sic] then, after these things are done, after these conditions are fulfilled, baptize them in the name of the Father, and of the Son, and of the Holy Ghost.

Does anyone ask why the Baptist churches condemn infant baptism? It is because their Lord commands them first to make disciples. "He that believeth and is baptized shall be save." Here the believing comes first; then baptism follows, as effect follows cause. John the Baptist preached repentance before baptism. Surely infants cannot experience repentance. John the Baptist further required confession of sin in those baptized. "Then went out to him Jerusalem, and all Judea, and all the region round about Jordan, and were baptized by him in Jordan, confessing their sins." (Matt. 3:5,6.) Can infants fulfill this condition? Philip told the eunuch he would baptize him, if he believed on the Lord Jesus with all his heart. It is said of the Corinthians, in Acts 18:8, that "many of the Corinthians hearing, believed, and were baptized." Notice the order: hearing, believing, being baptized. In Acts 2:41, we learn that "they that gladly received his word were baptized." Here we see the necessity of first receiving gladly the word before baptism ensues. When the Samaritans "believed Philip preaching the things concerning the kingdom of God, and the name of Jesus Christ, they were baptized, both men and women." The jailer at Philippi first believed, then he was baptized. First of all, the, we learn that only persons who can exercise saving faith in Christ ought to be baptized; and, secondly, that where there is no exercise of faith, there is no baptism. "Without faith it is impossible to please God."

II. Our text teaches the duty of all believers to be baptized.

"Go ye into all the world, and disciple all nations, baptizing them in the name of the Father, and of the Son, and of the Holy Ghost."

"Yes, but what is baptism?" says one. "I was baptized when I was an infant. I was sprinkled." DO you remember anything about it, then? "No." Did you believe when you were in infancy? "No." Then you were not baptized. "He that believeth and is baptized shall be saved." "But," says another, "I was baptized or christened- i.e., sprinkled, when I was grown up, and was conscious of the fact." Did you believe on Jesus then? "Yes, most emphatically. And was I not baptized?" No, emphatically no! "Then what is baptism? Can it not be sprinkling, pouring, or immersion?" Not all of them. Baptism can no more mean sprinkling, pouring, and immersion all at once than eating means sleeping, drinking, or hearing.

What, then, is baptism: or, What is it to baptize? In answering this question, we must not consult the ordinary mind, but we must take the words of the best scholars on this subject. But what kind of scholars? Shall they be Baptist scholars, or Pedobaptist scholars? I shall take the testimony of Pedobaptist scholars- those who practice sprinkling and christen their infants. For the most conclusive proof of the truthfulness of anything is found in the concessions of its opponents. We shall only mention as authorities men who love truth too well to attempt to lesson its teachings, though they do not practice it.

The word "baptize" is an untranslated word from the Greek. It was simply transferred into our language. Liddell and Scott, in their standard Lexicon, say that baptizo means "to dip in or under water." They add that in the case of ships this word means "to sink them." In not one place does this Lexicon speak of baptizo as meaning sprinkling or pouring. Noah Webster, who was not a Baptist, says in his Unabridged Dictionary that the word "baptism" is from the Greek baptisma or baptismos, which is further derived from baptizein, meaning "to dip in water."

Dr. Cunningham Geikie, of the Church of England, in his "Life of Christ," says of Christ's baptism by John: "Baptism was an ordinance of God, required by is prophet as the introduction of the New Dispensation. It was part of righteousness-that is, it was a part of God's commandments, which Jesus came into the world to show us the example of fulfilling both in the letter and the spirit. Moreover, he had not received the consecration of the Spirit, abiding in him, and had not yet assumed the awful dignity of the Messiah, but had hitherto been only the unknown villager of Nazareth. No subject is more mysterious than the 'increase in wisdom' which marked the Saviour [sic], as it does all other men, nor can we conjecture when it was that the full realization of his divine mission first rose before him. As yet there had been no indication of its having done so; for he had not yet manifested his glory, or appeared at all before men. Is it too much to believe that his baptism was the formal consecration which marked his entrance upon his great office? John resisted no longer; and, leading Jesus into the stream, the rite was performed. Can we question that such an act was a crisis in the life of our Lord? His perfect manhood, like that of other men, in all things except sin, forbids our doubting it. 'Holy and pure,' mark his words before sinking under the waters; he must have risen from them with the light of a higher glory in his countenance. His past life was closed, a new era had opened. Hitherto the humble villager, veiled from the world, he was henceforth the Messiah, openly working among men. It was the true moment of his entrance on a new life. Past years had been buried in the waters of Jordan. He entered them as Jesus, the Son of man; he rose from them the Christ of God."

Dean Alford, of the Church of England, says: "The baptism was administered by the immersion of the whole person." Kurtz, who belonged to the Lutheran Church, says in his "Church History": "Baptism took place by complete immersion." Dr. Philip Schaff, of Union Theological Seminary, New York, says: "Respecting the form of baptism, the impartial historian is compelled by exegesis and history, substantially, to yield the point to the Baptists, as is done, in fact, by most German scholars." Krause, another Pedobaptist scholar and church historian, says: "Baptism was performed by immersion in the name of the Trinity." One fact must impress us, and that is, that the scholars of Germany-that land of scholars-sustain the position maintained by Baptist. Guericke, in his "Church History," translated by Shedd, says: "Baptism was originally performed by immersion, in the name of the Trinity." Dr. Bunsen says, in his "Letters to Arndt," on the "Signs of the Times": "As regards their form of government, the Baptists are, as every one knows, Independents, who perform the rite of baptism, like the primitive Christians, by immersion."

Pope, in his Greek-German Dictionary defines baptizo, "to dip in, dip under." Chamber's "Encyclopedia," declares: "It is, however, indisputable that in the primitive church the ordinary mode of baptism was by immersion." Professor Whitney, a professor in Yale University, says that the word "baptize" is translated into German by the verb "taufen." Now, what is Professor Whitney's own definition for "taufen?" He says it means "to dip, immerse, plunge." Dr. Robinson's "Greek-English Lexicon of the New Testament," which was considered the most authoritative on New Testament Greek until Thayer's appeared, defines baptizo by the expression "to dip in, to sink, to immerse." He clearly makes the admission that the meaning of baptizo from the time of "Plato onward is everywhere to immerse, to sink, to overwhelm." The Greek language is not a dead language, as some suppose. It is still spoken by the modern Greeks. Surely they ought to know their own language, and the meaning of their own words. The modern Geeks declare that baptizo always means dipping, or immersing, and can mean nothing else. In corroboration of this fact, the Greek Church (in Greece and Russia), although it practices infant baptism, nevertheless always immerses or dips infants three times, for the Greek Church does not hold that its children can be baptized, according to the import of the word, without immersion. Stourdza, a native modern Greek, in a work published in 1816, declares that baptizo has but one signification. It signifies literally and invariably to plunge. "Baptism and immersion are therefore identical."

Professor E.A. Sophocles, of Harvard University, a native Greek, in his "Lexicon of the Greek, Roman, and Byzantine Periods," defines baptizo as signifying to "dip, immerse, sink, with figurative uses derived from this"; and he further declares that "there is no evidence that Luke and Paul, and the other writers of the New Testament, put upon this verb meanings not recognized by the Greek." A common complaint of the Greek Church against the Latin or Roman Catholic Church is that the Catholic Church must be held accountable for substituting sprinkling for immersion.

The reformers were convinced that a change ought to be made in the form of baptism. Luther said more than once: "Baptism is a Greek word, and may be translated immersion, as when we immerse something in water that it may be wholly covered. And it is almost wholly abolished (for they do not dip the whole children, but only pour a little water on them); they ought nevertheless to be wholly immersed... for that the etymology of the word seems to demand." He also declares that baptism "is rather a sign both of death and resurrection. Being moved by this reason, I would have those that are to be baptized to be altogether dip into the water, as the word means, and the mystery signifies." Calvin also spoke as freely in commenting upon the baptism of the eunuch, as follows: "They descended into the water. Here we perceive what was the rite of baptizing among the ancients, for they immersed the whole body into the waters; now the custom has become established that the minister only sprinkles the body or the head." Baptism in the original cannot mean sprinkling or pouring, for the words "sprinkling" and "pouring" occur many times in the New Testament, and they are not once translated thus from baptizo.

We have thus the testimony of some of the most eminent among scholars and reformers, conceding the Scripturalness [sic] of the Baptist position as to the ordinance which gives them their name. No Baptist is among them. Truth compels these men to pronounce against their practice, as in this matter it does all Pedobaptists whose scholarship entitles them to respect. The list could be multiplied many fold did not lack of space forbid. Our common English Bible, our King James' Bible, translated by seventy eminent men, not one of whom was a Baptist, will lead one aright, though he know not one letter of Greek. Thousands of men and women have joined the Baptist churches by their own unaided reading of the word of God. And thousands more will join it thus. Oh, that we could get everybody of every church to read the word of God for himself! Read the word of God for yourself. Read it with a view to discover truth and unearth error. Read it to find out your duty. Read it for instruction. Read it for your sanctification. "Search the Scriptures, for in them ye think ye have eternal life, and these are they which testify of me," Jesus said.

Let us notice for those who read nothing but their English Bibles that the expressions, circumstances, and places connected with the administration of baptism in the New Testament prove it to have been immersion. Beginning with Matt. 3: "In those days came John the Baptist preaching in the wilderness of Judea, and saying, Repent ye: for the kingdom of heaven is at hand. For this is he that was spoken of by the prophet Isaiah, saying, The voice of one crying in the wilderness, Prepare ye the way of the Lord, make his paths straight. And the same John had his raiment of camel's hair, and a leathern girdle about his loins; and his meat was locusts and wild honey. Then went out to him Jerusalem, and all the region round about Jordan, and were baptized of him in Jordan, confessing their sins."

We notice that John baptized where there was an abundance of water, and that he baptized in Jordan. Lieutenant Lynch, of the United States Navy, who traversed this river, says that "its width varies at different points from seventy-five to two hundred feet, and it's depth from three to twelve feet." At the traditional spot of our Lord's baptism, in the week preceding Easter, about seven or eight thousand pilgrims come, according to Dr. Broadus, "from all parts of the East, and there these thousands, men, women, and children, do actually immerse themselves and one another in the river-not as baptism (for they received that in fancy), but as a sacred bath at that holy spot." This same event occurs at the same spot every spring.

In Matt. 3:13, and following verses, we read: "Then cometh Jesus from Galilee to Jordan, unto John, to be baptized of him." The Lord Jesus went, it seems, about seventy miles for the express purpose of being baptized. "But John forbade him, saying, I have need to be baptized of thee, and comest [sic] thou to me? And Jesus answering, said unto him, Suffer it to be so now: for thus it becometh us to fulfil all righteousness. Then he suffered him. And Jesus, when he was baptized, went up straightway out of the water; and lo the heavens were opened unto him, and he saw the Spirit of God descending like a dove, and lighting upon him: and lo a voice from heaven, saying, This is my beloved Son, in whom I am well pleased." No one can read this passage carefully and not decide that our Lord was baptized in the river Jordan.

Notice now Mark 1:4-11: "John did baptize in the wilderness, and preach the baptism of repentance for the remission of sins. And there went out unto him all the land of Judea, and they of Jerusalem, and were all baptized of him in the river of Jordan, confessing their sins. And John was clothed with camel's hair, and with a girdle of skin about his loins; and he did eat locusts and wild honey; and preached, saying, There cometh one mightier than I after me, the latchet of whose shoes I am not worthy to stoop down and unloose. I indeed have baptized you with water: but he shall baptize you with [or rather, in] the Holy Ghost. And it came to pass in those days, that Jesus came from Nazareth of Galilee, and was baptized of John in Jordan. And straightway coming up out of the water, he saw the heavens opened, and the Spirit like a dove descending upon him. And there came a voice from heaven, saying, Thou art my beloved Son, in whom I am well pleased." John 3:23, reads: "And John also was baptizing in Enon, near to Salim, because there was much water there; and they came and were baptized." John the Baptist required an abundance of water for baptism. In the Acts, eight chapter, we have the baptism of the eunuch. Begin with the thirty-sixth verse: "And as they went on their way, they came unto a certain water: and the eunuch said, See, here is water; what doth hinder me to be baptized? And Philip said, If thou believest [sic] with all thine heart, thou mayest. And he answered and said, I believe that Jesus Christ is the Son of God. And he commanded the chariot to stand still: and they went down both into the water, both Philip and the eunuch; and he baptized him. And when they were come up out of the water, the Spirit of the Lord caught away Philip, that the eunuch saw him on more: and he went on his way rejoicing."

Can any one deny the fact of immersion from so plain an account? Read also the account of the conversion and baptism of the jailer and his house at Philippi, when Paul and Silas were so mercifully delivered. Turn to Acts, sixteenth chapter, and read from the thirtieth to the thirty-fourth verse: "And brought [i.e., the jailer] them out, and said, Sirs, what must I do to be save? And they said, Believe on the Lord Jesus Christ, and thou shalt be saved, and thy house. And they spake unto him the word of the Lord, and to all that were in his house. And he took them the same hour of the night, and washed their stripes; and was baptized, he and all his straightway. And when he had brought them into his house, he set meat before them, and rejoiced, believing in God with all his house."

What now are the facts in this case? First, the jailer took Paul and Silas to his house, where the apostle preached the word of God; secondly, the jailer took them out the same hour of the night, "and washed their stripes; and was baptized, he and all his, straightway"; thirdly, after the baptism, it is stated that the jailer again "brought them into his house," and "set meat before them and rejoiced in God with all his house."

The symbolical meaning of baptism indicates immersion. Ananias said to Paul: "Arise and be baptized and wash away thy sins, calling on the name of the Lord." Sprinkling would imply here, the use of too small an amount of water to be adequate for a washing.

In Rom. 6:3-4, we read: "Know ye not, that so many of us as were baptized into Jesus Christ were baptized into his death? Therefore we are buried with him by baptism into death: that like as Christ was raised up from the dead by the glory of the Father, even so we also should walk in newness of life." Here baptism is spoken of figuratively, symbolically, as a burial, "buried with him by baptism"; hence, when there is no burial, there can be no baptism.

Bloomfield, who is not a Baptist, says of these two passages of Scripture: "There is here plainly a reference to the ancient mode of baptism by immersion, and I agree with Koppe and Rosenmuller, that there is reason to regret that it should have been abandoned in most Christian churches, especially as it has so evidently a reference to the mystic sense of baptism."

Read now Col. 2:12: "Buried with him in baptism, wherein also ye are risen with him through the faith of the operation of God, who hath raised him from the dead."

Lightfoot, a Pedobaptist commentator, says of this verse: "Baptism is the grave of the old man and the birth of the new. As he sinks beneath the baptismal waters, the believer buries there, all his corrupt affections and past sins; as he emerges thence, he rises regenerate, quickened to new hopes and a new life." Bishop Wilson, another Pedobaptist commentator, says: "The expression 'buried with him in baptism' alludes to the ancient form of administering that sacred ordinance of the immersion or burial, so to speak, of the whole person in the water, after the example of the burial of the entire body of our Lord in the grave." We have then the authority of God's word for what baptism is. The opinions of learned men confirm this authority. It is, moreover, worthy of note, that while these scholars are Pedobaptists, no Baptist can be found who will concede the validity of sprinkling or pouring as New Testament baptism.

When Jesus was on earth, he said to one and another: "Follow me." Let all who would be truly enrolled among his disciples, follow him in baptism.

> "To Jordan's stream the Saviour [sic] goes,
> To do his Father's will;
> His breast with sacred ardor glows,
> Each precept to fulfill.

> "As from the water he ascends,
> What miracles appear!
> God, with a voice, his Son commends:
> Let all the nations hear.

> "Hear it, ye Christians, and rejoice,
> Let this your courage raise;
> What God approves, be this your choice,
> And glory in his ways."

"If ye love me," Jesus says, "keep my commandments." "But," says some one, "if sprinkling is not and cannot be baptism, how do you account for its beginning?" Luther, the great reformer, says it was not practice in the beginning. Calvin says the church felt authorized instituting a change. The scholars of the Church of Rome declare that the church had the right or authority to change an ordinance, and has changed the original rite for convenience. The church has the right to change an ordinance, of God. Think of it! We hold that no church, or bishop, or pope, or principality, or power under the canopy of heaven, is authorized to change a mandate of Almighty God. "Heaven and earth shall pass away, but not one jot or title of my word shall fail till all be fulfilled." "And if any man shall add unto these things, God shall add unto him the plagues that are written in this book: and if any man shall take away from the words of the book of this prophecy, God shall take away his part of the book of life, and out of the holy city, and from the things which are written in this book." (Rev. 22:18,19).

"Is baptism important after a man is converted?" exclaims some Christian. All of God's commandments are important. The least of them are essentially important. "Believe" and "be baptized" are the two commands which our ascended Lord left behind him for his church. Who shall say the one is essential and the other is not? Obey both. Obedience is better than mutilation. "Behold to obey is better than sacrifice, and to hearken than the fat of rams."

BIBLIOGRAPHY
References

Blog. Sterling Gardner: A feather in the Richmond Cap, 2019. Online. Internet. 19 Jan. 2019.

The Louisiana Historical Quarterly, Volume 30, 1947. Online. Internet. 19 Jan. 2019.

The Baptist Home Mission Monthly, Volumes 11-12, 1889. Online. Internet. 19 Jan. 2019.

Crisis Magazine, 1922: 176. Online. Internet. 21 Jan. 2019.

Encyclopedia Virginia. Virginia Foundation for the Humanities, 1 May. 2014. Web. 22 Jan. 2019., 2014.

Lincoln University Catalogue 1985-1987 (n.d.). Online. Internet. 27 Jan. 2019.

A call for a convention of the Colored Inhabitants of the State of New York. The Colored American, 1840. Online. Internet. 6 Mar. 2019.

Albany Evening Journal. "Colored Man's Temperance Convention", 1848: 2. Online. Internet. 8 Mar. 2019.

Albany Weekly Patriot, "Address to His Excellency Gov. Seward", 1843. Online. Internet. 7 Mar. 2019.

Alexander, Adele Logan. Parallel worlds. Charlottesville: University of Virginia Press, 2012.

Annual report. American Baptist Home Mission Society, 1885. Online. Internet. 21 Jan. 2019.

Bacote, Samuel William. Who's who among the colored Baptists of the United States. Kanas, 1913.

Bennett, Jessica. "noted Educators, Virginians All": How One Family Changed the Shape of African American Education". Presentation, Virginia, 2018.

Bentley, Altermese Smith. Seminole County. Charleston, SC: Arcadia, 2000.

Black Newspapers Publication: Frederick Douglass' Paper. "Our Correspondence", 1855. Online. Internet. 17 Mar. 2019.

Black Virginia: the Richmond Planet, n.d. Online. Internet. 30 Dec. 2018., https://blackvirginia.richmond.edu/items/show/68.

Blackmon, Douglas A. Slavery by another name. New York, NY: Anchor Books, 2008.

Blight, David W. Frederick Douglass' Civil War: Keeping Faith in Jubilee. Baton Rouge: Louisiana State University Press, 1989.

"Booker T. Washington Delivers the 1895 Atlanta Compromise Speech". Historymatters.gmu.edu, 2019. Online. Internet. 22 Jan. 2019., http://historymatters.gmu.edu/d/39/.

Boston Daily Globe. "No Protest of Vaughn, Says Commander Ingram", 1926: ProQuest Historical Newspapers pg. A27. Online. Internet. 8 Mar. 2019.

Brawley, Benjamin. History of Morehouse College 1882-1939. New York, N.Y.: McGrath, 1917.

Bureau of Freedmen, And Abandoned lands. Letter from Wm. J. Simmons. Anti-Slavery Reporter, ProQuest LLC, 1871.

Catalogue of the Officers and Students of Howard University, 1888. Online. Internet. 22 Jan. 2019.

Coates, Ta-Nehisi. "Slavery Made America". The Atlantic, 2014. Online. Internet. 6 Mar. 2019.

Committee, Shrewsbury Baptist Church Journey of History; on the 130th Anniversary, Congress. Message from the President of the United States, 1902.

Corey, Charles H. A history of the Richmond Theological Seminary. Richmond, Va.: J.W. Randolph, 1895.

Cutten, George. "Natural Checks or Higher Controls which". Presentation, Hamilton New York, 1935.

Cutten, George. "The Reconstruction of Democracy". Presentation, Hamilton New York, 1925.

Department of State. Early Appointments of Blacks in the Foreign Service, 1979.

Douglass, Frederick, and Philip Sheldon Foner. The life and writings of Frederick Douglass. New York: International Publishers, 1975.

Du Bois, W. E. B. The college-bred Negro. Atlanta, Ga.: Atlanta University Press, 1900.

Du Bois, W. E. B. The Souls of Black Folk. Chicago: Dodd, Mead, 1903.

"Durham Manifesto - Museum of Durham History". Museumofdurhamhistory.org, 2013. Online. Internet. 23 Jan. 2019., https://www.museumofdurhamhistory.org/blog/durham-manifesto/.

Dutch Reformed Records in selected states. 1639-2000 3rd edition, n.d. Online. Internet. 6 Mar. 2019.

"Equal Justice Initiative's report". Equal Justice Initiative's report, 2019. Online. Internet. 19 Jan. 2019., https://lynchinginamerica.eji.org/report.

Ferris, William Henry. The African abroad; or, His evolution in western civilization, by William H. Ferris. New Haven, Conn.: Tuttle, Morehouse & Taylor Co., 1913.

Flewellyn, Valada S. African Americans of Sanford. Charleston, SC: Arcadia Pub., 2009.

Foner, Eric. Reconstruction: America's Unfinished Revolution, 1863-1877. New York:

Perennial Classics, New York Harper Collins Publishers, Inc., 1988.

Foner, Philip Sheldon, and George Elizur Walker. Proceedings of the black state conventions, 1840-1865. Philadelphia: Temple Univ. Pr., 1980.

Garland Penn, Irvine. The Afro American Press, 1891. Online. Internet. 21 Jan. 2019.

Gates, Henry Louis, and Evelyn Brooks Higginbotham. African American National Biography. Oxford: Oxford Univ. Press, 2013.

Gavins, Raymond. The Perils and Prospects of Southern Black Leadership Gordon Blaine Hancock 1884-1970. Durham and London: Duke University Press, 1977.

General catalogue. Newton Centre, Mass., 1912.

Grose, Howard. "Missions". American Baptist Foreign Mission Society, 2019: 200. Online. Internet. 22 Jan. 2019.

"Hall of Fame Series Sunday Vespers". Florida Agricultural and Mechanical University (1962): 3. Online. Internet. 19 Feb. 2019.

Hall, Diana. "Slavery, The Underground Railroad and Resistance: Ontario's African-Canadian Past Before 1918", Normal School Upper Canada, 2011." Presentation, n.d.

Hamilton Literary & Theological Institute. The First Half Century of Madison University 1819-1869. New York: Sheldon & Co., 1872.

Hanson, Gayle. "Texas History | History of Texas | TexasHistory.com". Texas History. com, 2019. Online. Internet. 8 Mar. 2019. Available: https://texashistory.com/.

Haygood, Will. King of Cats: The life and times of Adam Clayton Powell, Jr.. Harper Collins, 2006.

"History and Mission of Tuskegee University". Tuskegee University, n.d. Online. Internet. 22 Jan. 2019., Available: https://www.tuskegee.edu/about-us/history-and-mission.

Howell, George, and John Munson. The History of the County of Schenectady, New York from 1662 to 1886. New York: W.W. Munsell & Co, 1886.

"John Brown Watson (1869–1942) - Encyclopedia of Arkansas". Encyclopediaofarkansas.net, 2019. Online. Internet. 24 Jan. 2019., Available: http://www.encyclopediaofarkansas.net/encyclopedia/entry-detail.aspx?entryID=333.

Krulikowski, Anne. "West Chester, Pennsylvania | Encyclopedia of Greater Philadelphia". Philadelphiaencyclopedia.org, 2017. Online. Internet. 17 Feb. 2019., Available: https://philadelphiaencyclopedia.org/archive/west-chester-pennsylvania/.

Lapp, Rudolph M. Blacks in Gold Rush California. Washington, DC: Georgetown University Press, 2013.

Madisonseis Vol 7, 1875: 13. Online. Internet. 19 Jan. 2019.

Madisonesis, 1874: 10. Online. Internet. 20 Jan. 2019.

"Minutes of the National Convention of the Colored Citizens" (1843). Online. Internet. 6 Mar. 2019.

Montesano, Philip M. Some aspects of the free Negro question in San Francisco. San Francisco: University of San Francisco, 1967.

New York Baptist Register. "Editorial Correspondence; Madison University Commencement", 1853. Online. Internet. 6 Mar. 2019.

New York Globe. "Stray Notes", 1884. Online. Internet. 21 Jan. 2019.

New York Recorder. "Schenectady Cabinet", 1853.

New York Tribune. "Colored People's Cosmopolitan Association, J.H.Townsend, Custom-House, Auditor's Department", 1866.

Office of the Historians, Bureau of Public Affairs, US Department of State. Spotlight on Dr. George Henry Jackson, 2012.

Page, Wilbur A. History of Union Baptist Church. Cincinnati: Selby Service/Roxy Press, 1978.

Painter, Nell Irvin. The History of White people. New York: W.W. Norton, 2010.

Pegues, A. W. Our Baptist ministers and schools. New York: Johnson Reprint Corp., 1892.

Petrulis, Jason. "A big Black Negro is Now in the Institution: Exhuming the History of Black Students in Antebellum Northern Universities". Presentation, University of Virginia, 2017.

Pierson, Arthur. Missionary Review of the World. vols. 18th ed. Funk & Wafnalls, 1895.

Powell, Adam Clayton. Adam by Adam. New York: Daily Press, 1971.

"Proceedings of the First State Convention of the Colored Citizens of the State of California. Held at Sacramento Nov. 20th, 21st, and 22d, in the Colored Methodist Church Sacramento: Democratic State Journal Print: 1855" (1855).

"Proceedings of the First State Convention of the Colored Citizens of the State of California, held at Sacramento Nov. 20th, 21st and 22nd in the Colored Methodist Church Sacramento". Democratic State journal Print (1855).

Proceedings of the National Education Convention. Phila, 1872. ProQuest Historical Newspapers: The Baltimore Afro-American, 1926.

Quarles, Benjamin, and William S McFeely. The Negro in the Civil War. New York, NY: Da Capo Press, 1989.

Reavis, Ralph. Virginia Union University & Virginia University of Lynchburg: Tow paths to Freedom, n.d.

Religious Herald. "Editoral", 1853.

Report of Auditor of Public Accounts to the General Assembly of Louisiana, 1875.

Reports of Committees: 30th Congress, 1st Session - 48th Congress, 2nd Session, Volume 8, 1879.

Reynolds, Mary C. Baptist missionary pioneers among Negroes. [Nashville, Tenn.]: [Sunday School Pub. Board], 1921.

Ripley, C. Peter. The Black abolitionist papers. Chapel Hill: University of North Carolina Press, 1991.

Ripley, Peter. The Black Abolitionist Papers Volume II Canada 1830-1865. Chapel Hill: The University of North Carolina Press Chapel Hill, 1986.

Roundtree, Alton G, and Paul M Bessel. Out of the shadows, The Emergence of Prince Hall Freemasonry in America: over 225 years of Endurance. Camp Springs, Md.: KLR Publishing, 2006.

Sadlier, Rosemary. Mary Ann Shadd: Publisher*Editor*Teacher*Lawyer*Suffragette. Toronto: Umbrella Press, 1995.

Simmons, William J, and Henry McNeal Turner. Men of Mark:Eminent, Progressive and Rising. vols. 1st ed. Cleveland Ohio: Geo. M. Rewell & Co., 1887.

Smith, Alice. "Historical Sketch of George B Cutten's Administration" (n.d.): 3,8,25,79. Online. Internet. 8 Mar. 2019.

Smith, Angry A, and Lucia B. Keys. Reminiscences of George W Hays, Hon. Cincinnati: Wm. P. Houston, Printing, 1913.

Smith, James. The History of Chenango and Madison Counties. Syracuse: D. Mason & Co, 1880.

"Southern Conference on Race Relations" (1942). Online. Internet. 23 Jan. 2019.

St. Petersburg Times. "3 FAMU buildings", 1956. Online. Internet. 24 Jan. 2019.

Staff. "Masonic (News)". Pacific Appeal, 1872. Online. Internet. 17 Mar. 2019.

Staff. "Texas State Convention". The Representative, 1871. Online. Internet. 17 Mar. 2019.

The City of New York. Passport of Jonas H. Townsend. New York City, 1849.

The First half century of Madison University, (1819-1869), or, The jubilee volume, containing sketches of eleven hundred livings and deceased alumni, with fifteen portraits of founders, presidents, and patrons ... New York: Committee of Alumni, 1872.

"The Gospel in all Lands". Methodist Episcopal Church, 1891. Online. Internet. 22 Jan. 2019.

The Independent Congregationalist, 1853. Online. Internet. 6 Mar. 2019.

The One Hundred and one Anniversary of the Theological Seminary. Hamilton NY: Colgate University, 1920. Online. Internet. 22 Jan. 2019.

The Pittsburg Courier. "Pitt and Navy Bar Colored Grid Star", 1926: ProQuest Historical Newspapers pg. 15. Online. Internet. 8 Mar. 2019.

The Weekly Anglo- African. "Col.4", 1864: 4. Online. Internet. 17 Mar. 2019.

The Weekly Anglo-African, 1860: page 4 col.4. Online. Internet. 8 Mar. 2019.

Thurman, Howard. With Head and Heart. Boston: Houghton Mifflin Harcourt, 1981.

Town Topics, Princeton NJ. "Man of the week", 1950. Online. Internet. 23 Jan. 2019.

"Underground railroad history: vigilance committee, the New York blog, Historical news and views from the Empire state". newyorkhistoryblog.org, n.d. Online. Internet. 8 Mar. 2019. Available: https://newyorkchistoryblog.org.

Vereen-Gordon, Mary, and Janet Smith Clayton. Morris College A Noble Journey. Hallmark Publishing Company, 1999.

Virginia Times- Dispatch, 1944. Online. Internet. 23 Jan. 2019.

"Virginia Union University | Virginia Union University". Vuu.edu, 2019. Online. Internet. 19 Jan. 2019. Available: https://www.vuu.edu/.

Waco School. Teacher's Monthly School Report for the Month of May, Freedman School. Waco, Texas, 1870.

Washington Post. "Obituary - Henry S. Robinson, Jr", 1976. Online. Internet. 27 Jan. 2019.

Weise, James Arthur. The History of the city of Albany, New York from the discovery of the great river in 1524 by Verrazano, to the present time. Albany: E.H.Bender, 1884.

White, Shane, and C. Peter Ripley. "The Black Abolitionist Papers, Vol. 4: The United States, 1847-1858". Journal of the Early Republic 12.2 (1992): 281.

Williams, George Washington. History of the Negro race in America from 1619 to 1880. New York: G.P. Putnam's Sons, 1883.

Wisbey, Peter, and Jennifer Haines. "Selected references to African-Americans, Slavery or the Underground Railroad" Seward Papers; -Frances Seward to William Henry Seward, May 28, 1857". Seward House Museum, 2004. Online. Internet. 8 Mar. 2019.

Work, Munore. Negro Year Book and Annual Encyclopedia. Negro Year Book Co, 1914.

Reprinted with Permission, Powell Letters, Special Collections and Archives, Colgate University Libraries.

Records of Richmond Theological Seminary, Virginia Union University Archives.

INDEX

Endnotes

CHAPTER I

1   Ta-Nehisi Coates, Slaver Made America, The Atlantic, June 24, 2014https://www.theatlantic.com/business/archive/2014/06/slavery-made-america/373288/.

2   *The History of Chenango and Madison Counties* by James H. Smith, D. Mason & CO. Syracuse New York 1880.

3   *Autobiography of Rev. Powell*, Special Collections and University Archives, Colgate University Libraries.

CHAPTER II

4   Excerpt from diary of Diary of Isaac K. Brownson relating to anti-slavery societies at Colgate, 1837, Isaac K. Brownson papers, A1065, Special Collections and University Archives, Colgate University Libraries.

CHAPTER III

5   Address to His Excellency Gov. Seward, January 26, 1843, Albany Weekly Patriot, Black Abolitionist Papers 1830-1865, 1981 ProQuest LLC.

6   Krulikowski, Anne, Rutgers University 2017, https://philadelphiaencyclopedia.org/archive/west-chester-pennsylvania/ Accessed 17 Feb 2019.

7   Bronson, Benjamin Franklin and Jirah Delano Cole, *The First Half Century of Madison University or the JUBLIEE VOLUME*, New York: Sheldon & Co., 1872.

8   Faculty Minutes May 26, 1842, Special Collections and University Archives, Colgate University Libraries.

9   Weise, Arthur James, *The history of the city of Albany, New York from the discovery of the great river in 1524, by Verrazano, to the present time/ Albany: E.H.Bender, 1884.*

10   UNDERGROUND RAILROAD HISTORY: VIGILANCE COMMITTEE, THE NEW YORK HISTORY BLOG, HISTORICAL NEWS AND VIEWS FROM THE EMPIRE STATES https:// newyorkhistoryblog.org.

11   Staff, Albany Weekly Patriot, Jan 26, 1843; Black Abolitionist Papers, ProQuest).

12   Minutes of the national Convention of Colored Citizens: Held at Buffalo, New York: Piercy & Reed, Printers, 1843, pg. 20, 21.

13   "Colored Man's Temperance Convention". Lenox Mass. July 18,1848, Albany Evening Journal (Albany, NY) 07-11-1848, Page [2].

14   The Black Abolitionist Papers, vol.4: The United States 1847-1858 S.White, C.Ripley 1992.

15   Lapp, *Blacks in Gold Rush California,* 13, 39, 194, 266.

16   Montesano, "Free Negro Question in San Francisco," 22–25; *AP,* 26 January, 3 October 1843 [4:0529, 0676]; *NSt,* 15 September 1848, 3, 10 August 1849; *Lib,* 30 March 1849; *IC,* 5 December 1849; FDP, 23 November 1855; *AAM,* March 1859; *WAA,* 22 October 1859, 24 March 1860, 28 December 1861; PA, 2 June 1863; *ESF,* 28 May 1869, 25 August 1872.

17   Proceedings of the First State Convention of the Colored Citizens of the State of California. Held at Sacramento Nov. 20th, 21st, and 22d, in the Colored Methodist Church Sacramento: Democratic State Journal Print: 1855.

18   The Black Abolitionist Papers Document 47, William H. Newby to Frederick Douglass 10 August 1854 pg. 234.

19   Black Newspapers Publication: FREDERICK DOUGLASS' PAPER Date: August 31, 1855] Title: OUR CORRESPONDENCE.

20   *NASS,* 16 May 1863 [14:0863–64]; David W. Blight, *Frederick Douglass' Civil War: Keeping Faith in Jubilee* (Baton Rouge, La., 1989), 101–21; Philip S. Foner, *The Life and*

Writings of Frederick Douglass, 5 vols. (New York, N.Y., 1975 3:390; *WAA,* 1 August 1863; Quarles, *Negro in the Civil War,* 188–89.

[21] Staff, New York Tribune, New York, New York, 10-31-1866, "Colored People's Cosmopolitan Association", J.H. Townsend, Custom-House, Auditor's Department; Page 8.

[22] The Weekly Anglo-African, 24 March, 1860, page 4, col 4.

[23] "Teacher's Monthly School Report for the Month of May, 1870, FREEDMAN SCHOOL, Signed Jonas H Townsend, Teacher"; "Report of School for Freeman In Waco, Texas for the Month of June 30[th]1870, Signed Jonas H Townsend, Teacher" In the TOWNSEND COLLECTION at The Local History Collection of the Gilbertsville Free Library, Gilbertsville, NY.

[24] Staff, THE REPRESENTATIVE, Galveston, "TEXAS STATE CONVENTION" August 26, 1871.

[25] Foner and Walker, *Proceedings of the Black State Conventions,*1:99,2:112–27, 132–65. The Black Abolitionist Papers Document 47, William H. Newby to Frederick Douglass 10 August 1854 pg. 234.

[26] C 1844 in Maine.

[27] Gayle Hanson, Archivist and Researcher, Texas History. ttexashistory.com .Prince Hall Grand Lodge of Texas and Its Jurisdiction.

[28] Alton G. Roundtree and Paul M. Bessel *"Out of the Shadows, The Emergence of Prince Hall Freemasonry in America: over 225 years of Endurance* KLR Publishing, LLC 2006).

[29] The organization that is over all the lodges in a specific jurisdiction, generally a state.

[30] Archivist, Adelphi Union Lodge No. 14, 454 West 15th Street, New York, NY 10032 "The History of Adelphi Union Lodge No. 14."

[31] The Year of Townsend's death is 1872. The month and day are in question. The place is variously report as WACO and Galveston.

[32] Staff, "MASONIC (NEWS)," PACIFIC APPEAL, 11 Nov. 1872, https://cdnc.ucr. edu/cgi-bin/cdnc?a=cl&cl=CL2.1846.11&e.

[33] PASSPORT Issued by the City of New York "this day of November 1849 to Jonas H Townsend, In the TOWNSEND COLLECTION at The Local History Collection of the Gilbertsville Free Library, Gilbertsville, NY.; Staff, The Pacific Appeal, MASONIC, San Francisco, Nov 9, 1872; Gates, Henry Louis JR and Evelyn Brooks Higginbotham, African American National Biography, OUP USA, 2013.

CHAPTER IV

[34] Colgate was known as Madison University when Simpson attended. There were three departments: academic, collegiate and theological. The academic department was called the Grammar School, a preparatory school before entering the collegiate and theological departments. Simpson entered the grammar school, graduated from the collegiate and theological departments.

[35] HOWELL, George Rogers, John H. Munsell; The History of the County of Schenectady, New York from 1762 to 1886,; W.W. Munsell & Co., Publishers, New York, 1886; p 170. Article appearing in a local paper at the time of his marriage to Harriet Bogart at Auburn.

[36] "A correspondent of the *New-York Recorder…" Schenectady Cabinet, 13 Sept. 1853."*

[37] *Dutch Reformed Church Records in Selected State, 1639-2000.* 3rd entry for 1812.

[38] " *A Call for a convention of the Colored Inhabitants if the State of New York;* THE COLORED AMERICAN" 11 July, 1840; *Public Meeting in Schenectady,* THE COLORED AMERICAN" 26 December 1840.

[39] Religious Herald 24 Feb. 1853.

[40] Petrulis, Jason, *A Big Black Negro is Now in the Institution": Exhuming the History of Black Students In Antebellum Northern Universities.* Cal Poly Pomona University, 2017.

References to Simpson's color, p's. 2,3,25,45,46,48

41   Religious Herald 31 March 1853.
42   Painter, Nell Irwin, The History of White People, W.W.Norton & Co., 2010. From his arrival at Colgate there were arguments as to whether Simpson was African-American or not. Census takers enumerated him as white and/or mulatto.
43   The Religious Herald.
44   Ibid
45   New York Baptist Register, Editorial Correspondence, Madison University Commencement 1853, August 25; and The Independent Congregationalist Sept. 8, 1853.
46   Cabinet, Schenectady NY 9-13-1853.
47   Smith, Angry A and Lucia B. Keys, *Reminiscences of George W. Hays, Hon.*, "UNION BAPTIST CHURCH, A fountain of service for our Lord." Cincinnati, Wm. P. Houston, Printing. 1913, 5-42.: Hamilton Literary & Theological Institute *The First Half Century of Madison University (1819-1969)*, New York: SHELDON & CO., 1872.
48   HOWELL, George Rogers, John H. Munsell; The History of the County of Schenectady, New York from 1662 to 1886,; W.W. Munsell & Co., Publishers, New York, 1886; p 170.
49   WISBEY, Peter and Jennifer Haines; "*Selected references to African-Americans, Slavery or the Underground Railroad*" Seward Papers ; -Frances Seward to William Henry Seward, May 28, 1857 : February 2004.
50   Page, Wilbur A., History of Union Baptist Church, Selby Service/Roxy Press Cincinnati, Ohio 1978).
51   Williams, George W., "*History of the Negro Race in America: 1619 to 1880 Negroes as Slaves, as Soldiers and as citizens.* G.P. Putnam's Sons 1883.
52   Committee; *SHREWSBURY BAPTIST CHURCH JOURNEY OF HISTORY*; on the 130th anniversary, p.1.
53   Shrewsbury a Black hamlet near Chatham, KENT COUNTY, Ontario. Upper Canada.
54   Sadlier, Rosemary; *Mary Ann Shadd: Publisher*Editor*Teacher*Lawyer*Suffragette*, Umbrella Prp.8ess, Toronto, On, 1995.
55   Also in West Chester, Rev Dyer A Nichols, Jonas Holland Townsend.
56   "At the close of the recent Session of the Normal School, at Toronto, Miss Emeline (sic) Shadd, as coloured lade, received the first prize of £ 5 10s; also a first class certificate. Miss Shadd is a sister of Miss M.A. Shadd..., daughter of Abram D. Shadd, Esq., of Raleigh Township, Kent Co., C.W. and formerly of West Chester, Pa., ---*Provincial Freeman.*"; TORONTO NORMAL SCHOOL, *JUBILEE CELEBRATION, TORONTO: WARWICK BROS & RUTTER, 1898.*
57   Hall, Diana, "*Slavery*, The Underground Railroad and Resistance: Ontario's African-Canadian Past Before 1918", Normal School Upper Canada, , 2011.
58   3. The Black Abolitionist Papers Volume II Canada 1830-1865. Peter Ripley, Editor, The University of North Carolina Press Chapel Hill and London @1986 The University of North Carolina Press).
59   *The FIRST HALF CENTRUY of MADISON UNIVERSITY (1919-1929 or the JUBILEE VOLUME, New York, SHELDON & CO.*, New York, Hamilton Literary & Theological Institute, 1972.
60   Foner, Eric, *Reconstruction: America's Unfinished Revolution, 1863-1877*, Perennial Classics, New York, HarperCollins Publishers, Inc., 1988.

CHAPTER V

61   Equal Justice Initiative's Report. (2019). Equal Justice Initiative's report. (online) Available at: https://lynchinginamerica.eji.org/report
62   Slavery by Another name-The Re-enslavement of Black Americans from the Civil

War to World War II by Douglas A. Blackmon, Anchor Books, 2008.

[63] Various records, Special Collections and University Archives, Colgate University Libraries.

CHAPTER VI

[64] Simmons, w. (1887). Men of Mark: Eminent, Progressive and rising. 1st ed. Cleveland Ohio: Geo. M. Rewell & CO., pg. 7.

[65] Ibid, pg. 30.

[66] Letter from Wm. J. Simmons to Office of the Commissioner, Bureau of Freedmen, And Abandoned Lands dated January1, 1871, Anti-Slavery Reporter, April 1, 1871, ProQuest LLC.

[67] Ibid, pg. 31.

[68] Letter from Wm. J. Simmons to Office of the Commissioner, Bureau of Freedmen, And Abandoned Lands dated January1, 1871, Anti-Slavery Reporter, April 1, 1871, ProQuest LLC.

[69] Ibid, pg. 33.

[70] Ibid, pg. 33.

[71] Ibid, pg. 33.

[72] Ibid, pg. 33.

[73] Ibid, pg. 35.

[74] Ibid, pg. 7.

CHAPTER VII

[75] Corey, C. (1895). *A History of the Richmond Theological Seminary*. Richmond, Va.: J.W. Randolph, pg. 52.

[76] Corey, C. (1895). *A history of the Richmond Theological Seminary*. Richmond, Va.: J.W. Randolph.

[77] Vuu.edu. (2019). *Virginia Union University | Virginia Union University*. [online] Available at: https://www.vuu.edu/ [Accessed 19 Jan. 2019].

[78] Anon, (2019). [Blog] *Sterling Gardner: A feather in the Richmond Cap.*

[79] Records of Richmond Theological Seminary Virginia Union University Archives.

[80] Letter from Sterling Gardner to Charles Corey, July 19, 1869, A008.B01.F03.021, Records of Richmond Theological Seminary, Virginia Union University Archives.

[81] Letter from Sterling Garner to Charles Corey, May 7, 1870, A008.B01.F04.015, Records of Richmond Theological Seminary, Virginia Union University Archives.

[82] Ibid

[83] Reprinted by permission, Virginia Union University Archives and Special Collections

[84] Ibid

[85] Ibid

[86] A1054 Box 2, Special Collections and University Archives, Colgate University Libraries.

[87] Madisonesis, vol. 6, No.7.pg. 10, January 1874, Colgate University Student Newspapers, Special Collections and University Archives, Colgate Libraries.

[88] Madisoneis Vol. 7 no. pg. 13, Special Collections and University Archives, Colgate University Libraries.

[89] Records of Richmond Theological Seminary, Virginia Union University Archives.

[90] American Baptist Home Mission Society. The Baptist Home Mission Monthly. New York: American Baptist Home Mission Society, 1878-1909, page 295.

[91] Report of Auditor of Public Accounts to the General Assembly of Louisiana. (1875).

[92] Reports of Committees: 30th Congress, 1st Session - 48th Congress, 2nd Session, Volume 8. (1879), Pg. 75.

[93] Anon, (1947). The Louisiana Historical Quarterly, Volume 30.

[94] Anon, (1889). The Baptist Home Mission Monthly, Volumes 11-12, pg. 242.

[95] A. W. Pegues, Our Baptist ministers and schools (New York: Johnson Reprint Corp.,

1892, pg. 301.

96   Mary C Reynolds, *Baptist missionary pioneers among Negroes* ([Nashville, Tenn.]: [Sunday School Pub. Board], 1921).

97   Letter from Joseph E. Jones to Charles Corey, November 25, 1872, A008.B01. F06.017, Records of Richmond Theological Seminary Virginia Union University Archives.

98   *The Crisis*, 1922 vol. 25, pg. 176.

99   Irvine Garland Penn, *The Afro American Press*, 1891, online, Internet, 21 Jan. 2019.

100   The Baptist Home Mission Monthly Vol. 2, 1880.

101   Letter from Joseph E. Jones to Charles Corey, June 28, 1893, A008.B01.F27.004, records of Richmond Theological Seminary, Virginia Union University Archives.

102   *The Crisis* was first published in 1901 and founded by W.E.B. Du Bois as the official publication of the NAACP as a journal on civil rights, history, politics, and culture.

103   *The Crisis* , pg. 176, Vol. 25 n.4 Feb 1923.

104   Black Virginia: the Richmond Planet, 1894-1909, accessed Dec. 30, 2018, https:// blackvirginia.richmond.edu/items/show/68).

105   Records of Richmond Theological Seminary, Virginia Union University Archives.

106   Letter from D. N. Vassar to Charles Corey, January 27, 1877, A008.B01.F11.010, Records of Richmond Theological Seminary, Virginia Union University Archives.

107   Ralph Reavis, Virginia Union University & Virginia University of Lynchburg: Two Paths to Freedom n.d. online, Internet, 21 Jan 2019.

108   Noted Educators, Virginians All": How One Family Changed the Shape of African American Education by Jessica Bennett, Virginia Forum 2018.

109   Annual Report (American Baptist Home Mission Society, 1885). Pg. 25.

110   A. W. Pegues, Our Baptist ministers and schools (New York; Johnson Reprint Corp. 1892), pg. 218-221.

111   William Henry Ferris, The African aboard; or His evolution in western civilization,(New Haven, Conn.: Tuttle, Morehouse & Taylor Co., 1913), pg. 788.

112   New York Globe, "Stray Notes", Oct., 18, 1884.

113   The obituary in *The Crisis*, May 1917, p. 31,32.

CHAPTER VIII

114   Pegues, A.W. Our Baptist ministers and schools (New York; Johnson Reprint Corp., 1892 pg. 277-280.

115   57th Congress, Message from the President of the United States, 1902, pg.128.

116   Department of State, Early Appointments of Blacks in the foreign service, 1979, pg. 31,32.

117   Munore Work, Negro Year Book and Annual Encyclopedia (Negro Year Book Co. 1914, pg. 153.

118   *The Crisis*, Feb. 1914 p. 170.

119   Adele Logan Alexander, Parallel worlds (Charlottesville: University Press, 2012).

120   Office of the Historians, Bureau Public Affairs, US Department of State, Spotlight on Dr. George Henry Jackson, 2012 http://historyatstate.tumblr.com/post/112149978083/ spotlight-on-dr-george-henry-jackson.

121   Adele Logan Alexander, Parallel worlds (Charlottesville: University Press, 2012).

122   https://www.history.com/topics/black-history/niagara-movement.

123   General Catalogue 1913, Special Collections and University Archives, Colgate University Libraries.

124   General catalogue (Newton Centre, Mass. 1912)He died in 1881. Catalogue of the Officers and Students of Howard University, March 1887 to March 1888, online, Internet, 22 Jan. 2019 pg.15.

125   Special Collections and University Archives, Colgate University Libraries.

[126] General catalogue (Newton Centre, Mass. 1912).

[127] A literary society formed in 1840 that met weekly.

[128] Arthur Pierson, Missionary Review of the World vols. 18th ed (Funk & Wagnalls, 1895).

[129] Howard Grose, "Missions", American Baptist Foreign Mission Society, 1923, online, Internet 22 Jan. 2019.

[130] General Catalogue, Special Collections and University Archives, Colgate University Libraries.

[131] The Baptist Home Mission Monthly vol 1-2 p. 31, 91.

[132] Student Newspaper, Madisonensis, vol. 14, no 2, Oct. 15, 1881,pg. 9 Special Collections and University Archives, Colgate University Libraries.

[133] Altermese Smith Bentley, Seminole County (Charleston, SC: Arcadia, 2000, pg. 25).

[134] Valada S. Flewellyn, African Americans of Sanford (Charleston, SC: Arcadia Pub., 2009, pg. 110).

CHAPTER IX

[135] https://www.tuskegee.edu/about-us/history-and-mission.

[136] "Booker T. Washington Delivers the 1895 Atlanta Compromise Speech", Historymatters. gmu.edu.2019, online, Internet, 22 Jan. 2019, Available: http://historymaters.gmu.edu/d/39/.

CHAPTER X

[137] Samuel Howard Archer collection. Archives Division, Auburn Avenue Research Library on African-American Culture and History, Atlanta-Fulton Public Library System.

[138] Archer, S.H., The Disenfranchisement of the Negro, 1901, A1014, Student Oratorical and Essay Contests, Special Collections and University Archives, Colgate University Libraries.

[139] The Roland Oratorical Prize was awarded to a member of the senior class for their excellency in public speaking set up by Eugene A. Roland'1884. and he was a Kingsford Declamation Speaker.

[140] Archer, S,H., "The Ethical Ideal in American Life", 1902, , Student Oratorical and Essay Contest, Special Collections and University Archives, Colgate University Libraries.

[141] See Chapter X Appendix, pgs. 203-205.

[142] Letters from the Members of the Class of 1902 Colgate University, Special Collections and University Archives, Colgate University Libraries.

[143] The Torch Atlanta, Georgia, 1923 (Morehouse Yearbook-Faculty Photo); Samuel Howard Archer Collection, Archives Division, Auburn Avenue Research Library on African-American Culture and History, Atlanta-Fulton Public Library System.

[144] Bulletin: Morehouse College: A Liberal Arts College for Negro Men, Atlanta, Georgia; Samuel Howard Archer Collection, Archives Division, Auburn Avenue Research Library on African-American Culture and History, Atlanta-Fulton Public Library System.

[145] Corresp. 1932-39 (Vertical File/CCMC A-1Folder); Samuel Archer President Collection. Archives Research Center, Atlanta University Center Robert W. Woodruff Library.

[146] Program: Funeral Rites for Samuel Howard Archer Sale Hall, Morehouse College, January 19, 1941 Samuel Howard Archer Collection, Archives Division, Auburn Avenue Research Library on African-American Culture and History, Atlanta-Fulton Public Library System.

[147] Box 1 Folder 9, Samuel Howard Archer Collection, Archives Division, Auburn Avenue Research Library on African-American Culture and History, Atlanta-Fulton

Public Library System.

148 Howard Thurman, With Head and Heart: The Autobiography of Howard Thurman, Houghton Mifflin Harcourt, 198, pg. 35.

149 Ibid, pg. 38.

150 Ibid, pg. 38.

151 Ibid, pg. 39-40.

CHAPTER XI

152 Raymond Gavins, The Perils and Prospects of Southern Black Leadership, Gordon Blaine Hancock 1884-1970 (Durham and London: Duke University Press, 1977 pg. 18.

153 The One Hundred and First Anniversary of the Theological Seminary, Special Collections and University Archives, Colgate University Libraries.

154 Southern Conference on Race Relations, Durham N. C. October 1942.

155 "Durham Manifesto- Museum of Durham History" http://www. museumofdurhamhistory.org/blog/durham-manifesto/.

156 The Perils and Prospects of Southern Black Leadership-Gordon Blaine Hancock 1884-1970 Raymond Gavins, Duke University Press Durham and London 1977.

157 Southern Conference on Race Relations, Durham, N.C., October 20, 1942.

158 The Perils and Prospects of Southern Black Leadership-Gordon Blaine Hancock 1884-1970 Raymond Gavins, Duke University Press Durham and London 1977.

159 The Perils and Prospects of Southern Black Leadership-Gordon Blaine Hancock 1884-1970 Raymond Gavins, Duke University Press Durham and London 1977 pg. 18.

160 WWI Draft Registration card.

CHAPTER XII

161 25th Reunion Book class of 1903, Special Collections and University Archives, Colgate University Libraries.

162 The Crisis, Vol. 28, No1, May 1924 pg. 27.

163 Everett Booker Jones, Class notes 1930, Special Collections and University Archives, Colgate UniversityLibraries.

164 St. Petersburg Times, Feb. 22, 1956.

165 Florida Agricultural And Mechanical University, Hall of Fame Series, Sunday Vespers, FAMU Liv Library, 8 April 1962, pg. 4.

166 St. Petersburg Times, Feb. 22, 1956.

167 Student Newspapers, Colgate Madisonensis, Tuesday Nov. 14, 1914, p. 4, Special Collections and University Archives, Colgate University Libraries.

168 Ibid

169 Brawley, Benjamin Griffith, 1882-1939, History of Morehouse College 19701917.

170 (source http//: thesiac.com).

CHAPTER XIII

171 Miss Alice Smith, Historical Sketch of George B. Cutten's Administration 1922 September 1, A1058, George B. Cutten papers, Special Collections and University Archives, Colgate University Libraries pg. 8

172 Ibid, pg. 25.

173 No Protest of Vaughn, Says Commander Ingram, Boston Daily Globe, October 28, 1926; ProQuest Historical Newspapers; The Boston Globe, pg. A27.

174 Pitt and Navy Bar Colored Grid Star- The Pittsburgh Courier, Oct. 30, 1926; ProQuest Historical Newspapers; Pittsburgh Courier pg. 15).

175 Afro- American (1893-1988); Nov 6, 1926; ProQuest Historical Newspapers: the Baltimore Afro-American pg.5).

176 COLGATE SPECIAL COLLECTIONS.

CHAPTER XIV

[177] Miss Alice Smith, Historical Sketch of George B. Cutten's Administration 1922 September 1, A1058, George B. Cutten papers, Special Collections and University Archives, Colgate University Libraries, pg. 3.

[178] George B Cutten papers, Special Collections and University Archives, Colgate University Libraries.

[179] Student Newspapers, The Colgate Maroon, Special Collections and University Archives, Colgate University Libraries.

[180] Student Newspapers, The Colgate Maroon Vol 66, no 15, "Dr. Schmitt speaks on Jewish Question p. 1, Special Collections and University Archives, Colgate University Libraries.

[181] Miss Alice Smith, Historical Sketch of George B. Cutten's Administration 1922 September 1, A1058, George B. Cutten papers, Special Collections and University Archives, Colgate University Libraries.

[182] George B. Cutten, The Reconstruction of Democracy, October 7, 1922, A1002, President Office Records, Special Collections and University Archives, Colgate University Libraries.

[183] George B. Cutten, Natural Checks or Higher Controls Which?, September 25, 1935, President Office Records, Special Collections and University Archives, Colgate University Libraries.

[184] Ibid

[185] Ibid

[186] Ibid

[187] Ibid

[188] Ibid

[189] Ibid

[190] George Barton Cutten, The Reconstruction of Democracy, October 7, 1922, A1002, President's Office Records, Special Collections and University Archives, Colgate University Libraries.

[191] Ibid

CHAPTER XV

[192] The Telegraph, March 10, 1950- Around the Town.

[193] *Crisis Magazine,* May 1922.

[194] Colgate Maroon Vol. LIV- October 5, 1921- Special Collections and University Archives, Colgate University Libraries.

[195] Smith, H. M., Letter from H. M. Smith to W. E. B. Du Bois, April 30, 1921. W. E. B. Du Bois Papers (MS 312). Special Collections and University Archives, Colgate University Libraries

[196] Lincoln University catalogue 1985-1987.

[197] Student Newspapers, The Colgate Scene, July 1988 pg.9, box A1283, Special Collections and University Archives Colgate University Libraries.

[198] Obituary in Washington Post, June 25, 1976.

[199] The term 'Uncle Tom' is used as a derogatory epithet for an excessively subservient **person**, particularly when that **person** perceives their own lower-class status based on race.

[200] *King of Cats: The life and Times of Adam Clayton Powell,* Jr. by Will Haygood, Harper Collins Publishers, Inc. 2006.

[201] History, art & Archives, U.S. House of Representatives, "Powell, Adam Clayton, Jr.," https://history.house.gov/People/Detail?19872.

[202] Ibid

[203] Ibid, pg. 81.

[204] https://www.thecrimson.com/article/1956/3/1/thePowell-amendment-pwhen-president=eisenhowers/ & The Powell Amendment Voting Cycle: An Obituary, John. B. Gilmour, Legislative Studies Quarterly Vol. 26. No. 2 (May 2001), pp. 249-262).

[205] Special Collections and University Archives, Colgate University Libraries.

[206] Chapter 15 - 1930, 25th Reunion Class Notes, Special Collections and University Archives, Colgate University Libraries.

[207] Ibid

[208] Letter to President Case from Adam Clayton Powell, dated April 30, 1947, Powell letters, Special Collections and University Archives, Colgate University Libraries.

[209] Letter to President Case from Robert Bruce dated May 2, 1947, Powell letters Special Collections and University Archives, Colgate University Libraries.

[210] Ibid

[211] Ibid

[212] Ibid

[213] Ibid

[214] Letter from President Case to Adam Clayton Powell, dated May 11, 1947, Powell Letters, Special Collections and University Archives, Colgate University Libraries.

ABOUT THE AUTHOR

Diane Ciccone was a member of the first class of women at Colgate University. After Colgate she went on to law school and has been a practicing attorney, arbitrator, mediator, and administrative law judge in New York City.

Judge Ciccone became re-engaged with Colgate after realizing that the current students had no historical reference of African American attendance at Colgate in the recent past. She became a mentor, an early president of the Alumni of Color, served on the Alumni Council, and Board of Trustees. In 2016, the University named its first residential commons in her honor.

Her daughter also graduated from Colgate and Diane lives in New Jersey with her husband, Daryl McMillan.

"I felt this book was important to bring into the light the rich legacy of the early African American men who attended Colgate and went on to be a vital part of the transformation of this nation."

This is Diane's first published book, however she has written extensively on her rich African American roots in Central New York. She has produced and hosted her own TV show on Princeton Community TV. Diane also wrote and produced the award winning documentary film "Act of Faith," a film documenting the first integrated planned housing development in New Jersey.

"Diane Ciccone brings together an impeccable array of talents for her book, *Into the Light*: a film maker's eye, nuanced descriptions, an ear for crisp prose, and a historian's zest for discovery. In addition, she celebrates the indomitable will of the nineteenth century first Black male students at Colgate University, reminding us that even having borne repression, they became leaders in the human and civil rights struggles. This is a lesson for these times."

Cecelia Hodges Drewry, Ph.D.
Lecturer, Rank of Associate Professor (Retired)
Assistant Dean of the College
Princeton University

"A well-crafted, thoroughly researched study of African American men who attended Colgate University from 1840-1930. Highly sensitive to the national contexts and filled with fascinating connections, this book will reward its primary audience of Colgate alumni and extends to readers interested in the history of black men at America's colleges."

Graham Russell Gao Hodges
George Dorland Langdon, Jr. Professor of History and
Africana Studies, Colgate University

"Through a meticulous and judicious research, Judge Diane Ciccone has crafted a fabulous book about the life of the earliest Black men at Colgate University, who went on to make significant contributions to society that are still unknown and unrecognized to this day. In a very powerful way, Judge Ciccone has carved out a place in the history of Colgate University and in the annals of America for these ignored and uncelebrated Colgate alumni to be finally known. She has woven beautifully the stories of their 'silenced voices' to highlight their unacknowledged achievements. For far too long, the faculty, administrators, and trustees of the university have often questioned whether alumni of color make contributions to society at all. *Into the Light* responds with a resounding 'Yes!' This is the untold story that Colgate should embrace fully and take pride in, in spite its own history of race relations that the earliest Black men endured courageously and students of color continue to experience. In many ways, this book is also the story of America's attitude towards race, injustice and power that Black people have defied at every corner to claim their human dignity and place in society. This book will inspire generations of students at Colgate and beyond to be brave, courageous, resilient, focused, optimistic, and to keep their eyes on the prize, but also to commit themselves to the progress of their people, thereby contributing to the creation of a broader and more inclusive vision of America as the result of their great Colgate education."

Harvey J. Sindima, Ph.D., Presidential Scholar
Professor of Philosophy and Religion
Colgate University, Hamilton, New York

"I have worked with Diane Ciccone, Esq. and I have been positively impacted as a result of my relationship with her. From the beginning, she welcomed me my freshman year at Colgate, as an older sister figure. After graduation, I worked as secretary in her alumni organization presidency. Diane enjoys being a scholar and has enthralled many by sharing her findings regarding Colgate's cultural past. Her interest was in writing about the part of Colgate's history that would matter to me, a history which includes information about the 'firsts' of students of color, specifically of Black students, and where we all fit in both American history and in Colgate's history.

Buckle up and stay tuned, as Diane has unearthed some pretty astounding information about Colgate which sheds light on what I gained there. It seems my Dad inherently knew it would be significant for me to have a Colgate life."
Angela Moody Robinson, Ed.D.
Colgate class of 1977
Student Access & Educational Equity, Rutgers University (Retired)

"Too often, Colgate students (of color and not of color) find themselves questioning the worthiness and validity of our presence. Knowing our history and the people who laid a path for us to attend is a testament to our right to be here."
Kia Edwards, Colgate 2010
Product Marketing Associate

"Diane Ciccone's compilation of the histories about the first African Americans to attend Colgate University will provide much needed insight into the challenges, triumphs, and contributions of the men who used their education to disprove the stereotypes about the intellectual abilities of African Americans. This masterful work shares evidence and proof of the existence of people of color who were part of the early history of American higher education."
Veronica McFall, Colgate 1989
Assistant Director of Alumni Relations for Affinity and Identity Programs, Colgate University

"*Into The Light* provides not only a comprehensive look into the experiences of Blacks who have attended Colgate, but also an in-depth look of those experiences both historically and culturally. It is refreshing to observe these occurrences through the eyes of a Black intellectual; having history once again written with through the lens of historical and cultural honesty. I salute you!!"
Cheryl Larrier Jemmott,
Former Director of Adoptions for the City of New York

"*Into the Light: The Early African American Men of Colgate University Who Transformed a Nation* matters because the men it chronicles matter. Diane Ciccone has done Colgate a great and necessary service in bringing this important history to light."
Kyle Bass,
Playwright, Burke Endowed Chair in Regional Studies, Colgate University

To order additional copies
please visit
www.bolderspiritpublish.com

Made in the USA
Middletown, DE
19 May 2019